A-Level Chemistry

CloudLearn Ltd

Specification code: 7405

First Teaching: 2015

First Assessment: 2017

A Level Chemistry

Published and distributed by: UKDLP LTD

First published in July 2015

Edition Number: 2015/01

© UKDLP LTD

Printed under license by CloudLearn Ltd

Disclaimer

The authors of this text believe the contents of this course to be accurate and correct. While all possible care has been taken in producing this work, no guarantee can be given.

Contents

Introduction

You have chosen to study A-Level Chemistry. In order to successfully complete the A-Level Chemistry course from AQA, you will need to pass the three A-Level written examinations, and undertake a series of practicals. These must be conducted under supervision at an examination centre and should never be attempted at home. You can register to sit these at any examination centre that will accept you as an external candidate, although we know the following should accept you:

3A Tutors Ltd.
1A High Street
Staple Hill
Bristol
BS16 5HA
www.3at.org.uk
Tel: 0117 9109931

English Maths Science Tuition and Educational Centre
40 Showell Green Lane
Sparkhill
Birmingham
B11 4JP
Tel: 0121 771 1298
Fax: 0872 110 7502
e-mail: info@englishandmaths.com
Website: www.englishandmaths.com

London Brookes College
40/42 The Burroughs
Hendon
London
NW4 4AP
Tel: 020 8202 2007
E-mail: info@londonbrookescollege.co.uk
Website: http://www.londonbrookescollege.co.uk/

Please note that we are not affiliated with these centres and we only suggest them as centres where we know students can take their practical assessments.

In this course we have endeavoured to provide you with enough information to allow you to complete the written exams, but you will need to liaise with your chosen exam centre for further details regarding the practicals.

None of the experiments detailed in this course should be attempted at home, but only under supervised laboratory conditions.

Assessment

In this course, at the end of certain topics, you will find either a TMA (Tutor Marked Assignment) or an instruction to contact your tutor in order to receive the TMA.

When your tutor has e-mailed a past paper TMA to you, you should print it out, complete it under examination conditions, scan it and e-mail it back to your tutor.

In order to sit your exams and the practicals, you will need to contact an examination centre and organise this for yourselves.

Once again I would like to remind you that **the organising of the practical work is your responsibility**. Your examination centre will provide you with all of the information you need on these practicals, including more details on what you should expect to do during the practical assessment.

Details of the written exams can be found on the following page.

The practical tests are set and do not change every year; they are detailed in the specification, and we will give you information about them as we progress through the course.

Core Content

The A-Level Chemistry consists of 3 topics:

Topic 1 – Physical Chemistry

Topic 2 – Inorganic Chemistry

Topic 3 – Organic Chemistry

The formal assessment for A-Level Chemistry is as follows:

Paper 1	+ Paper 2	+ Paper 3
What's assessed	**What's assessed**	**What's assessed**
• Relevant Physical chemistry topics (sections 3.1.1 to 3.1.4, 3.1.6 to 3.1.8 and 3.1.10 to 3.1.12) • Inorganic chemistry (Section 3.2) • Relevant practical skills	• Relevant Physical chemistry topics (sections 3.1.2 to 3.1.6 and 3.1.9) • Organic chemistry (Section 3.3) • Relevant practical skills	• Any content • Any practical skills
How it's assessed	**How it's assessed**	**How it's assessed**
• written exam: 2 hours • 105 marks • 35% of A-level	• written exam: 2 hours • 105 marks • 35% of A-level	• written exam: 2 hours • 90 marks • 30% of A-level
Questions	**Questions**	**Questions**
105 marks of short and long answer questions	105 marks of short and long answer questions	40 marks of questions on practical techniques and data analysis 20 marks of questions testing across the specification 30 marks of multiple choice questions

Timescales

The practicals will likely be held in the Spring of every year (starting in 2017).

The written exams are held in May/June every year (starting in 2017).

You need to confirm the specific dates with your chosen examination centre, and we always recommend you book early for both practicals and the written examinations.

Students must take all written exams and practicals in the same year; it is not permissible to take some exams one year and some the following year.

Course structure

The course is written systematically to cover the AQA specification, and, as a result, there are times when a particular issue or subject is discussed in more than one section. This is not an error but reflects the specification, which also does this. This should not in any way harm your learning but should actually enhance it as it gives you the opportunity to learn/revise a key issue in several different areas of the course.

THE PERIODIC TABLE

Group

Period	1	2												3	4	5	6	7	0
1							1 **H** Hydrogen 1												4 **He** Helium 2
2	7 **Li** Lithium 3	9 **Be** Beryllium 4												11 **B** Boron 5	12 **C** Carbon 6	14 **N** Nitrogen 7	16 **O** Oxygen 8	19 **F** Fluorine 9	20 **Ne** Neon 10
3	23 **Na** Sodium 11	24 **Mg** Magnesium 12												27 **Al** Aluminium 13	28 **Si** Silicon 14	31 **P** Phosphorus 15	32 **S** Sulfur 16	35.5 **Cl** Chlorine 17	40 **Ar** Argon 18
4	39 **K** Potassium 19	40 **Ca** Calcium 20	45 **Sc** Scandium 21	48 **Ti** Titanium 22	51 **V** Vanadium 23	52 **Cr** Chromium 24	55 **Mn** Manganese 25	56 **Fe** Iron 26	59 **Co** Cobalt 27	59 **Ni** Nickel 28	63.5 **Cu** Copper 29	65 **Zn** Zinc 30		70 **Ga** Gallium 31	73 **Ge** Germanium 32	75 **As** Arsenic 33	79 **Se** Selenium 34	80 **Br** Bromine 35	84 **Kr** Krypton 36
5	86 **Rb** Rubidium 37	88 **Sr** Strontium 38	89 **Y** Yttrium 39	91 **Zr** Zirconium 40	93 **Nb** Niobium 41	96 **Mo** Molybdenum 42	99 **Tc** Technetium 43	101 **Ru** Ruthenium 44	103 **Rh** Rhodium 45	106 **Pd** Palladium 46	108 **Ag** Silver 47	112 **Cd** Cadmium 48		115 **In** Indium 49	119 **Sn** Tin 50	122 **Sb** Antimony 51	128 **Te** Tellurium 52	127 **I** Iodine 53	131 **Xe** Xenon 54
6	133 **Cs** Caesium 55	137 **Ba** Barium 56	139 **La** Lanthanum 57	179 **Hf** Hafnium 72	181 **Ta** Tantalum 73	184 **W** Tungsten 74	186 **Re** Rhenium 75	190 **Os** Osmium 76	192 **Ir** Iridium 77	195 **Pt** Platinum 78	197 **Au** Gold 79	201 **Hg** Mercury 80		204 **Tl** Thallium 81	207 **Pb** Lead 82	209 **Bi** Bismuth 83	210 **Po** Polonium 84	210 **At** Astatine 85	222 **Rn** Radon 86
7	223 **Fr** Francium 87	226 **Ra** Radium 88	227 **Ac** Actinium 89																

Key

Relative atomic
mass
Symbol
Name
Atomic number

A-Level Chemistry

Topic 1

Physical Chemistry

Topic 1

Section 1 – Atomic Structure

Introduction

The chemical properties of elements depend on their structure and in particular on the arrangement of electrons around the nucleus. The arrangement of electrons in orbitals is linked to the way in which elements are organised in the Periodic Table. Chemists can measure the mass of atoms and molecules to a high degree of accuracy in a mass spectrometer. The principles of operation of a modern mass spectrometer are studied.

1.1.1 – Fundamental particles

As with every aspect of science, our knowledge of chemistry and of the fundamental particles of chemistry have changed and evolved over a long period of time.

For the purposes of A-Level, atoms are made up of three fundamental particles:

- Protons
- Neutrons
- Electrons

These are called sub-atomic particles.

Protons and neutrons are always located in the nucleus of the atom, with the electrons orbiting around them in what are variously called "shells", "orbitals" or "energy levels".

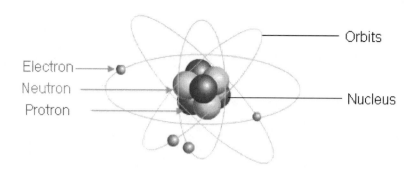

The physical characteristics of these particles are as follows:

Particle	Charge (C)	Mass (kg)	Location
Protons	+ 1.602 x 10-19	1.673 x 10-27	Nucleus
Neutrons	None	1.675 x 10-27	Nucleus
Electrons	- 1.602 x 10-19	0.911 x 10-30	Orbit Around Nucleus

Note that charge (C) is measured in coulombs.

The values for charge and mass in the above table are incredibly small, so they are normally represented as follows:

Particle	Charge	Relative Mass
Protons	+	1
Neutrons	None	1
Electrons	-	1/1840

Activity 1 – How many electrons would be needed to equal the mass of one neutron?

Answer to Activity 1:

The mass of an electron is 1/1840 and therefore you would need 1840 electrons to equal the weight of just one neutron (or, indeed, one proton).

Atoms are complex to draw, particularly when they are large, and there are a great many sub-atomic particles to represent. The illustration of the nitrogen atom below is typical:

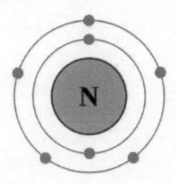

The protons and neutrons are not illustrated (you will see how to calculate their number later) and the electrons are represented as dots in different shells.

1.1.2 – Mass number and isotopes

Protons, Neutrons & Electrons

<u>Electron Shells</u>

As we noted above, electrons orbit the nucleus in one of a number of electron shells. These shells provide order and structure to their movement and location. Ultimately, there can be quite a large number of shells. Consider zinc, for example:

30: Zinc   2,8,18,2

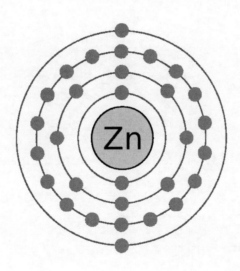

Activity 2 – How many electrons does zinc have, and in how many shells?

Answer to Activity 2:

Zinc has 30 electrons in 4 shells. The outer shell contains 2 electrons.

Electrons orbit the nucleus in what are often described as shells (or orbitals or energy levels). The energy of a shell is directly proportional to the distance from the nucleus. The further away the electron is from the nucleus, the higher the energy level. Each shell can only hold a fixed maximum number of electrons before it becomes full.

The next rule is that lower energy levels fill up with electrons before higher energy ones. This means that the shell closest to the nucleus fills first, then the next one and so on.

If there is an incomplete shell, as frequently there are in atoms, it will be the one furthest from the nucleus.

The shells are often labelled with the letter n before them, so:

- n1 is the closest shell to the nucleus
- n2 is the next closest (and so on)

The following is a table of shell numbers and the number of electrons each shell can hold:

Shell No.	Electrons
1	2
2	8
3	18
4	32

Below is an illustration of the shells and the numbers of electrons they can hold:

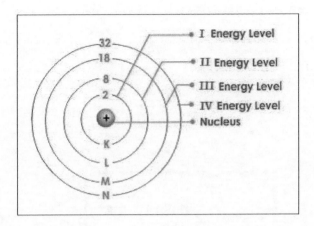

Activity 3 – Look at the illustration of zinc earlier. How many electrons are in its n3 shell?

Mass Number, Atomic Number and Isotopes

There are two basic pieces of data associated with every atom:

- Atomic Number
- Mass Number

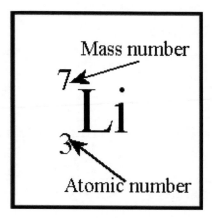

The mass number and the atomic number can sometimes be presented in different places in the Periodic Table. In the illustration above, the mass number is shown above and the atomic number is below. They can also sometimes be the opposite way round (i.e. atomic number on top). Just remember that the mass number is always greater than the atomic number (the exception being hydrogen, where both are 1).

The Atomic Number is the number of protons in the nucleus.

The Atomic Number is also the number of electrons in an Atom.

The Mass Number is the number of protons and neutrons in the nucleus.

Every element in the periodic table has a different atomic number. If you have an unidentified atom which you experiment upon and discover it has 16 protons, you would know that the atomic number was therefore 16, and by looking at the periodic table you could identify it as sulphur.

Activity 4 – Look at the following atom and calculate the number of protons and neutrons that are in its nucleus.

$$\text{mass number} \quad {}^{39}_{19}\text{K} \quad \text{atomic number}$$

Answer to Activity 4:

The element with the symbol K is potassium. Its atomic number is 19, and therefore it has 19 protons.

Its mass number is 39, therefore 39-19 = 20 neutrons.

Remember the mass number = protons + neutrons. Therefore if you know the number of protons (from the atomic number), then calculating the number of neutrons is quite simple.

Isotopes

Isotopes are atoms with the same atomic number but a different mass number than the element; this means that isotopes vary in the number of neutrons they have in the nucleus. Isotopes have the same number of electrons and protons, however; therefore the electrical charge of the isotope is no different from the normal atom.

Consider carbon: its normal mass number (looking at the periodic table) is 12; therefore normal carbon is sometimes called 'carbon-12'. It also has two isotopes, illustrated in the diagram below, called 'carbon-14' and 'carbon-13'.

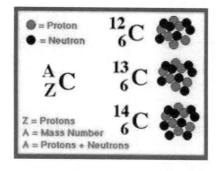

Three important things to remember are that isotopes are:

- Atoms with the same number of protons, but a different number of neutrons
- Isotopes of the same element that react chemically in exactly the same way. For example, carbon-12, carbon-13 and carbon-14 all react in exactly the same way
- Isotopes of the same element differ in atomic mass because of the different number of neutrons in the nucleus

Mass Spectrometry

A time of flight (TOF) mass spectrometer is complex piece of equipment that can measure the relative atomic mass of an atom or the relative molecular mass of a substance.

We use the term "relative" because the mass is relative to the mass of carbon-12; you will learn more about this later in the course.

Carbon-12 is considered to have a mass of EXACTLY 12 (there are no units). No other isotope has an exact whole number as its mass. This is because the mass of protons and neutrons is not exactly 1.

A mass spectrometer can be used by scientists to determine the masses of a given substance, but it also determines the relative amount of that material in the sample. For example, it will tell you if something is 95% carbon, 5% hydrogen. So a sample of an unknown material can be analysed and the machine will determine the constituent parts to that substance, and therefore what it is.

Activity 5 – Can you think of an example where this could be useful?

Answer to Activity 5:

In truth, there are thousands of potential applications for such a piece of technology. One would be in law enforcement to test an unknown substance to see if it is an illegal drug or something harmless. Another would be in a planetary space probe to identify elements in space.

A Time-of-Flight Mass Spectrometer works by accelerating an ionised sample and calculating mass per charge based on how long each 'object' is in flight for. Since every 'object' receives equal force, according to Newton's Second Law, the acceleration of each 'object' will be inversely proportional to its mass.

The sample is first ionised by bombarding it with electrons, which also causes fragmentation to form smaller groups of atoms. Ions tend to have +1 charge since a bombarding electron will knock an electron out of an atom's shell. So 'mass per charge' can generally be taken as simply 'mass'.

The ions are then accelerated by Electromagnetic Field and travel through a vacuum area called the Drift Region, before being detected by the Ion Detector.

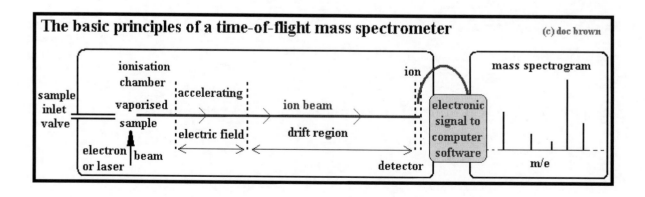

Why Does It Need a Vacuum?

It is important that the ions produced in the ionisation chamber do not have an impact on any air molecules as they pass through the machine, as this would change the results dramatically.

Ionisation Process

The vaporised sample passes into the ionisation chamber where the electrically heated metal coil gives off electrons. These electrons are attracted to the electron trap, which has a positively charged plate.

The particles in the sample, either atoms or molecules, are therefore bombarded with a stream of electrons, and some of the collisions are energetic enough to remove one or more electrons from the sample to produce positively charged ions.

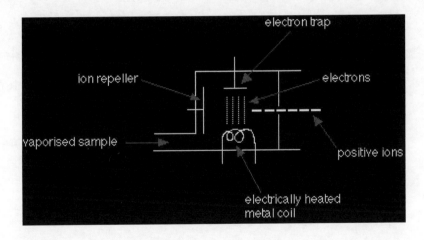

Most of the positive ions formed will carry a charge of 1^+ because it is much more difficult to remove further electrons from an already positive ion; although a small percentage, around 5%, do carry a 2^+ charge.

These ions are then directed out of the ionisation chamber by a "repeller", which is another metal plate carrying a slight positive charge.

Acceleration of the Ion Stream

As the positive ions leave the ionisation chamber, they pass through three slits. These slits have the effect of creating a beam of ions, as those not part of the beam are stopped by the plate that the slits are cut into.

Detection

Only the ions in stream B will reach the detector. When the ions reach the detector, they hit a wall where they collect electrons and are therefore essentially neutralised. Eventually, they are removed from the mass spectrometer by a vacuum pump.

When an ion hits the metal plate at the detector, its charge is neutralised by an electron migrating from the metal onto the ion. That leaves a space amongst the electrons in the metal, and the electrons in the wire that connects to the metal plate move along to fill it.

A flow of electrons in the wire is detected as an electric current, which can be amplified and recorded; the more ions that impact on the detector plate, the greater the current.

Activity 6 – How do you think you know the amount of a substance?

A read out might look like the following:

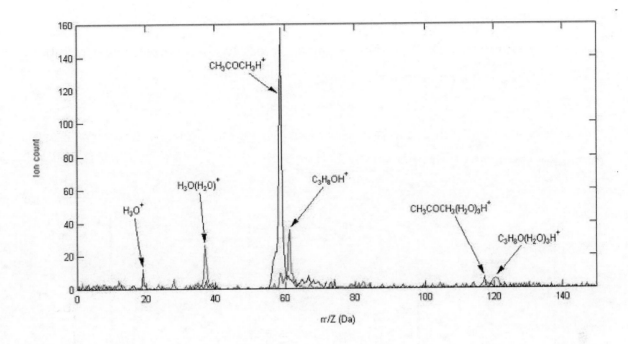

A mass spectrum can be used to identify the isotopes than make up an element. Different isotopes are detected separately in the detector because they have a different mass.

The following is the mass spectrum of a sample of chlorine illustrating two isotopes, Cl^{35} and Cl^{37}, and their relative abundance in the sample:

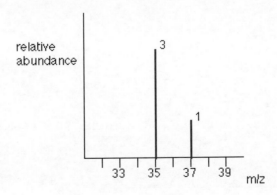

There are two basic types of mass spectrometry:

- High Resolution – Detects relative atomic mass up to 5 decimal places.
- Low Resolution – Detects relative atomic mass to the nearest whole number. This is the more common of the two.

From a mass spectrograph of the isotopes of an element in a sample, we can calculate the relative atomic mass of the sample easily.

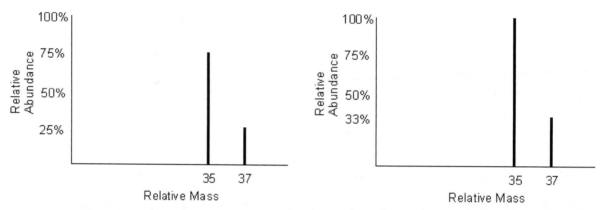

Consider these two graphs for a moment. Sometimes the mass spectrograph will be of the form on the right. In this graph the largest isotope will be adjusted to 100% and the others have their relative abundance adjusted to suit. So we see that Cl^{37} is 33% of the sample. The more typical, and in many ways more useful form, is that on the left. Here we see the following:

- Cl^{35} – 75% of sample
- Cl^{37} – 25% of sample

The relative atomic mass of chlorine in this sample can be calculated as follows:

$$\frac{(75 \times 35) \ + \ (25 \times 37)}{100} = \textbf{35.5}$$

The relative atomic mass for this sample of chlorine is, therefore, 35.5.

Activity 7 – Calculate the relative atomic mass of uranium from the graph.

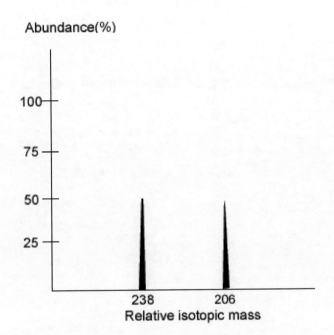

Answer to Activity 7:

$$\frac{(50 \times 238) + (50 \times 206)}{100} = \mathbf{222}$$

The relative atomic mass for the above illustrated sample of uranium would be 222.

1.1.3 – Electron configuration

Electron Arrangement

We must now look at electrons and how they are arranged in greater detail than we did earlier.

Electrons orbit the nucleus in shells, sometimes called energy levels because it takes a different amount of energy to occupy each one.

Each shell can hold a different number of electrons. The closest can contain the fewest, and the number increases with every succeeding shell:

Shell No.	Electrons
1	2
2	8
3	18

Shell three can contain 8 in some circumstances, but don't worry about that. For this course, it contains 18.

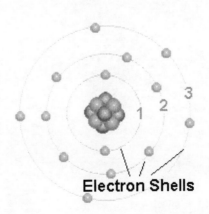

Electron Shells

For A-Level, you need to understand the configuration of electrons up to a total of 36.

Note that you will sometimes see these shells called k, l and m. This tends to be an older notation; we will generally use 1, 2 and 3.

Each shell has a number of subshells within it.

Subshells are labelled:

- s
- p
- d
- f

In terms of the numbers of subshells:

- Shell 1 contains 1 subshell
- Shell 2 contains 2 subshells
- Shell 3 contains 3 subshells

Below is an illustration of the shapes of the orbitals:

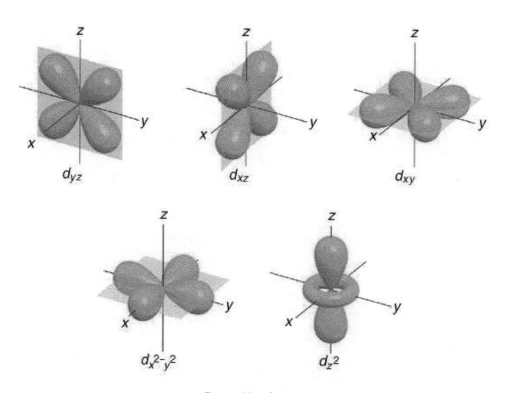

Don't worry too much about the shapes of the orbitals; just remember and understand that the electrons orbit the nucleus in different configurations, each of which has a different energy.

These different orbitals are the subshells.

By means of a recap then, the main shells are called:

- 1
- 2
- 3
- 4

The subshells within those are called:

- s
- p
- d
- f

Not all of the main shells have all of the subshells. This is because the first shell, for example, can only contain 2 electrons and they exist in the first subshell. The first shell contains only 1 subshell.

The illustration below shows the shell and subshell, its relative distance from the nucleus and how many electrons each subshell can contain (in blue text in brackets after the name of the shell).

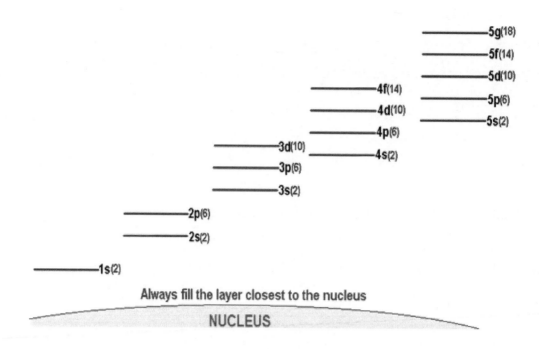

Always fill the layer closest to the nucleus

NUCLEUS

You only need to know about the first 4 shells in this course but be aware that there are more.

- Shell 1 has 1 subshell (1s)
- Shell 2 has 2 subshells (2s & 2p)
- Shell 4 has 4 subshells (4s, 4p, 4d & 4f)

Activity 8 – How many subshells does shell 3 have? Name them.

Answer to Activity 8:

Shell 3 has 3 subshells (3s, 3p & 3d).

Any single sub-orbital can only contain 2 electrons, so:

- Shell 1 contains 1 x s subshell
- Shell 2 contains 1 x s subshell and 3 x p subshells (because it contains 8 electrons in total)
- Shell 3 contains 1 x s subshell, 3 x p subshells and 5 x d subshells (because it contains 18 electrons in total)

Shell number	Maximum Number of Electrons
1	2 ($1s^2$)
2	8 ($2s^2, 2p^6$)
3	18 ($3s^2, 3p^6, 3d^{10}$)
4	32 ($4s^2, 4p^6, 4d^{10}, 4f^{14}$)

Shell (energy level)	1	2		3			4			
Subshells	S	s	p	s	p	d	s	p	d	F
No. of orbitals	1	1	3	1	3	5	1	3	5	7
Total in that subshell	2	2	6	2	6	10	2	6	10	14
Total number of electrons	2	8		18			32			

How these shells and subshells are filled is the next issue to examine.

Shells and subshells with the lowest energy are filled first. This means that the lowest energy level shell is filled first, then the next, and within those, the lowest energy level subshell is filled first.

It is not quite as simple as you might think, however, as, for example, the 4s subshell fills before the 3d subshell. Study the illustration below. It shows the order in which shells and subshells fill, starting with 1s.[1]

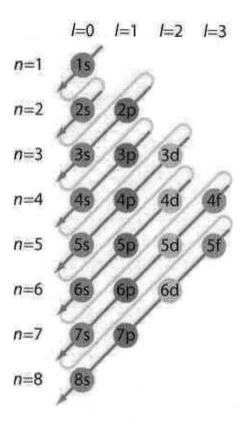

[1] Remember you only need go up to the 4th shell.

Orbitals of the same energy level fill with a single electron before they begin to pair up. These are sometimes illustrated by using arrows to represent the electrons:

Element	Total Electrons	Orbital Diagram					Electron Configuration
		1s	2s	2p		3s	
Li	3	↑↓	↑				$1s^2 2s^1$
Be	4	↑↓	↑↓				$1s^2 2s^2$
B	5	↑↓	↑↓	↑			$1s^2 2s^2 2p^1$
C	6	↑↓	↑↓	↑ ↑			$1s^2 2s^2 2p^2$
N	7	↑↓	↑↓	↑ ↑ ↑			$1s^2 2s^2 2p^3$
Ne	10	↑↓	↑↓	↑↓ ↑↓ ↑↓			$1s^2 2s^2 2p^6$
Na	11	↑↓	↑↓	↑↓ ↑↓ ↑↓		↑	$1s^2 2s^2 2p^6 3s^1$

H (+1)   ↑
          1s

He (+2)   ↑↓   Filled shell, inert gas
          1s

Li (+3)   ↑↓ ↑   Active!
          1s 2s

Be (+4)   ↑↓ ↑↓
          1s 2s

B (+5)   ↑↓ ↑↓ ↑ __ __
          1s 2s 2p

C (+6)   ↑↓ ↑↓ ↑ ↑ __
          1s 2s 2p

N (+7)   ↑↓ ↑↓ ↑ ↑ ↑
          1s 2s 2p

O (+8)   ↑↓ ↑↓ ↑↓ ↑ ↑
          1s 2s 2p

F (+9)   ↑↓ ↑↓ ↑↓ ↑↓ ↑   Active!
          1s 2s 2p

Ne (+10) ↑↓ ↑↓ ↑↓ ↑↓ ↑↓   Stable 2s2p octet, inert gas.
          1s 2s 2p

Na (+11) ↑↓ ↑↓ ↑↓ ↑↓ ↑↓ ↑   __ __   Active!
          1s 2s 2p   3s 3p

Mg (+12) ↑↓ ↑↓ ↑↓ ↑↓ ↑↓ ↑↓ __ __
          1s 2s 2p   3s 3p

Look at nitrogen in the above illustration. There are 3 p subshells and 1 electron in each of them. Oxygen has 1 more electron and there are no more p subshells to begin to fill, so the extra electron will form a pair in one of those three p orbitals.

Shorthand

There is a useful and widely used shorthand method of writing the electron configuration. Let us look at sodium. The electron configuration is:

- $1s^2\ 2s^2\ 2p^6\ 3s^1$

$1s^2$ – This tells us three things:

1 – Refers to shell no. 1
s – Refers to the subshell
^{2} – Refers to the number of electrons in that subshell

$2p^6$ – Tells us:

2 – Refers to shell no. 2
p – Refers to the subshell
^{6} – Refers to the number of electrons in that subshell

Activity 9 – Write out the electronic configuration of calcium (20 electrons) in shorthand.

Answer to Activity 9:

$1s^2$ $2s^2\,2p6$ $3s^2\,3p6$ $4s^2$

If you got this wrong, it is probably because you filled the 3d subshell. The 4s subshell fills before the 3d subshell because it has a lower energy level.

The diagram below is a reminder of how energy levels fill and the order in which they fill.

Follow the arrow that points to 3p; you will see the next energy level it points to (the next that is filled) is 4s, then return to the top and fill 3d.

The order the subshells fill is as follows, remember you only need to learn up to shell 4:

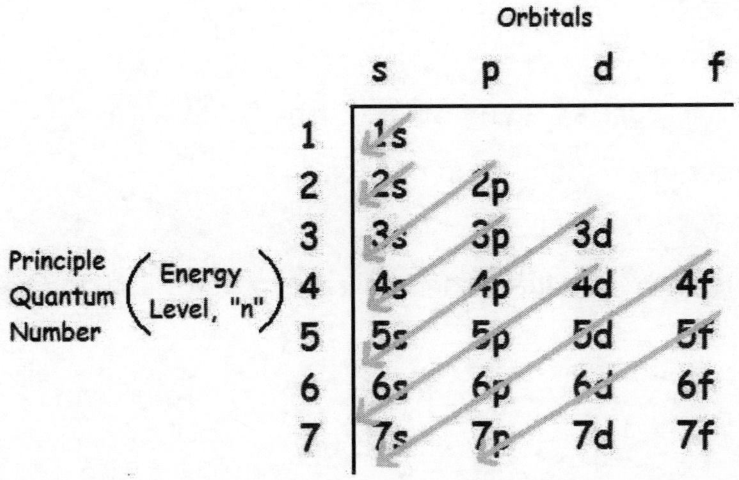

Orbitals

	s	p	d	f
1	1s			
2	2s	2p		
3	3s	3p	3d	
4	4s	4p	4d	4f
5	5s	5p	5d	5f
6	6s	6p	6d	6f
7	7s	7p	7d	7f

Principle Quantum Number (Energy Level, "n")

Order: 1s 2s 2p 3s 3p 4s 3d 4p 5s 4d 5p 6s 4f 5d 6p 7s 5f 6d 7p

Ionisation Energy

Electrons can be removed from atoms by bombarding the atom with a beam of electrons; you might remember that this is what occurs in a mass spectrometer.

If the beam of electrons is fired from something like an electron gun, then the amount of energy it takes to remove electrons from the sample atoms can be measured. This value is called the ionisation energy.

Ionisation energy is the energy required to remove 1 mole of electrons from 1 mole of atoms in the gaseous state. Ionisation energy is measured in kJ mol^{-1}. It is typically abbreviated to IE.

The amount of energy required to remove the first electron can be measured, as can the amount of energy required to remove the second, third etc.

The amount of energy required to remove the first electron is called the first ionisation energy. The amount of energy it takes to remove the second electron from a 1$^+$ ion is called the second ionisation energy.

- The first IE would produce a 1$^+$ ion
- The second IE would produce a 2$^+$ ion from a 1$^+$ ion
- The third IE would produce a 3$^+$ ion from a 2$^+$ ion

It is important that you understand that the second ionisation energy is NOT measured by the following experiment:

$$Na \rightarrow Na^{2+} + 2e^-$$

The second ionisation energy is the energy required to remove the second electron, not the first two, as is occurring in the above equation.

The following is a periodic table showing the trends in ionisation energy:

INCREASING IONIZATION ENERGY

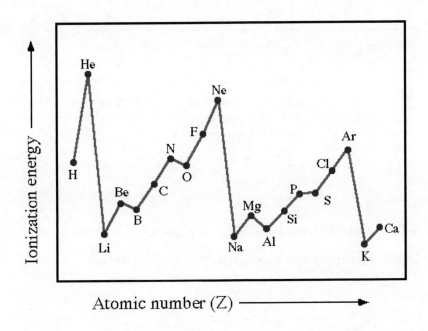

The following shows the relative values for the first 20 elements:

Activity 10 – Draw the equation that would measure the second ionisation energy of iron.

Answer to Activity 10:

$$Fe^+ \rightarrow Fe^{2+} + e^-$$

This equation takes an iron ion with 1 electron removed (hence a 1^+ charge), and removes the second electron.

The shells closest to the nucleus contain the electrons that are hardest to remove (take the most energy) and, generally speaking, the ones furthest from the nucleus take the least energy to remove.

Study the graph below.

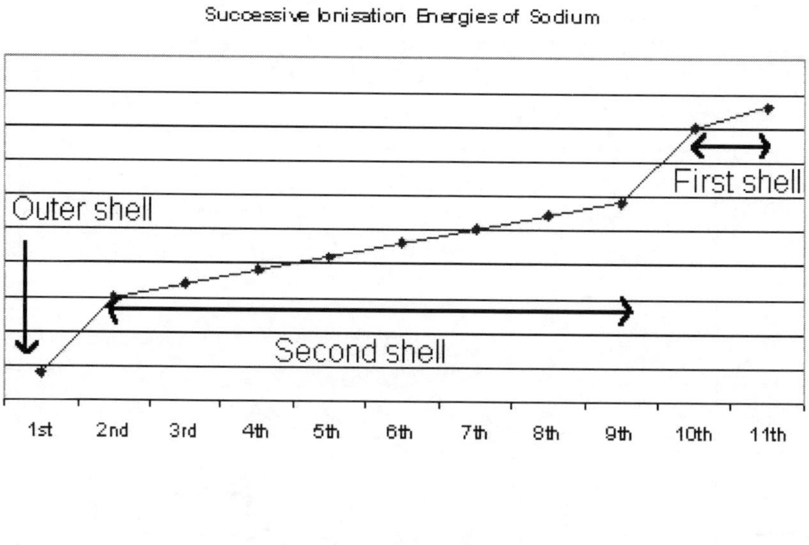

Successive Ionisation Energies of Sodium

Activity 11 – Think about what you know about electron shells and attempt to explain the information in the above graph.

Answer to Activity 11:

The tables suggest the following:

- The 1 electron furthest away from the nucleus is relatively easy to remove, requiring very little energy, because the atomic radius is large and there is a lot of shielding from other electrons between it and the attractive pull of the nucleus.
- The 8 electrons closer to the nucleus are harder to remove (those in shell 2). They are closer to the nucleus, and the atomic radius is reduced.
- The electrons closest to the nucleus are the hardest to remove because of the influence of the positive charge of the nucleus itself.
- As the charge increases, the energy required to remove successive electrons also increases. This is because the additional charge makes it harder to remove successive electrons.

There are always jumps in the amount of energy required to remove electrons as we move between shells, and there is always a steady increase in energy required within a shell. For example, it takes a little more energy to remove the 6th than the 5th electron, despite them both being in shell 2, but there is a great jump between the 9th and 10th electrons, as this moves from the second shell to the first, which is the closest to the nucleus.

Trends in Ionisation Energies

There are trends across a period on the periodic table (periods go from left to right). These trends can tell us about the electrons and which energy levels and subshells they occupy. There is a general increase in IE across the period, but there are slight drops too.

Activity 12 – Look at the table of 1st ionisation energies below and think about why there is a drop in 1st IE between magnesium and aluminium, and then again between phosphorus and sulphur.

Write out the electron configuration. It will help.

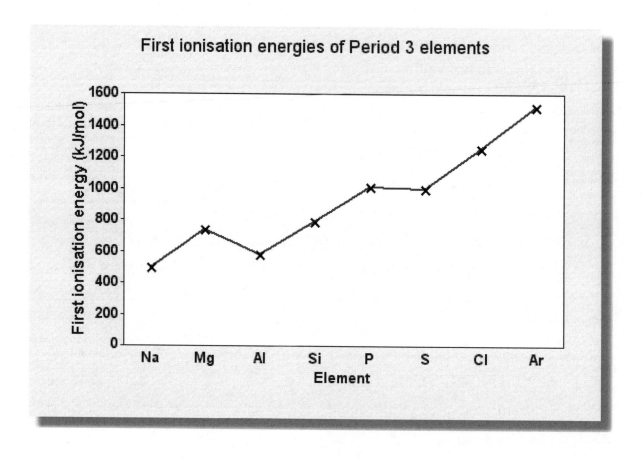

Answer to Activity 12:

Consider the electron configuration of phosphorus and sulphur:

- Phosphorus – $1s^2$ $2s^2$ $2p^6$ $3s^2$ $3p^3$
- Sulphur – $1s^2$ $2s^2$ $2p^6$ $3s^2$ $3p^4$

Now look at their arrangement:

	phosphorus				sulphur		
sub-level				sub-level			
3p	↑	↑	↑	3p	↑↓	↑	↑
3s	↑↓			3s	↑↓		
2p	↑↓	↑↓	↑↓	2p	↑↓	↑↓	↑↓
2s	↑↓			2s	↑↓		
1s	↑↓			1s	↑↓		

With phosphorus, the outermost shell, 3p, contains 3 electrons. Remember that the p subshell can contain 6 electrons, organised in 3 pairs. In the case of phosphorus, they would each be orbiting singly, as they only pair up when they are forced to.

With sulphur, the outer shell, 3p, contains 4 electrons. This means that 2 of those electrons would be paired. Electrons **repel** each other, and therefore a paired electron like this will be slightly easier to remove than one of the single ones from phosphorus. Therefore the 1st IE for sulphur is slightly lower than that of phosphorus.

There is also a trend in IE down a group in the periodic table (down being from top to bottom of a group).

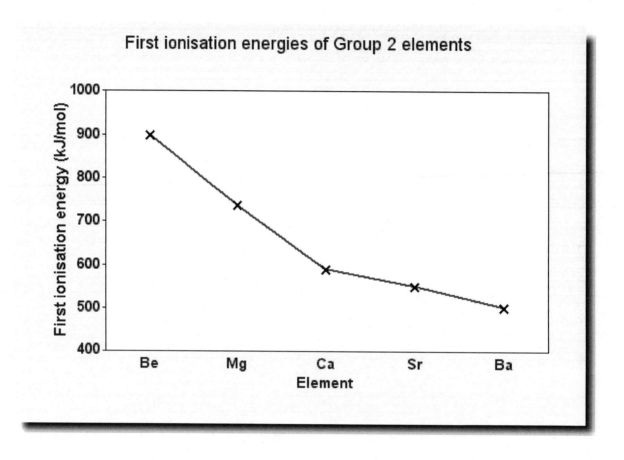

The general trend here is for a decrease in 1st IE as you go down the group.

Activity 13 – Why is there a trend of reducing 1st IE down a group?

Answer to Activity 13:

This trend is partly because the outermost electron is further away from the nucleus with every step down a group (because there are more electrons in more shells as you move down a group). This increase in atomic radius means that the outermost electrons are further away from the attractive influence of the nucleus with each step down a group. Secondly, and connected to this, there are physically more electrons between the outer electron and the nucleus with every step down, increasing the amount of shielding from the nucleus, and reducing the amount of energy it takes to pull the outer electron away.

This trend is the same in any group.

1.2 – Amount of Substance

Introduction

When chemists measure out an amount of a substance, they use an amount in moles. The mole is a useful quantity because one mole of a substance always contains the same number of entities of the substance. An amount in moles can be measured out by mass in grams, by volume in dm^3 of a solution of known concentration and by volume in dm^3 of a gas.

1.2.1 – Relative atomic mass and relative molecular mass.

Relative Atomic Mass

Atoms are so minute that they cannot be measured or weighed with the normal measuring tools; similarly we do not use the normal units of measurement.

Instead of weighing an atom directly, the mass of any given atom is determined by a comparison of its mass to the mass of an atom of carbon-12.

Given that everything is compared against the mass of carbon-12, we assume that carbon-12 has a mass of exactly 12. There are no units of measurement for this as it is a relative weight and not an actual measurement of mass.

Using this system, therefore, an atom with a mass of 6 would be exactly half as heavy as carbon-12, and an atom with a mass of 36 would be exactly three times as heavy as carbon-12.

The most abundant element in the universe is hydrogen, which has a relative atomic mass of 1. It is a simple calculation, therefore, to say that it would take 12 atoms of hydrogen to weigh the same as one atom of carbon. (In this context, when we say carbon, we are referring to carbon-12.)

Relative atomic mass is usually abbreviated to either RAM or Ar.

The atomic mass of the elements shown on many periodic tables is not a whole number; this is because the relative atomic mass of an element is the weighted average mass of all of the isotopes of that element.

A weighted average means that you need to take into account the relative quantities of each different isotope.

For example, carbon actually has three isotopes in different quantities:

- Carbon-12 (the most abundant isotope, and for this reason when we use 'carbon' here we mean 'carbon-12' unless otherwise stated)
- Carbon-13
- Carbon-14

Another example is chlorine, which has two isotopes:

- Chlorine-35
- Chlorine-37

In order to calculate the relative atomic mass of chlorine (the average mass of a sample of chlorine), you cannot simply take the average between the different masses of the isotopes, but you must also take into account the relative abundance of each isotope.

A sample of naturally occurring chlorine would contain the isotopes in the following relative abundances:

- ^{37}Cl – 25%
- ^{35}Cl – 75%

Activity 14 – Calculate the relative atomic mass of chlorine using the above data.

Answer to Activity 14:

From the relative abundance data, we can assume that for every four atoms of chlorine we have, three will be of the ^{35}Cl isotope and one will be of the ^{37}Cl isotope.

Therefore, if we had 100 atoms of chlorine, 75 would be ^{35}Cl and 25 would be ^{37}Cl.

Therefore:

Mass of ^{35}Cl: 75 x 35 = 2625

Mass of ^{37}Cl: 25 x 37 = 925

Total Mass: 2625 + 925 = **3550**

RAM of Cl: $\dfrac{3550}{100}$ = 35.5

The RAM of Chlorine = 35.5

You could look at RAM (or Ar) in two other ways too:

$$Ar = \frac{\text{Average mass of 1 atom of an element}}{1/12^{th}\text{ the mass of an atom of } C^{12}}$$

or

$$Ar = \frac{\text{Average mass of 1 atom of an element x 12}}{\text{Mass of an atom of } C^{12}}$$

Relative Molecular Mass

Molecules are dealt with in the same way as atoms, by comparing them to the mass of C^{12}.

The relative molecular mass (RMM or Mr) of a molecule is the mass of that molecule compared to $1/12^{th}$ the Ar of an atom of C^{12}.

$$Mr = \frac{\text{Average mass of 1 molecule}}{1/12^{th} \text{ the mass of an atom of } C^{12}}$$

or

$$Mr = \frac{\text{Average mass of 1 molecule x 12}}{\text{Mass of an atom of } C^{12}}$$

You can calculate the relative molecular mass of a substance by adding together the relative atomic mass of every atom in the molecule.

Consider methane, for example:

One molecule of methane (CH_4) contains one atom of carbon and four atoms of hydrogen. Its Mr is, therefore, calculated as follows:

Carbon = 12
Hydrogen = 1
Hydrogen = 1
Hydrogen = 1
Hydrogen = 1

Mr of Methane is 12+1+1+1+1 = 16

Consider a more complex molecule, calcium sulphate ($CaSO_4$):

Calcium = 40

Oxygen = 16 (x 4)

Sulphur = 32

Mr of calcium sulphate is 40+16+16+16+16+32 = 136

Activity 15 – Calculate the Mr of calcium hydroxide: $Ca(OH)_2$

Answer to Activity 15:

The Mr of calcium hydroxide is:

Calcium = 40
Oxygen = 16 (x 2)
Hydrogen = 1 (x2)

Mr of calcium hydroxide is 40+16+16+1+1 = 74

The term 'relative formula mass' (RFM) is typically used when looking at ionic compounds, but it is essentially the same as Mr.

1.2.2 – The mole and the Avogadro Constant

Moles

Many students find moles confusing, but a mole is simply a specific mass of a particular substance. You can have a mole of water, half a mole of carbon dioxide or 10 moles of sucrose and so forth. In order to calculate the mass of 1 mole of any substance, first calculate the RFM (relative formula mass) of that substance and add the units of mass (grams). For example:

Calculate the mass of 1 mole of water (H_2O)

First calculate the Mr:

Oxygen = 16
Hydrogen = 1 (x2)

Mr of water: 16+1+1 = 18

1 mole of water would therefore weigh 18g

Calculate the mass of 1 mole of hydrochloric acid (HCl)

First calculate the Mr:

Hydrogen = 1
Chlorine = 35.5

Mr of hydrochloric acid: 1 + 35.5 = 36.5

1 mole of hydrochloric acid would therefore weigh 36.5g

The first stage in molar calculations is always to have the correct formula; if the formula is wrong, you have no chance of a correct calculation.

There are two basic calculations you can make with moles:

1) Calculate the mass of a mole of a substance (as we did above)
2) Calculate the number of moles of a substance in a sample of a measureable mass

If you are unsure of the first, then look back over the previous pages. We will now turn to the second. If you have a given mass of a substance (water, for example), you can work out the number of moles present by applying the following formula:

Number of Moles   =   Mass (g)
                               Mass of 1 Mole (g)

If you had 500g of water, how many moles would there be?

Use the formula just quoted:

Number of Moles of water   =   Mass (g)
                                        Mass of 1 Mole (g)

Therefore:

Number of Moles of water   =   500 g
                                        18g

(NB: 1 mole of water has a mass of 18g)

Therefore:

Number of Moles of water in a 500g sample   =   27.78

Activity 16 – How many moles are there in 1 kg (1000g) of glucose?

Answer to Activity 16:

First of all you need to calculate the RFM of glucose. We did this earlier (calculating RFM that is), but here is a reminder:

Carbon = 12

Hydrogen = 1

Oxygen = 16

RFM of Glucose: (12 x 6) + (1 x 12) + (16 x 6) = 180

Therefore:

1 mole of glucose has a mass of 180g

Then use the formula:

Number of Moles of glucose   =   Mass (g)

                                                    Mass of 1 Mole (g)

Therefore:

Number of Moles of glucose   =   1000g

                                                    180g

Therefore:

Number of Moles of glucose in 1kg   =   5.56

Avogadro Constant

The Avogadro Constant is the number of atoms of carbon in a 12g sample of ^{12}C. The Avogadro Constant is 6.022×10^{23}.

1 mole of ^{12}C would contain 6.022×10^{23} atoms of carbon and have a mass of 12g.

We can say:

- 1 mole of any element will (by definition) contain 6.022×10^{23} atoms
- 1 mole of any compound will (by definition) contain 6.022×10^{23} molecules of that substance

However:

- 1 mole of oxygen would therefore contain 6.022×10^{23} atoms of oxygen (but would have a mass of 16g)
- 1 mole of sodium chloride would contain 6.022×10^{23} molecules of sodium chloride (but would have a mass of 58.5g)
- 1 mole of electrons would contain 6.022×10^{23} electrons

The Avogadro Constant is 6.022×10^{23} and can refer to atoms, molecules, ions or electrons (you will not be expected to remember this number, it will be given in the exam).

1.2.3 – The ideal gas equation

The volume of a given mass of any gas varies with changes in temperature and pressure.

The ideal gas equation defines the relationship between these key physical characteristics for a gas.

In reality, no gas obeys the ideal gas equation exactly, but they are all close to it, especially at room temperature and pressure. For many areas of chemistry, it is useful to imagine a gas that would obey this equation; this would be an ideal gas.

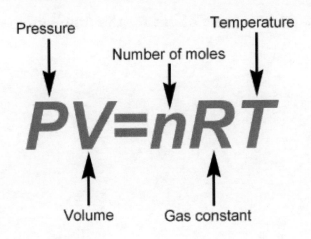

The gas constant = 8.31 $JK^{-1}mol^{-1}$

Units of the ideal gas equation:

- p must be in pascals (Pa) (Nm^{-2})
- V must be in cubic metres (m^3) (1cm^3 is 1 x10^{-6} m^3)
- T must be in Kelvin (K) (just add 273 to the temperature in °C)
- R must be in $JK^{-1}mol^{-1}$ (8.31)
- n = number of moles of gas

Rearranging the equation:

The ideal gas equation can be used to calculate a number of values, including the volume of one mole of gas at any temperature and pressure, if you first rearrange the equation.

The rearranged equation would be:

$$V = \frac{nRT}{p}$$

Activity 17 – Calculate the volume of gas for the following parameters:

- **T = 24°C (297K)**
- **p = 60,000 Pa**
- **n = 1**

Answer to Activity 17:

Use the equation:

$$V = \frac{nRT}{P}$$

Therefore:

$$V = \frac{1 \times 8.31 \times 297}{60,000}$$

V = 0.0411345 m^3

To convert to cm^3 x the answer by 10^6

$$V = 0.0411345 \times 10^6$$

V = 41,135 cm^3

Activity 18 – Now try and calculate the number of moles for the following parameters:

- T = 23°C (296K)
- V = 0.0342 m^3
- p = 82,000 Pa

Answer to Activity 18:

The ideal gas equation is:

$$V = \frac{nRT}{p}$$

This first needs to be rearranged to make n the subject:

$$n = \frac{pV}{RT}$$

Therefore:

$$n = \frac{82,000 \times 0.0342}{8.31 \times 296}$$

$$n = \frac{2804.4}{2459.76}$$

n = 1.14 mol

NB You need to be able to conduct calculations using the ideal gas equation but you will not be expected to remember the value of the gas constant (R) - this will be given to you if needed in the exam.

1.2.4 – Empirical and molecular formula

An empirical formula represents the simplest ratio of the elements in a compound. For example, the formula for glucose is:

- $C_6H_{12}O_6$

But the empirical formula would be:

- CH_2O

The empirical formula tells us that, however large the compound is and whatever the actual formula, for every one carbon atom, it will contain two hydrogen atoms and one oxygen atom.

Therefore:

- $C_8H_{16}O_8$

Will also have the empirical formula:

- CH_2O

Another example:

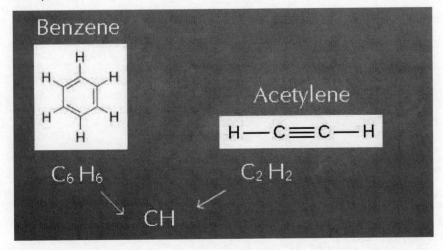

An empirical formula can be calculated by:

- Finding the mass of each element present (by experimentation)
- Calculating the number of moles of each element

$$\text{Moles} = \frac{\text{Mass of element}}{\text{Mass of 1 mol of element}}$$

- Converting the moles of each element into a whole number ratio

Example calculation:

Suppose we react exactly 16g of hydrogen with 128g of oxygen.

You can by now work out the number of moles of each:

No. moles of hydrogen = 16/1 (i.e. mass/Ar)

= 16

No. of moles of oxygen = 128/16

= 8

Ratio of moles reacting together = 16:8 = 2:1

Simplest formula = H$_2$O

Activity 19 – Calculate the empirical formula for a substance containing the following materials:

- C - 80g
- H - 13.34g
- O - 106.66g

Answer to Activity 19:

No. moles of carbon $= \dfrac{80}{12}$

Moles C = 6.67

No. moles of hydrogen $= \dfrac{13.34}{1}$

Moles H = 13.34

No. moles of oxygen $= \dfrac{106.66}{16}$

Moles O = 6.66

Ratio of moles	Carbon	:	Hydrogen	:	Oxygen
	$\dfrac{3.33}{3.33}$	:	$\dfrac{6.67}{3.33}$	:	$\dfrac{3.33}{3.33}$

Ratio of moles	Carbon	:	Hydrogen	:	Oxygen
	1	:	2	:	1

Empirical formula = CH$_2$O

Note that this method also works if you are given percentage composition by mass: just change the grams to % and the calculation is the same.

Molecular Formulae

The molecular formula is the actual formula of the material you are investigating.

For example, as we saw above:

- $C_6H_{12}O_6$ is the molecular formula for glucose
- CH_2O is the empirical formula

Activity 20 - Calculate the empirical formula for a substance containing the following:

- **Carbon – 85.7%**
- **Hydrogen – 14.3%**

Assume you have 100g of the substance.

Answer to Activity 20:

The Ar is equivalent to the atomic weight taken from the periodic table, and is as follows:

- Carbon – 12
- Hydrogen – 1

If we have 100g of substance (whatever that is) then we can work out the empirical formula as follows:

First calculate the mass of each element present:

Carbon: 85.7% of 100g = 85.7g

Hydrogen: 14.3% of 100g = 14.3g

Now calculate the number of moles of each element:

Moles of carbon = 85.7/12

$$= 7.14 \text{ moles}$$

Moles of hydrogen = 14.3/1

$$= 14.3 \text{ moles}$$

Ratio of carbon : hydrogen = 7.14 : 14.3

$$= 1 : 2$$

The empirical formula would therefore be **CH_2**

When we come to study chemical bonding, you will realise that a molecule of CH_2 would be very unstable, and the actual compound is far more likely to be C_2H_4 (ethane) or larger (for example, propene, C_3H_6), as illustrated below:

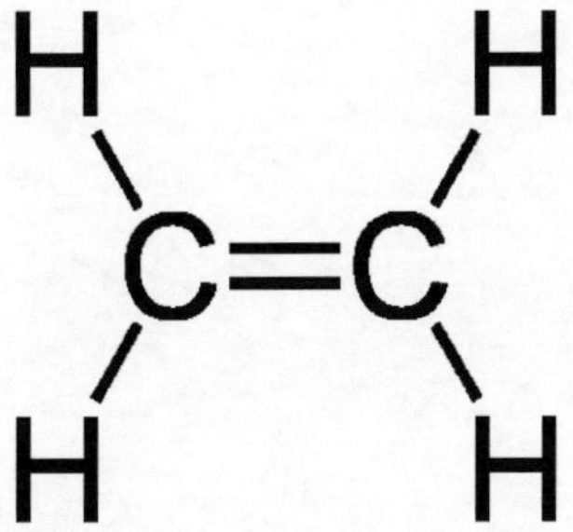

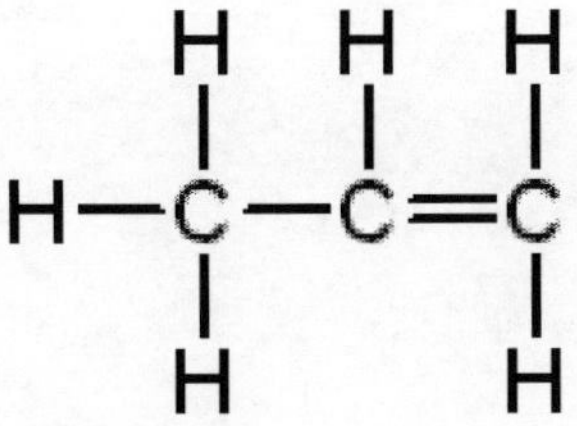

$$\begin{array}{ccc} H & & H \\ \diagdown & & \diagup \\ & C=C & \\ \diagup & & \diagdown \\ H & & H \end{array}$$

$$H-\underset{\underset{H}{|}}{\overset{\overset{H}{|}}{C}}-\underset{\underset{H}{|}}{\overset{\overset{H}{|}}{C}}=\overset{\overset{H}{|}}{\underset{\underset{H}{|}}{C}}$$

1.2.5 – Balanced equations and associated calculations

Over the course of the A-Level, you must become familiar with writing chemical equations. In this section we present an introduction which you can build upon through the remainder of the course.

A chemical equation is a written representation of a chemical reaction.

One of the most basic and important reactions to life on earth is respiration which is the process of converting glucose or other similar organic chemicals into energy. This process is critical in order for the organism to repair itself, to grow, to reproduce and to move. It can be represented as follows:

$$\text{Glucose} + \text{Oxygen} \longrightarrow \text{Carbon Dioxide} + \text{Water} \ (+ \text{Energy})$$

$$C_6H_{12}O_6 + 6O_2 \longrightarrow 6CO_2 + 6H_2O \ (+ \text{Energy})$$

The first equation details the substances that react together, and what they produce, in words. The second is the actual chemical equation, showing the molecules in reaction. This is the type of equation you must become accustomed to using.

The equation shows that one molecule of glucose reacts with 6 molecules of oxygen to produce 6 molecules of carbon dioxide and 6 molecules of water (along with energy).

$$C_6H_{12}O_6 + \mathbf{6}O_2 \longrightarrow \mathbf{6}CO_2 + \mathbf{6}H_2O \ (+ \text{Energy})$$

<u>Balancing Equations</u>

Chemical equations need to be balanced. There needs to be the same amount of every atom on the left of the equation (the chemicals that are reacting together) as there is on the right (the chemicals that you end up with).

You cannot, therefore, have more oxygen at the end of a reaction than at the start, although the oxygen can be in a different form, for example, as carbon dioxide (CO_2).

Consider the equation for the combustion of methane:

$$CH_4 + 2O_2 \longrightarrow CO_2 + 2H_2O$$

On the left, we have:

- 1 atom of carbon
- 4 atoms of hydrogen
- 4 atoms of oxygen (remember 1 molecule of oxygen is made up of 2 atoms, and there are 2 molecules)

On the right of the equation, we have:

- 1 atom of carbon
- 4 atoms of oxygen (2 in CO_2 and 2 in $2H_2O$)
- 4 atoms of hydrogen

Add up what we have on the left and on the right and you will see that there are the same number of atoms of each element, even though the oxygen that we had at the start is now combined with carbon and hydrogen to make carbon dioxide and water.

This equation is balanced.

Activity 21 – Are the following equations balanced?

$$Fe + Cl_2 \longrightarrow FeCl_3$$

$$Zn + HCl \longrightarrow ZnCl_2 + H_2$$

$$Cu + AgNO_3 \longrightarrow Cu(NO_3)_2 + Ag$$

If not, how might they become balanced?

Answer to Activity 21:

They are obviously not balanced. The first equation has too much chlorine on the right hand side. The second one has too much chlorine and hydrogen on the right hand side. The third has too much nitrogen and oxygen (NO_3) on the right hand side.

You need to balance equations by adding to the number of molecules on either side until the total number of atoms of every substance is equal on each side.

The above equations can be balanced as follows:

$$2Fe + 3Cl_2 \longrightarrow 2FeCl_3$$

$$Zn + 2HCl \longrightarrow ZnCl_2 + H_2$$

$$Cu + 2AgNO_3 \longrightarrow Cu(NO_3)_2 + 2Ag$$

You will become a lot more familiar with these throughout this course: just make sure you are aware of the concept of balancing equations.

Ionic Equations

In some instances, we can simplify an equation by considering the ions that are present. Sometimes there are ions that do not take part in the overall reaction. When an acid reacts with an alkali, the product is always a salt and water.

Consider the following reaction:

$$HCl(aq) + NaOH(aq) \rightarrow NaCl(aq) + H_2O(l)$$

The ions present, given the aqueous solutions, would be:

From HCl:

- H^+
- Cl^-

From NaOH:

- Na^+
- OH^-

From NaCl:

- Na^+
- Cl^-

We should write out the ions on each side of the equation to demonstrate which are on both sides:

$$H^+_{(aq)} + Cl^-_{(aq)} + Na^+_{(aq)} + OH^-_{(aq)} \rightarrow Na^+_{(aq)} + Cl^-_{(aq)} + H_2O_{(l)}$$

We can see that there are both Na^+ and Cl^- ions on either side of the equation; we can assume, therefore, that they take no meaningful part in the reaction. For this reason, they are often called spectator ions.

Symbols Indicating State

You should now be starting to understand chemical equations and be happy with the concept of balancing them, ensuring that you have the same number of atoms of every element at the end of the reaction as you had at the beginning of the reaction.

We can add to the chemical equations one other piece of information: the state of the material. State refers to what form that material takes, i.e.:

- Liquid (l)
- Gas (g)
- Solid (s)
- Aqueous solution (aq)

You will be familiar with the solid, liquid and gas states, but perhaps not the aqueous solution. An aqueous solution occurs when a substance is in a solution, with water being the solvent.

State symbols are not always written in chemical equations, but when they are, they occur after the molecules they refer to. For example:

$$2NaOH(aq) + FeCl_2(aq) \rightarrow 2NaCl(aq) + Fe(OH)_2(s)$$

For the exams, you should include them where you can.

Calculations

We can use balanced equations to calculate the amount of product that is produced in a given reaction. For example:

Consider the reaction between magnesium and excess hydrochloric acid.

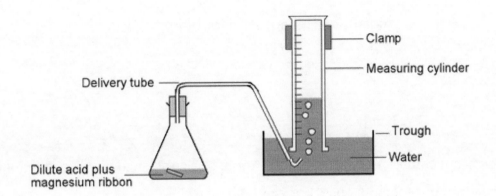

If we have the following conditions:

- 0.5g magnesium
- 26^{0}C (299K)
- 92,000 kPa

First, look at the periodic table for the atomic weight of the reacting materials.

- Mg = 24.3
- H = 1
- Cl = 35.5

Then work out the equation for the reaction that is occurring:

$$Mg(s) + HCl(aq) \rightarrow MgCl_2(aq) + H_2(g)$$

Activity 22 – Balance the above equation.

Answer to Activity 22:

$$Mg(s) + 2HCl(aq) \rightarrow MgCl_2(aq) + H_2(g)$$

Next, consider the number of moles that are involved in the reaction:

$$Mg(s) + 2HCl(aq) \rightarrow MgCl_2(aq) + H_2(g)$$

Moles =	1	2	1	1

We know from earlier in the course that 1 mole of a substance has a mass equal to the atomic weight of that substance. For example:

A mole of magnesium = 24.3g because the Ar of magnesium is 24.3 (and you know this by looking at the periodic table)

In this experiment we have 0.5g of magnesium, therefore:

$$\text{Mol Mg} = \frac{0.5}{24.3}$$

Mol = 0.0206

So we know that there are only 0.0206 moles of magnesium taking part in our reaction.

The chemical equation for the reaction tells us that:

- 1 mol Mg reacts to form 1 mol H_2

We know, therefore:

- 0.0206 mol Mg must react to produce 0.0206 mol H_2

The next part is to calculate the volume of gas using the ideal gas equation:

$$Mg(s) + 2HCl(aq) \rightarrow MgCl_2(aq) + H_2(g)$$

$$V = \frac{nRT}{p}$$

Remember that R is a constant $= 8.31 JK^{-1}mol^{-1}$

T was one of our parameters at the start $= 299K$

Using the ideal gas equation then, we can calculate the volume of gas produced by the reaction:

$$V = \frac{nRT}{p}$$

$$V = \frac{0.0206 \times 8.31 \times 299}{92,000}$$

$$V = 0.000556 \ m^3$$

$$V = 556 \ cm^3$$

Concentrations from Titrations

Titrations can be conducted to calculate the concentration of a solution. For example, we can react an acid with an alkali.

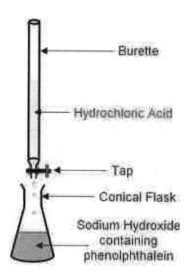

We would need to know two things before we start:

- The concentration of the acid
- The chemical equation for the reaction

A titration experiment is conducted in a series of steps:

- Fill the burette with an acid of known concentration
- Measure accurately the amount of alkali using a Volumetric Pipette
- Add the alkali to a conical flask
- Add a few drops of a suitable indicator solution
- Record the starting volume and then add the acid to the alkali until the indicator solution changes colour. Record the volume of acid used
- Repeat the experiment until you get two concordant results

Titration calculation:

Consider a titration experiment to calculate the concentration of sodium hydroxide using hydrochloric acid. The parameters are as follows:

- 38.00cm^3 sodium hydroxide
- 27.00cm^3 hydrochloric acid
- HCl concentration was 0.14 mol dm^{-3}

First, write the balanced chemical equation for the reaction:

$$NaOH(aq) + HCl(aq) \rightarrow NaCl(aq) + H_2O(l)$$

Then look at the number of moles involved in the reaction:

$$NaOH(aq) + HCl(aq) \rightarrow NaCl(aq) + H_2O(l)$$

Moles =   1   1   1   1

We know, therefore, that in this reaction 1 mole of acid will react with 1 mole of alkali to produce 1 mole of product.

$$\text{No. mol in solution} = \frac{M \times V}{1000}$$

Therefore:

$$\text{No. mol HCl} = \frac{27.00 \times 0.14}{1000}$$

We know that no. mol NaOH = no. mol HCl

We must, therefore, have $\frac{27 \times 0.14}{1000}$ mol of NaOH in the $38cm^3$ NaOH solution

Note that the concentration of a solution is the number of moles in $1000cm^3$.

Therefore the concentration of the alkali $= \frac{27 \times 0.14}{1000} \times \frac{1000}{38}$

$= 0.00378 \times 26.32$

= 0.0995 mol dm^{-3}

Atom Economy and Percentage Yield

When we have a balanced equation for a particular chemical reaction, we can calculate the theoretical amount of product that can be produced from the reaction; this is the yield.

It is only ever theoretical because in the real world other things interfere and you seldom get your maximum theoretical yield.

There are many reasons for this. For example, there may be impurities, or the temperature or pressure may not be perfect.

Atom Economy

The atom economy can be calculated directly from the balanced equation. It is:

% Atom economy = Mass of desired product x 100
                        Total mass of reactants

It is important to note that the mass of DESIRED product is used in the calculation; any unwanted by-products must be ignored if the calculation is to be accurate.

Consider the following industrial process:

Sodium hydroxide is reacted with chlorine to produce sodium chlorate (NaOCl, this is household bleach). A number of unwanted by-products are also produced.

The chemical equation for the reaction is:

$$2NaOH + Cl_2 \rightarrow NaCl + H_2O + NaOCl$$

Moles =   2   1   1   1   1

Activity 23 – Calculate the mass of substance involved in the reaction. Use the number of moles as your starting point.

Answer to Activity 23:

Calculate the atomic weight for each of the reactants from the information on the periodic table.

$$2NaOH + Cl_2 \rightarrow NaCl + H_2O + NaOCl$$

Mr (therefore weight)   40g   71g   58.5g   18g   74.5g

Remember to take into account the number of moles. Therefore the mass involved in the reaction is:

$$2NaOH + Cl_2 \rightarrow NaCl + H_2O + NaOCl$$

Mr   80g   71g   58.5g   18g   74.5g

Now, calculate the atom economy:

% Atom economy = $\dfrac{\text{Mass of desired product}}{\text{Total mass of reactants}} \times 100$

Remembering that sodium chlorate is the only desired product, therefore:

% Atom economy = $\dfrac{74.5}{151} \times 100$

= 49.3%

This figure tells us that only 49.3% of the reactants produce product, the rest is essentially wasted as unwanted by-product (which may be useable for something else, of course).

Activity 24 – Calculate the % atom economy for the following reaction (ethene being the desired product):

$$C_2H_5OH \longrightarrow C_2H_4 + H_2O$$

Answer to Activity 24:

$$C_2H_5OH \rightarrow C_2H_4 + H_2O$$

Moles	1	1	1
Mr	46g	28g	18g

% Atom economy = $\dfrac{\text{Mass of desired product}}{\text{Total mass of reactants}}$ x 100

Atom economy = $\dfrac{28}{46}$ x 100

= 60.9%

Yield of a Reaction

The yield of a reaction is different from the atom economy because:

- atom economy is the proportion of reactants that are converted into useful products, rather than waste products
- yield is the actual amount of product produced in real life situations

Again we need to know the reaction that is occurring, but as long as we know the equation accurately, we can calculate the amount of product that we should get from a given amount of reactants if the reaction runs to completion (i.e. if all of the reactants are used in the process).

Consider the laboratory reaction between potassium iodide and lead nitrate:

$$2KI(aq) + Pb(NO_3)_2(aq) \rightarrow PbI_2(s) + 2KNO_3(aq)$$

Moles	2	1	1	2
Mr	332g	331.2g	461g	202.2g

If we react:

- 13.28g of KI with
- 13.24g $Pb(NO_3)_2$

we should produce:

- 18.44g PbI_2

In reality, not all of the reactants would react. Some would be left in the beaker or on the filter paper that you use to separate out the solid lead iodide. The reaction, therefore, is not 100% efficient.

$$\% \text{ Yield} = \frac{\text{No. moles of product}}{\text{Theoretical max. no. moles of product}} \times 100$$

Or:

$$\% \text{ Yield} = \frac{\text{Mass of product}}{\text{Theoretical max. mass of product}} \times 100$$

Activity 25 – If you had produced 10.2g of solid lead iodide from your laboratory reaction, what would be the % yield?

Answer to Activity 25:

Remember that:

% Yield = $\dfrac{\text{Actual yield}}{\text{Theoretical yield}}$ x 100

Or:

% Yield = $\dfrac{\text{Mass of product (actual yield)}}{\text{Max. mass of product (theoretical yield)}}$ x 100

Therefore:

Yield = $\dfrac{10.2}{18.44}$ x 100

Yield = 55.31%

Required Practical 1:

Make up a volumetric solution and carry out a simple acid-base titration.

1.3 - Bonding

The physical and chemical properties of compounds depend on the way in which the compounds are held together by chemical bonds and by intermolecular forces. Theories of bonding explain how atoms or ions are held together in these structures. Materials scientists use knowledge of structure and bonding to engineer new materials with desirable properties. These new materials may offer new applications in a range of different modern technologies.

1.3.1 – Ionic bonding

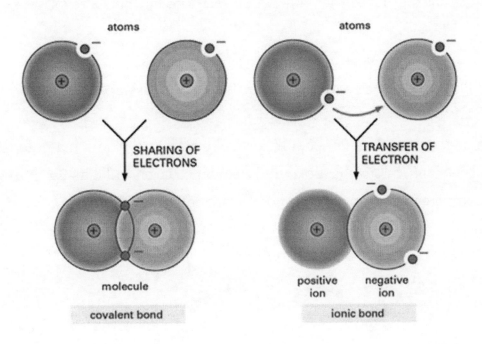

Metals have either 1, 2 or 3 electrons in their outer shells. The easiest way for them to form full shells is to lose these outer electrons. An ionic bond is formed when one atom loses an electron(s) and another atom gains that electron(s).

- Ionic bonds occur between metals and non-metals
- Electrons are transferred from the metal to the non-metal
- Ions are formed, both positive and negative

Consider the reaction between sodium (metal) and chlorine (non-metal):

First, you must identify these two elements on the periodic table and determine how many electrons they have. Then draw these electrons into shells as follows:

- Sodium has 11 electrons arranged $1s^2, 2s^2, 2p^6, 3s^1$
- Chlorine has 17 electrons arranged $1s^2, 2s^2, 2p^6, 3s^2, 3p^5$

Sodium, therefore, will be looking to lose an electron to gain a full outer shell (the second shell) and chlorine is looking to gain an electron to fill its 3p subshell. Thus, these atoms create the perfect situation for an ionic bond.

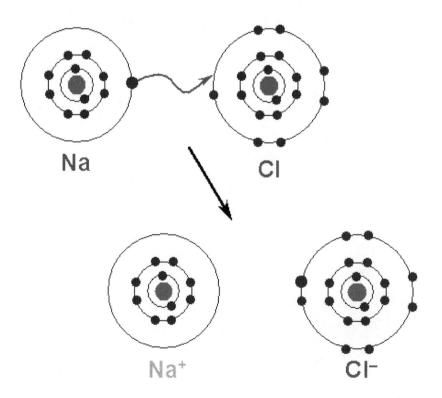

Sodium loses an electron, which is transferred to chlorine. The resulting ions Na$^+$ and Cl$^-$ form a very strong electrostatic ionic bond.

- The sodium ion is positively charged because it has lost a negatively charged electron
- The chlorine ion is negatively charged because it has gained a negatively charged electron

An ionic bond is the result of electrostatic attraction between oppositely charged ions in a lattice.

Properties of ionic bonds:

- Solid at room temperature
- Giant structures
- High melting points
- Electrically conductive when in solution or molten, but not whilst in solid state
- Ionic compounds are brittle solids

You will learn more about their structures later in this course.

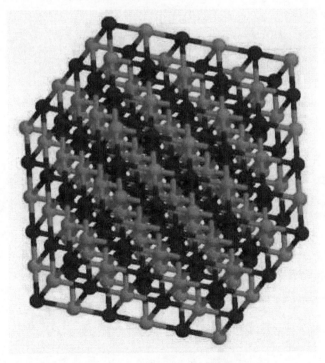

You also need to be aware of the formulae for some common compound ions:

Sulphate:

SO_4^{2-}

Hydroxide:

OH^-

Nitrate:

NO_3^-

Carbonate:

CO_3^-

Ammonium: NH_4^+

1.3.2 – Nature of covalent and dative covalent bonds

<u>Covalent Bonding</u>

In ionic bonding, we described the bond as electrostatic, which is to say that there is a strong electrical attraction between positively and negatively charged ions.

All bonds that hold chemicals together are electrostatic in nature, but in a covalent bond the electrostatic attraction occurs between the positively charged nucleus of each atom and a pair (or more than one pair) of shared negatively charged electrons.

The sharing of a single pair of electrons is called a single bond, but there are double and triple bonds where two or three pairs of electrons are shared.

Consider the simplest atom, hydrogen. It contains a single electron. In order to fill its first shell, it needs to acquire an electron. It can do this by sharing its electron with another hydrogen atom to form H_2:

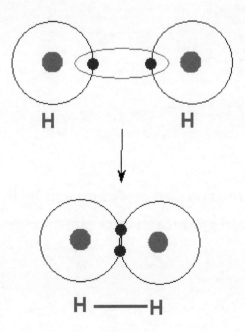

Consider also, chlorine. From the periodic table, you will see that a chlorine atom has 17 electrons.

These electrons are arranged (ignoring subshells for the moment):

- 2, 8, 7

To form stable substances, it needs an extra electron in its outer shell. In order to achieve this, it can react with another chlorine atom and share one of its outer electrons, thus forming a shared pair:

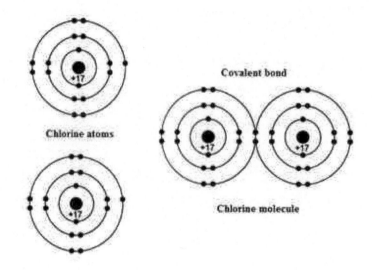

Chlorine atoms

Covalent bond

Chlorine molecule

Activity 26 – Consider the reaction of carbon and hydrogen. Draw the covalent bonds that would form to produce a stable substance (methane).

Answer to Activity 26:

Methane

Chemical formula: CH_4

Electrons:

- Hydrogen: 1
- Carbon: 2, 4

Carbon needs 4 electrons to fill its outer shell and will form a covalent bond with 4 atoms of hydrogen in order to do this.

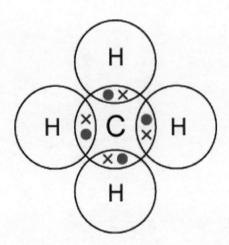

Activity 27 – How can nitrogen become a stable compound by reacting with another nitrogen atom? Draw the resulting structure.

Answer to Activity 27:

Nitrogen in its most stable form is N_2 (diatomic nitrogen)

Electrons in nitrogen:

- Nitrogen: 2,5

Nitrogen needs 3 electrons to fill its outer shell, and will in this case form a covalent bond with another nitrogen atom.

We mentioned earlier that covalent bonds could involve more than a single pair, and could be double or triple bonds. In this case, there is a triple covalent bond to form stable N_2.

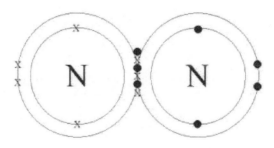

Properties of covalently bonded substances:

- Unless the substance is a Giant Covalent Structure, they are either gases, liquids or solids with low melting and boiling points (because there is only weak attraction between molecules)
- Poor conductors of electricity
- Solutions do not conduct electricity

Coordinate Bonding

A covalent bond consists of the sharing of a pair (or more than one pair) of electrons, with a single electron being provided by each atom forming the bond.

In some cases, however, one of the atoms can provide both electrons to the covalent bond; this is called a coordinate bond, or sometimes a dative covalent bond.

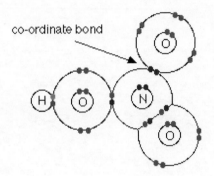

In the above illustration, the nitrogen atom provides both electrons to the bond with one of the oxygen atoms. This bond is, therefore, a coordinate bond.

1.3.3 Metallic bonding

Most metals are solids at room temperature (mercury being an obvious exception) and are hard. They also tend to have high melting points, which are a result of the strong bonds within the structure, holding the atoms together.

A metal is similar in structure to graphite. Every atom (or ion) in the metal has a spare electron in its outer shell. In the solid state, this outer electron is free to move around the structure. As it does this, it is described as being 'delocalised'. A metallic crystal, therefore, is a structure of atoms surrounded by delocalised electrons.

In a metallic crystal, the electrons are free to travel throughout the structure. That is why it is called a 'sea' of delocalised electrons; every atom/ion will provide an electron to this sea. This sea of delocalised electrons allows metals to conduct electricity.

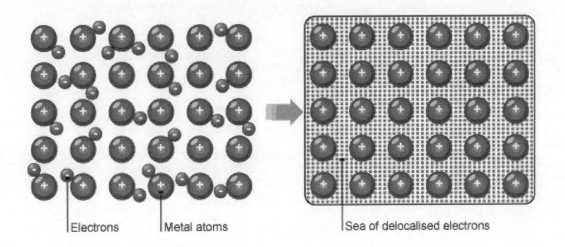

Electrons   Metal atoms   Sea of delocalised electrons

Most metallic elements, when in the solid state, will provide one electron to the sea, but not all. Some will provide two, but the effect is the same: the creation of a sea of delocalised electrons around the stable atoms/ions. Remember that the structure of a metal is regular, much like that depicted below:

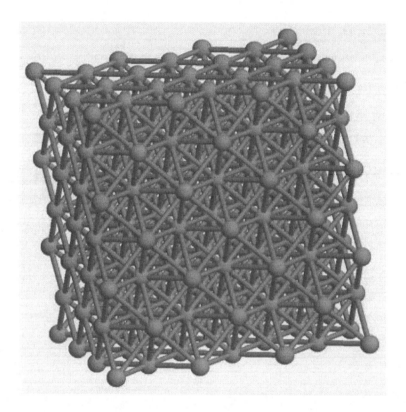

Metals tend to be malleable. If a force is applied to a metal it will become misshapen, but then return to its original shape when the force is removed. Metals, therefore, have some elastic properties.

Consider a building made from steel reinforced concrete; large skyscrapers sway slightly in strong winds, but they return to their original shape when the force of the wind is removed.

If a much larger force is applied, however, the shape of the sample of metal can change permanently. Metals can be worked into many shapes, from wire to car bodies, for example.

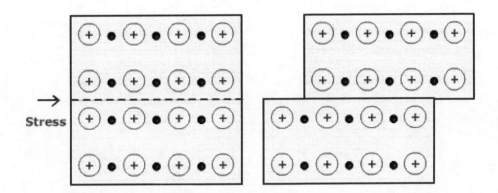

The change in the shape of a metal is brought about because the force that is applied is strong enough that it will cause some of the particles in the structure to permanently slide past their neighbours.

The regularity of the structure of metal makes this easier. This would not happen in diamond, for example, as the atoms of carbon are far too interconnected and could not slide past one another in this way.

1.3.4 – Bonding and physical properties

Ionic Crystals

All ionic compounds exist as giant, three-dimensional crystalline lattices of tightly packed, and well ordered, positive and negative ions. The sodium chloride lattice is represented below:

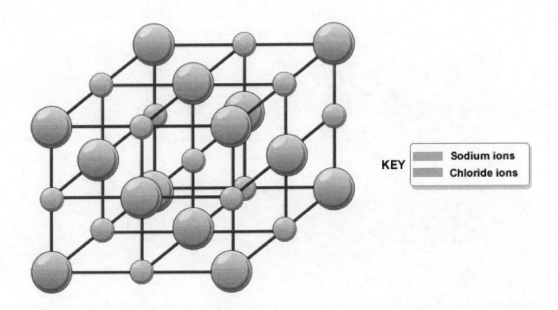

These three-dimensional lattices are not molecules. Molecules always have a fixed number of every atom; the size of an ionic lattice varies, and it depends on the amount of material present (i.e., 5g or 5kg of the same ionic compound will produce a different size lattice).

The lattice is held together by the electrostatic attraction of the different ions. This attraction is very strong, as with a single lithium chloride molecule, and can lead to structures that are very hard and have very high melting and boiling points.

You are expected to be able to draw a three-dimensional representation of this compound, showing the sodium and chloride ions.

Metallic Crystals

We already looked at these earlier in the course, but by way of a reminder:

Metals exist as a lattice of positive ions in a sea of delocalised electrons. The attraction of positive to negative exists throughout the lattice. Metals generally have a high melting point, and this is a result of these strong metallic bonds.

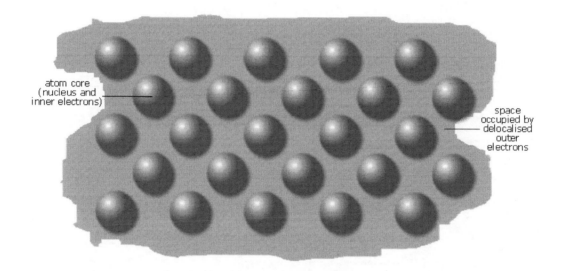

Remember that the structure of a metal is regular, much like that depicted below:

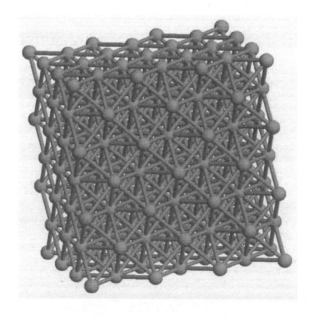

Molecular Crystals

Molecular crystals consist of molecules held in a regular structure by one or more of the three types of intermolecular forces.

In molecular crystals, covalent bonds within the molecules hold the atoms together, but they do not act between the molecules.

Given that intermolecular forces are much weaker than covalent, ionic or metallic bonds, molecular crystals have low melting points and low enthalpies of fusion (this is the energy required to change the state of a substance from a solid to a liquid).

Molecular crystals (of which iodine, I_2, is a good example) generally have the following properties:

- Crystals that are soft and easy to break apart
- Low melting points
- Often sublime to form gases, particularly true in the case of I_2
- They do not conduct electricity

Macromolecular Crystals

These are formed in substances with large molecules where the covalent bonds extend throughout the compounds, creating a giant structure held together by strong bonds. Macromolecular structures generally have high melting points.

Activity 29 – In your own words, describe the three intermolecular forces.

<u>Diamond & Graphite</u>

Some molecules are very simple structures, others are huge and complex.

Molecules always contain a fixed number of atoms bonded together, either by ionic or covalent bonds. Many of these are small but some can be very large indeed, like DNA or some rubbers and plastics (collectively called polymers: more on these later). However big the molecule, it will have a specific number of atoms.

Having said this, giant structures can exist where the number of atoms (or ions) is not fixed. One such substance is diamond. Diamond is pure carbon; that is to say, it only contains carbon. In diamond, each carbon atom is bonded with 4 other carbon atoms to form a tetrahedral structure.

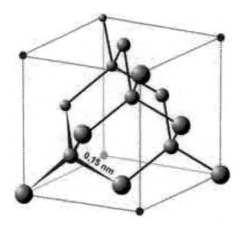

This structure can become enormous because each individual carbon atom continues to seek a stable outer shell and therefore continues to form bonds with other carbon atoms. When a new carbon atom bonds with the existing structure, then 3 bonding locations become available (remember that carbon needs 4 electrons to complete its outer shell, therefore it can make up to 4 bonds).

The structure can become vast as a result, but it is not a molecule, as the number of atoms is not fixed or constant.

In terms of physical properties, diamonds are extremely hard with a very high melting point. These properties are the result of the very strong carbon-carbon covalent bond that forms the basis of the structure. The fact that every bond in the structure is this identical carbon-carbon bond makes its properties even more remarkable.

This property of hardness can be utilised in industry, in diamond tipped drills or saw blades, for example.

Diamonds do not conduct electricity. This is because the electrons are tightly held together and there is no freedom of movement of electrons (electricity is essentially the movement of electrons).

Diamond also cannot be dissolved by any solvent yet discovered. In order for a diamond to dissolve, its carbon-carbon bonds would have to be broken, and they are simply too strong for this to happen.

Graphite is rather different to diamond. It is the same in that it is entirely carbon, but its structure, and therefore its properties, are completely different. Instead of a three-dimensional carbon-carbon lattice, as in diamond, graphite is a series of carbon layers.

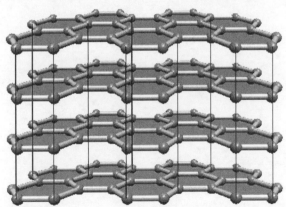

Imagine a great many sheets of paper stacked one on top of the other: graphite is much the same. Any individual layer of graphite is very strong because of the carbon-carbon bond, but the layers can be separated easily. This is because the forces holding those layers together (Van der Waals bonds) are very weak. The result is that graphite is a very soft material.

Graphite is so soft that it has something of a greasy feel, and can be used as a dry lubricant. Graphite only becomes harder if it is mixed with something, e.g. graphite can be mixed with clay in order to form the substance (known as graphite) that we use in pencils.

Graphite, like diamond, has a very high melting point and is similarly insoluble. This is because, although the layers can easily be separated, the bonds between the carbon atoms are still very strong.

Unlike diamond, graphite conducts electricity. This is because in graphite each carbon atom is only bonded with 3 others. You already know that carbon requires 4 extra electrons to be stable, and each of these 3 bonds are single bonds, so how is graphite stable if every carbon atom has one space remaining in its outer shell? The answer is not immediately obvious, but all those spare electrons have a degree of freedom and travel throughout each layer. This free movement of electrons is what allows graphite to conduct electricity.

For A-Level chemistry, you need to be aware of the structures of the following:

- Ice
- Graphite
- Diamond
- Sodium chloride
- Magnesium
- Iodine

We have looked at the first three already, we will now briefly look at the remaining three structures.

Sodium Chloride

Sodium chloride forms an ionic crystal structure with strong electrostatic attractions between the Na^+ and Cl^- ions.

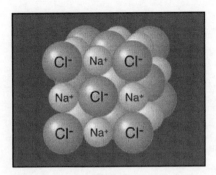

Magnesium

This forms a metallic crystalline structure, as it is a lattice of positive ions that exist within a sea of delocalised electrons.

Iodine

This forms a molecular crystal structure, as the iodine atoms are covalently bonded, and weak intermolecular forces hold the molecules together in a crystalline structure.

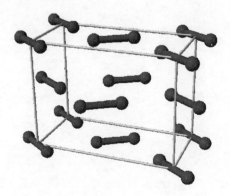

1.3.5 – Shapes of simple molecules and ions

We can predict the shape of a simple molecule that is composed of covalent bonds by understanding a couple of important points:

- Each pair of electrons will repel all other pairs of electrons (because of the negative charge)
- Given this, each pair of electrons will take up a position as far apart from all other electrons as they can get

This is the basis of electron pair repulsion theory.

As you know, electron pairs can exist as:

- shared pairs
- lone pairs

This is illustrated in ammonia below:

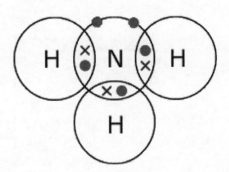

This shows that the nitrogen atom in ammonia has a lone pair (not bonded with anything) and three shared pairs of electrons (bonded with the hydrogen atoms).

Bond Angles in Substances with Shared Pairs of Electrons

Different molecules have different bond angles, and we will not examine these. The basic shapes for molecules are as follows:

Linear	2 pairs	$180°$
Trigonal planar	3 pairs	$120°$
Tetrahedral	4 pairs	$109°28'$
Trigonal bipyramidal	5 pairs	$90°$ $120°$
Octahedral	6 pairs	$90°$

© scienceaid.co.uk

For the purposes of the exam, you should quote the tetrahedral structure as having a bond angle of 109.5°.

Two Pairs of Electrons

If there are two pairs of electrons in the outer shell of an atom, they will push the other as far away from themselves as possible. They will, therefore, exist on opposite sides of an atom. For example, beryllium chloride:

Linear   2 pairs 180° —X—

Three Pairs of Electrons

A substance with three pairs of electrons would exist in a trigonal planar structure. For example, nitrogen trioxide:

Trigonal   3 pairs 120° X
planar

Four Pairs of Electrons

A substance with four pairs of shared electrons would take up a tetrahedral structure, for example, methane. For the purposes of the exam, you should quote this as 109.5°.

Tetrahedral   4 pairs $109^\circ 28'$ X

Five Pairs of Electrons

A substance with five pairs of shared electrons would adopt a trigonal bipyramidal structure. For example, phosphorous pentafluoride:

Trigonal   5 pairs
bipyramidal

90°

X   120°

Six Pairs of Electrons

A substance with six pairs of electrons would adopt an octahedral shape, with each bond at 90°. An example of this would be sulphur hexafluoride:

Octahedral   6 pairs

90°

X

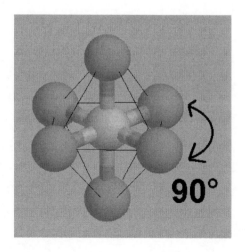

90°

Bond Angles in Substances with Lone Pairs of Electrons

One Lone Pair

As we saw earlier, in ammonia the nitrogen has four pairs of electrons in its outer shell; one of these is a lone pair (it is not bonded to anything else). This lone pair will have an effect on the bond angle, and therefore the shape of the molecule, because of its repulsive effect on the other electron pairs. In a substance with a single lone pair, the bond angle will be 107.5°.

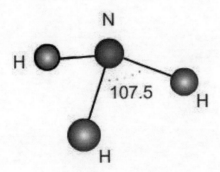

Two Lone Pairs

In a substance with two lone pairs, e.g. water, the bond angle would be 104.5°. Water has a bent line shape:

$$:O:$$
$$104.5°$$
$$H \qquad H$$

The fundamental difference between shared pairs and lone pairs in terms of bond angle is that, with a shared pair of electrons (taking ammonia as an example), they are attracted to the nucleus of both the nitrogen and hydrogen atoms. The lone pair on the nitrogen atom is only attracted to the nucleus of that atom.

The result of this is that the lone pair is pulled closer to the nitrogen nucleus and therefore exerts a greater "push" on the shared pairs, pushing them further away from the lone pair and reducing the bond angle between the shared pairs slightly.

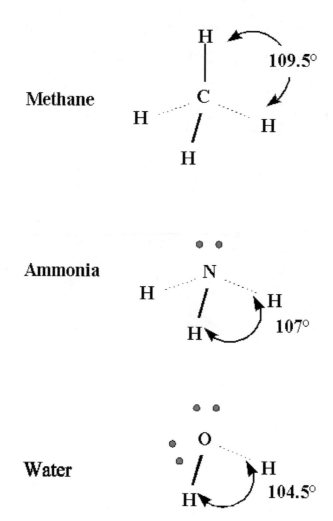

1.3.6 - Bond polarity

The force that holds molecules together is essentially an electrical attraction. It is the different electrical charge between the positive and negative ions.

With an ionic bond, this is easy to see. An electron is transferred from one atom to another, creating two ions that are then attracted together.

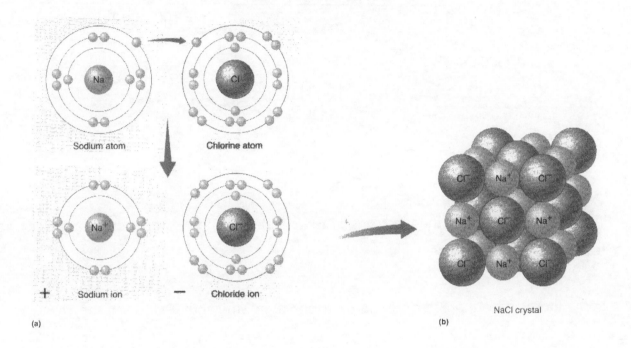

(a)   (b)

Electronegativity occurs within a covalent bond. This is because, despite the electrons being shared, they will not be shared evenly. Larger atoms will exert more of a pull on the electron because of the large positive charge from the greater number of protons in their nucleus.

The electrons will therefore be slightly displaced towards that atom, creating electronegativity in the bond.

Consider the example of water, H_2O.

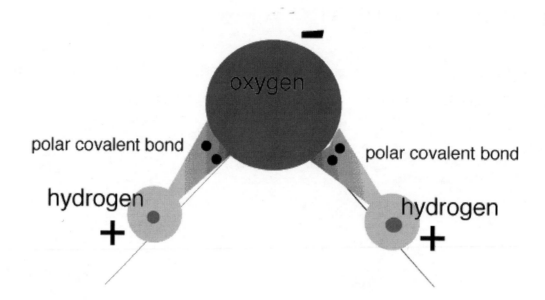

The oxygen will attract the electrons of the covalent bonds towards itself and away from the hydrogen atoms.

Some atoms have a greater pull on electrons than others; that is to say they have a greater electronegativity.

When we consider electrons in terms of bonding, we should think of charge clouds. The term electron density is often used to describe how the negative charge is distributed in the molecule.

The Pauling scale is used to measure electronegativity and its scale runs from 0 to 4:

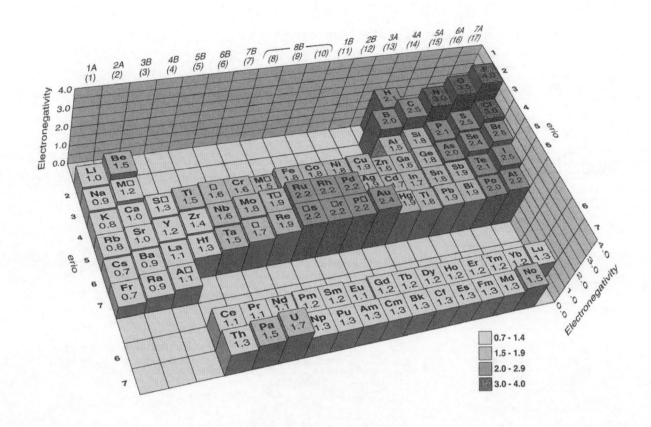

The noble gases (on the extreme right) do not have a Pauling scale number as they, generally speaking, do not form covalent bonds.

Electronegativity depends on a number of factors:

- The charge of the nucleus
- The distance between the nucleus and the outer electrons
- The shielding effect of the nuclear charge by the inner electrons

Polarity of Covalent Bonds

Polarity will occur in a covalent bond when there are atoms of two different elements with different Pauling numbers bonding together.

If we have a bond between two chlorine atoms, for example, they both have the same electronegativity so the electrons in the covalent bond will be exactly shared.

When the covalent bond is between two different atoms with different Pauling numbers, the bond will be closer to the most electronegative atom.

This can be illustrated using water as an example, with the oxygen atom being more electronegative than the hydrogen atoms.

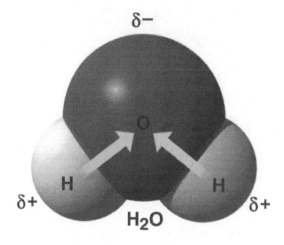

We discussed this briefly above. Oxygen has a greater electronegativity (3.5) than hydrogen (2.1) and will therefore attract electrons towards it, creating a polar covalent bond.

The important thing about this bond is that it will create a small negative charge on the oxygen (because the electrons are closer to it) and a small positive charge on the hydrogen atoms.

1.3.7 – Forces between molecules

Atoms within molecules are held together by strong covalent, ionic or metallic bonds.

Molecules, and indeed other individual atoms, are attracted together by much weaker forces. These are called intermolecular forces.

If these intermolecular forces are strong enough, then the substance will exist as either a liquid or a solid.

There are three main types of intermolecular forces:

- Van der Waals forces   Weakest
- Dipole-dipole forces
- Hydrogen bonding   Strongest

Van der Waals Forces

Even if the overall charge of a substance is neutral, all atoms and molecules consist of positive and negative charges. These positive and negative charges produce weak attractions between molecules.

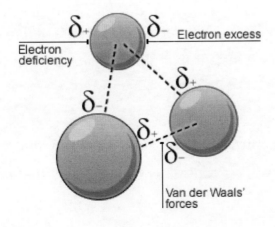

In order to understand how van der Waals forces develop and operate, you must be comfortable understanding electron orbits; you should now revise that section before proceeding.

At any given moment in time, the electrons could be located anywhere around the orbit of an atom, and given that they are in constant motion, their position changes all the time.

Wherever they are in their orbit they will create temporary dipoles, that is to say there will be more of a negative charge at the point in the orbit where they are located, and more of a positive charge away from them (i.e. a greater pull from the protons in the nucleus).

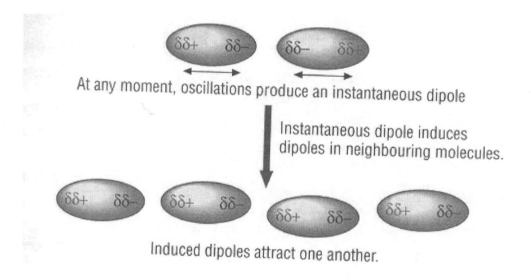

At any moment, oscillations produce an instantaneous dipole

Instantaneous dipole induces dipoles in neighbouring molecules.

Induced dipoles attract one another.

At any given instant, one atom or molecule will be attracted to another because of this temporary dipole, the next instant that dipole will change position and the attraction will cease.

At that point, another attraction will form between that molecule and another, however. This process will be constantly repeating, as the electrons are in constant motion.

Remember the following about van der Waals forces:

- They act between all atoms and molecules all of the time
- They act in addition to other intermolecular forces
- The dipole effect is caused by the movement of the electron cloud, so the more electrons present, the stronger the forces involved

Larger atoms and molecules therefore have higher van der Waals forces and thus will have higher boiling points. Note that van der Waal's forces are sometimes called induced dipole bonds.

Dipole – Dipole Forces

These forces exist only between certain types of molecule, and they are stronger than van der Waals forces.

These forces exist between molecules which have permanent dipoles.

For example, hydrogen chloride has a permanent dipole because chlorine is more electronegative than hydrogen, and so a permanent dipole charge is established.

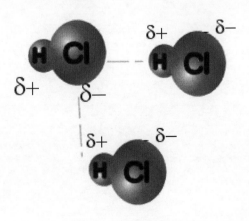

London dispersion forces

The London dispersion force is the weakest intermolecular force. It is a temporary attractive force that results when the electrons in two adjacent atoms occupy positions that make the atoms form temporary dipoles.

Unequal sharing of electrons causes rapid polarisation and counter-polarisation of the electron cloud forming short lived dipoles. These dipoles interact with the electron clouds of neighboring molecules forming more dipoles.

The attractive interaction of these dipoles are called dispersion or London Dispersion forces. These forces are weaker than other intermolecular forces. They do not extend over long distances. The strength of these interactions within a given molecule depends directly on how easily the electrons in the molecules can move (i.e. be polarised). Large molecules in which the electrons are far from the nucleus are relatively easy to polarise, and therefore possess greater dispersion

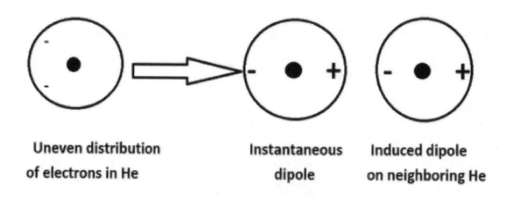

| Uneven distribution of electrons in He | Instantaneous dipole | Induced dipole on neighboring He |

Hydrogen Bonds

Hydrogen bonds have some of the characteristics of a dipole – dipole bond, and some of a covalent bond. They are also the strongest of the intermolecular bonds.

Hydrogen bonds form when a hydrogen atom is located between two strongly electronegative atoms (in the case of water, these are oxygen atoms).

We also need a strongly electronegative atom with a lone pair of electrons covalently bonded to a hydrogen atom. Water is a perfect example. Oxygen is much more strongly electronegative than hydrogen.

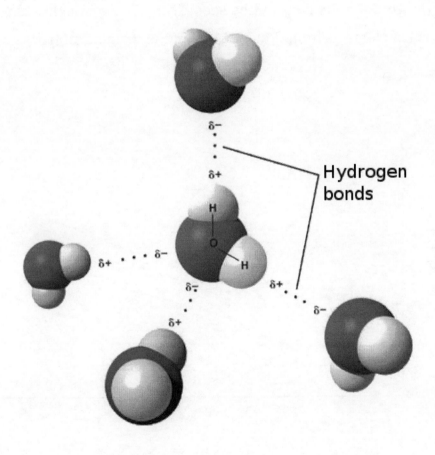

There are two reasons why this hydrogen bond is much stronger than a normal dipole-dipole bond:

- The oxygen atoms have a lone pair of electrons
- In the example of water, the hydrogen atoms are very deficient in electrons because hydrogen is much less electronegative than oxygen

The hydrogen bond forms because the lone pair of electrons on another water molecule are attracted to the heavily electron deficient hydrogen atoms of the first water molecule.

The Importance of Hydrogen Bonds

The effect of hydrogen bonding can be seen clearly in the boiling point of hydrides (graph below) of elements from groups 4 to 7 of the periodic table:

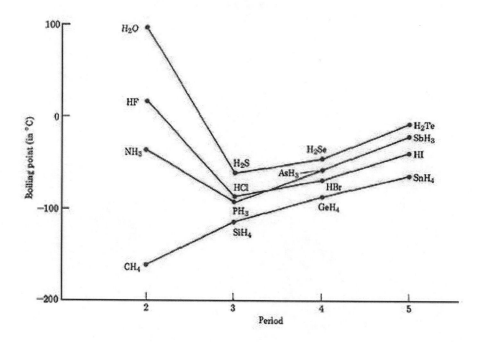

Hydrogen bonds are only around 10% as strong as a covalent bond, but despite this their effect is very significant.

Their relative weakness means that they can form and break under conditions where covalent bonds would not do so.

When we consider water, the hydrogen bonds that form in its liquid state form and break easily as the molecules are in motion.

When water freezes to form ice, the molecules are no longer free to move, and the hydrogen bonds hold the molecules in a fixed position. A three dimensional structure similar to diamond forms.

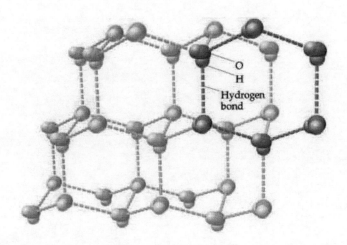

In order for the molecules to fit into this structure, they need to be slightly less closely packed than they are in water, and this is why water expands when it freezes.

This also means that ice is less dense than water and therefore floats. Floating ice serves to insulate ponds and rivers in the winter and helps fish and other aquatic animals to survive the cold.

This property would have helped life survive during the many ice ages that the earth has seen. It is also a sobering thought that it is hydrogen bonds that maintain water as a liquid at normal temperatures, and liquid water is vital to all life on earth. We could say, therefore, that life would not exist on earth without hydrogen bonds.

1.4 - Energetics

The enthalpy change in a chemical reaction can be measured accurately. It is important to know this value for chemical reactions that are used as a source of heat energy in applications such as domestic boilers and internal combustion engines.

1.4.1 – Enthalpy change

In terms of energy, there are essentially two types of reaction:

- Exothermic – Reactions that release energy during the reaction process
- Endothermic – Reactions that take in energy during the reaction process

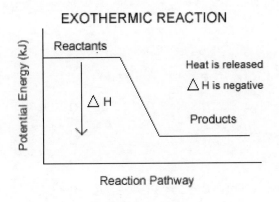

The illustration above is a graphical representation of an exothermic reaction. That is to say, energy is released during the reaction process. You can see that the energy level of the reactants is higher than the energy level of the products; the only conclusion is that the difference was released during the reaction (therefore the reaction is exothermic).

Activity 43 – Draw a graph for an endothermic reaction.

Answer to Activity 43:

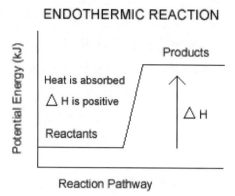

In this case, you can see that the reactants have a lower energy level than the products, indicating that energy must have been taken in during the reaction; it is therefore endothermic.

In the above two illustrations, the term ΔH refers to the energy change during the reaction. You will frequently see this referred to as 'enthalpy change'; enthalpy simply means the energy in the system.

ΔH is always either a positive number or a negative number. To understand which one it ought to be, you must always think of the enthalpy change from the perspective of the substances themselves.

- When the ΔH is negative, this means the reactants have lost energy. When this is the case, the reaction is exothermic.
- When the ΔH is positive, the reactants have gained energy during the reaction. In this case, the reaction would be endothermic.

Take, for example, the reaction between hydrogen gas and oxygen gas to form water:

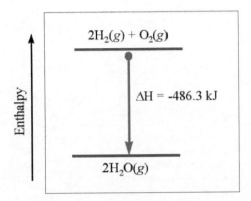

The enthalpy change (ΔH) is negative, which means that the products have a lower energy level than the reactants; this can only occur during an exothermic reaction.

Note also that the units of measurement are kJ mol^{-1} (kilojoules per mol).

In the above illustration, 486.3 kJ mol^{-1} of energy are released during the reaction.

Enthalpy changes are measured at standard conditions i.e.:

- 100 kPa
- Standard temperature (e.g. ΔH_{298})

There are two other key definitions that you need to be familiar with:

- Standard enthalpy of combustion (ΔH_c) – This is the enthalpy change when 1 mole of substance is completely burned in oxygen under standard conditions (100kPa and 298K), with all reactants and products in their standard states.
- Standard enthalpy of formation (ΔH_f) – This is the enthalpy change when one mole of compound is formed from its constituent elements under standard conditions, with all reactants and products in their standard states.

1.4.2 - Calorimetry

Calorimetry is an experimental technique that is used to determine the energy involved in a chemical reaction.

A calorimeter can be extremely expensive, or it can be extremely cheap. The experiment we describe will be one capable of being conducted in a laboratory at minimal cost.

A simple calorimeter can consist of a polystyrene cup (polystyrene is used because it is a very good insulator) covered with a cardboard lid. The lid has a hole cut into it to allow a thermometer into the contents. A stand and clamp can be used to hold the thermometer in place during the experiment.

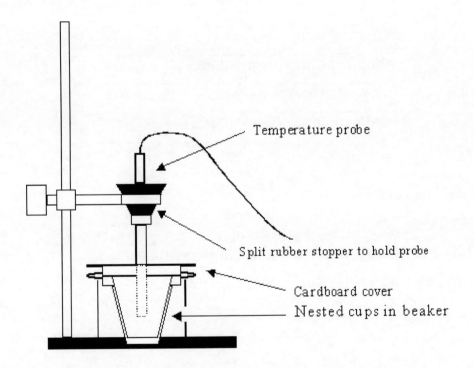

A large amount of dilute sulphuric acid should be poured into the cup, perhaps 75ml. This volume is not critical provided there is an excess of the dilute acid. An excess means that not all of it will be used up during the reaction.

The initial temperature of this acid should then be measured and recorded.

A dish should be weighed on a set of very accurate scales and the weight of the empty dish recorded.

A small amount (around 0.1g) of magnesium powder should then be poured onto the dish. The dish should then be re-weighed and the weight recorded.

The difference between these two weights is the weight of the powder.

The magnesium should then be dropped into the dilute acid and the lid replaced on the cup (this also acts as insulation). The temperature rise should be measured and the maximum temperature recorded.

The recorded results could look something like those in the table below:

Weight of dish	7.42
Weight of dish + magnesium	7.54
Initial temperature	14.3
Maximum recorded temperature	28.2

Activity 44 – Calculate:

- **The mass of magnesium used in the experiment**
- **The temperature rise during the experiment**

Answer to Activity 44:

Weight of magnesium = Weight of dish + magnesium – Weight of dish

Weight of magnesium = 7.54 – 7.42

Weight of magnesium = **0.12g**

Temperature rise = Maximum temperature – Initial temperature

Temperature rise = 28.2 – 14.3

Temperature rise = **13.9°C**

Activity 45 – Write the equation for the reaction that you think is occurring.

Answer to Activity 45:

The reaction is:

$$Mg(s) + H_2SO_4(aq) \rightarrow MgSO_4(aq) + H_2(g)$$

We can use the information we gathered from the experiment, along with what we know of the chemical reaction taking place from the chemical equation, to calculate how much heat is given out when 1 mole of magnesium reacts with 1 mole of dilute sulphuric acid.

The equation for the calculation of the heat given out, when you know exactly the mass of the substances involved and the temperature rise, is:

$$q = m \times c \times \Delta T$$

or:

Enthalpy change = mass x specific heat capacity x temperature change

Specific heat capacity is something you have not yet encountered. It is the amount of energy (heat) that it takes to raise the temperature of 1 gram of a substance by 1K.

The specific heat capacity of water is $4.18 \text{ Jg}^{-1}\text{K}^{-1}$.

When conducting calculations involving aqueous solutions, you can (almost always) assume that the specific heat capacity of the solution is the same as for water, unless told differently.

The mass in the equation is the mass of the solution (the dilute sulphuric acid).

Using the equation above:

Enthalpy change = mass x specific heat capacity x temperature change

Enthalpy change = 75 x 4.18 x 13.9

Enthalpy change = 4,358J

Or:

= 4.358kJ

In the equation, note that we have assumed that 75ml of dilute acid would weigh 75g.

This is halfway there...

Remember 1 mole of magnesium weighs 24.3g, from the atomic mass that you can get from the periodic table.

If 0.12g of Mg reacts to produce kJ, how much energy would 24.3g of Mg produce?

If 0.12g Mg produces 4.358kJ

Then:

24.3g Mg produces $\underline{24.3}$ x 4.358
                    0.12

= 882.495kJ mol^{-1}

In this reaction, if the observed data were accurate, the heat evolved would be:

ΔH = 882.495kJ mol^{-1}

One important note: the data we have used was hypothetical and not the result of experimentation. We have used these data only for the purposes of demonstrating the calculations. The actual experimental heat evolved during this reaction is rather lower than this. You do not need to remember the number, just how to conduct the calculations.

N.B. You are not expected to remember the value for specific heat capacity c.

Required Practical 2:

Measurement of enthalpy change.

1.4.3 – Application of Hess's Law

For some reactions, the enthalpy change cannot be measured directly. In order to calculate these, we need to take a more indirect approach.

In this approach, we use the enthalpy changes that we *can* measure to calculate the enthalpy changes that we *cannot*. To do this we use Hess's Law.

Hess's Law states that the enthalpy change for a chemical reaction is the same, whatever route is taken from reactants to products.

Application of Hess's Law

Ethyne (C_2H_2) can be converted to ethane (C_2H_6) by two different routes. How, therefore, can we find the enthalpy change of the reaction?

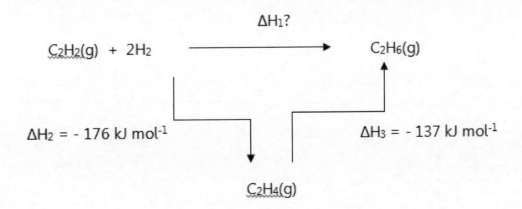

Route 1:

$$C_2H_2(g) + 2H_2 \rightarrow C_2H_6(g) \qquad \Delta H = ?$$

Route 2:

This is a two stage process:

$$(\Delta H_2) \; C_2H_2(g) + H_2 \rightarrow C_2H_4(g) \qquad \Delta H = -176 \text{ kJ mol}^{-1}$$

$$(\Delta H_3) \; C_2H_4(g) + H_2 \rightarrow C_2H_6(g) \qquad \Delta H = -137 \text{ kJ mol}^{-1}$$

Hess's Law tells us that the enthalpy change for route 1 is equal to the total enthalpy change occurring in the reaction. Therefore:

$$\Delta H_1 = \Delta H_2 + \Delta H_3$$

Therefore:

$$\Delta H_1 = (-176) + (-137)$$

$$\mathbf{\Delta H_1 = -313 \text{ kJ mol}^{-1}}$$

Using Enthalpy Changes of Combustion ΔH_c

Remember:

The standard enthalpy of combustion is the enthalpy change when 1 mole of a substance is completely burned in oxygen under standard conditions, with all reactants and products in their standard states.

Let us look again at the reaction we have just used:

$$C_2H_2(g) + 2H_2 \rightarrow C_2H_6(g)$$

This time, however, we will look at the enthalpy change of combustion. To do this, we will look at the combustion enthalpies of the three molecules in the reaction:

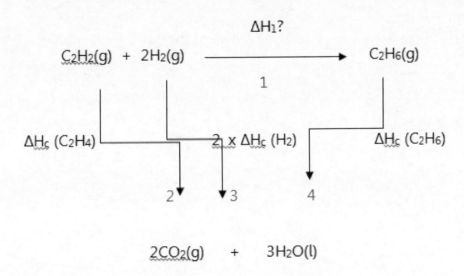

We know from experimentation that the enthalpies of combustion are as follows:

- $C_2H_2(g)$ = - 1301 kJ mol^{-1}
- $H_2(g)$ = - 286 kJ mol^{-1} (note, x2 = - 572 kJ mol^{-1})
- $C_2H_6(g)$ = - 1560 kJ mol^{-1}

To calculate the enthalpy change of reaction 1, we must move around the reaction with the block arrows as follows:

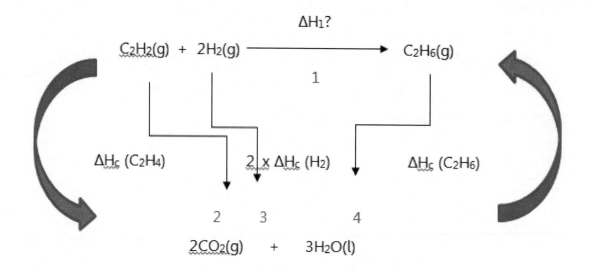

Therefore:

$$\Delta H_1 = \Delta H_c \text{ of reaction } 2 + 3 + \text{ the reverse of the } \Delta H_c \text{ for reaction } 4$$

It is the reverse of the enthalpy of combustion of reaction 4 because we are forming the substance rather than combusting it.

Therefore:

$$\Delta H_1 = -1301 + -572 + 1560$$

$$\boldsymbol{\Delta H_1 = -313 \text{ kJ mol}^{-1}}$$

Note again that this figure is the same as those for the enthalpy of formation, again as you would expect from Hess's Law.

1.4.4 – Bond enthalpies

Look at the graph below for a moment.

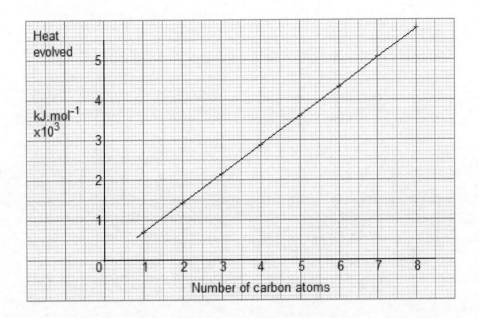

Methane is the simplest alkane (CH_4). Every subsequent alkane has an extra CH_2 group bonded to it; that is to say one extra C-C bond and two extra C-H bonds.

From the graph, we can see that the bond energies increase at a fixed rate for every extra carbon atom. This suggests that we can assign a definite amount of energy to a particular bond: a bond enthalpy.

You know that a carbon-carbon bond is covalent, and energy is required to break (dissociate) that bond. The **bond dissociation energy** is the energy required to break a covalent bond with all species (chemicals) in the gaseous state. The same amount of energy is given out as when the bond forms.

The same bonds, C-H for example, will have slightly different bond enthalpies in different compounds, and for calculations we use the **mean bond enthalpy**, usually called simply the **bond energy**.

Using Mean Bond Enthalpies to Calculate the Enthalpy Change of a Reaction

We can use the concept of mean bond enthalpies to calculate the enthalpy change of a reaction. Consider:

Ethane + Chlorine → Chloroethane + Hydrogen Chloride

$$C_2H_6(g) + Cl_2(g) \rightarrow C_2H_5Cl(g) + HCl(g)$$

We can use average bond enthalpy tables to calculate the enthalpy change of the reaction.

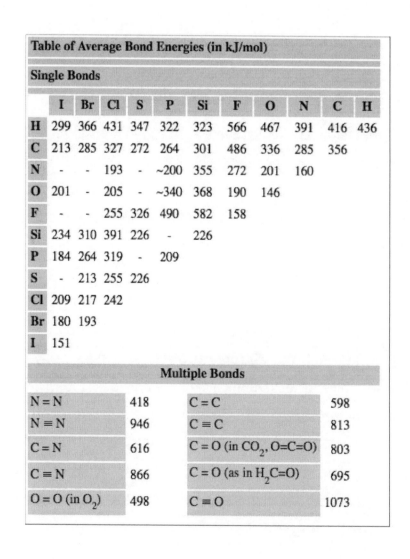

Table of Average Bond Energies (in kJ/mol)

Single Bonds

	I	Br	Cl	S	P	Si	F	O	N	C	H
H	299	366	431	347	322	323	566	467	391	416	436
C	213	285	327	272	264	301	486	336	285	356	
N	-	-	193	-	~200	355	272	201	160		
O	201	-	205	-	~340	368	190	146			
F	-	-	255	326	490	582	158				
Si	234	310	391	226	-	226					
P	184	264	319	-	209						
S	-	213	255	226							
Cl	209	217	242								
Br	180	193									
I	151										

Multiple Bonds

$N=N$	418	$C=C$	598
$N \equiv N$	946	$C \equiv C$	813
$C=N$	616	$C=O$ (in CO_2, O=C=O)	803
$C \equiv N$	866	$C=O$ (as in $H_2C=O$)	695
$O=O$ (in O_2)	498	$C \equiv O$	1073

There are two methods of using this data.

First, calculate the bond energy of every bond on either side of the reaction, and then calculate the difference:

Reactants:

- 6 x C-H = 6 x 416 = 2496 kJ mol^{-1}
- x C-C = 1 x 356 = 356 kJ mol^{-1}
- x Cl-Cl = 1 x 242 = 242 kJ mol^{-1}

Total = 3094 kJ mol^{-1}

Products:

- 5 x C-H = 5 x 416 = 2080 kJ mol^{-1}
- x C-C = 1 x 356 = 356 kJ mol^{-1}
- x C-Cl = 1 x 327 = 327 kJ mol^{-1}
- x H-Cl = 1 x 431 = 431 kJ mol^{-1}

Total = 3194 kJ mol^{-1}

Therefore:

3094 kJ mol^{-1} is taken in and 3194 kJ mol^{-1} is given out during the reaction.

Net Enthalpy change is therefore:

3094 - 3194

-100 kJ mol^{-1}

Activity 46 – Would this be an exothermic or an endothermic reaction?

Answer to Activity 46:

It would be exothermic because there is more energy given out than taken in.

The second method is something of a shortcut:

With this method you only consider, and therefore only calculate, the bonds that are broken and formed in the reaction. This has the advantage of being briefer, but you need to take care that you include all of the bonds that are involved.

Activity 47 – Calculate the bond enthalpy for the reaction:

Ethane + Bromine → Bromoethane + Hydrogen bromide

using the shortcut method and see how it compares with the first method.

Answer to Activity 47:

Using this method, the calculation is rather shorter.

Bonds broken	Bonds Formed
Br-Br = 193	H-Br = -366
C-H = 416	C-Br = -285
609 +	-651

$$= - 42 \text{ kJ mol}^{-1}$$

1.5 - Kinetics

The study of kinetics enables chemists to determine how a change in conditions affects the speed of a chemical reaction. Whilst the reactivity of chemicals is a significant factor in how fast chemical reactions proceed, there are variables that can be manipulated in order to speed them up or slow them down.

1.5.1 – Collision theory

Reactions can only ever occur when two particles come into contact. The particles need to impact with each other with sufficient energy to enable the reaction to occur.

At the start of any reaction, the rate of reaction is much faster because there are simply more reactant particles available and more impacts occurring.

As the reaction progresses, the reactant particles in the solution are used up and therefore the number of collisions between the reactants declines. This is called collision theory.

Low concentration = Few collisions   High concentration = More collisions

Not all the impacts that occur do so with enough energy to cause a reaction. In fact, the majority of collisions result in no reaction at all. This is because, in order for a reaction to occur, the activation energy needs to be met.

Activation Energy

Sometimes reactions do not occur because they do not generate the required activation energy or, in other words, the collisions that occur do not generate the required energy.

The activation energy is very simply defined as the amount of energy required for a given reaction to occur.

The illustration below shows the activation energy required by an exothermic reaction:

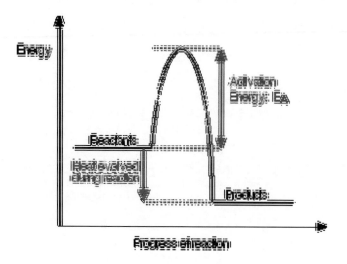

The reactants begin at a given energy level (as shown in the illustration). They require an input of energy (activation energy) for the reaction to begin. Once that energy is there, the reaction will progress, and more energy may be evolved during the process than was required initially (in an exothermic reaction, that is).

Activity 48 – Draw a graph for the activation energy required for an endothermic reaction.

Answer to Activity 48:

Activation energy is still required, but with an endothermic reaction less energy is emitted than is taken in.

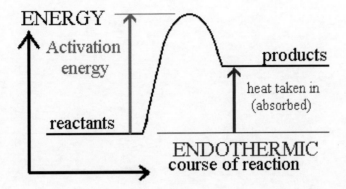

1.5.2 – Maxwell-Boltzmann distribution

You will remember from earlier in the course that within any gas or liquid the particles are in motion. Some of them will be moving very slowly, and some very quickly, but most will be somewhere in between.

A particle's energy depends upon its speed, and therefore the particles in any gas or liquid will have a range of energies.

If we plot a graph of particle energy against the proportion of a substance with that energy level, we get a Maxwell-Boltzmann Distribution.

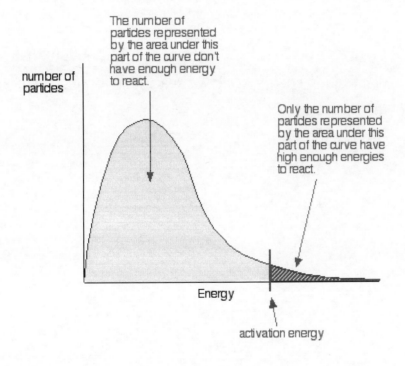

This distribution tells us:

- No particles have zero energy
- Most particles have an intermediate energy, around the peak of the graph
- A few particles have very high energies (towards the right of the graph). There is no upper limit

We know that not all collisions result in a reaction, and that for a reaction to occur the activation energy needs to be met.

The below distribution illustrates that only a few particles at the high energy end of the distribution have sufficient energy to cause a reaction to occur.

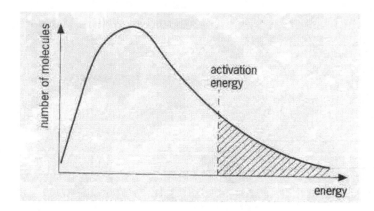

The number of particles to the extreme right of the distribution, that is to say those with the required activation energy to allow a reaction to occur, can be affected by the temperature of the reaction.

1.5.3 – Effect of temperature on reaction rate

The rate of a reaction can be measured by the rate at which a *reactant* is used up, or the rate at which a *product* is formed.

Chemical reactions can only happen if reactant particles collide with enough energy. The more frequently particles collide, and the greater the proportion of collisions with enough energy, the greater the rate of reaction.

Different reactions can happen at different rates. Reactions that happen slowly have a low rate of reaction. Reactions that happen quickly have a high rate of reaction. For example, the chemical weathering of rocks is a very slow reaction: it has a low rate of reaction. Explosions are very fast reactions: they have a high rate of reaction.

Reactants and products

There are two ways to measure the rate of a reaction:

1. Measure the rate at which a *reactant* is used up
2. Measure the rate at which a *product* is formed

The method chosen depends on the reaction being studied. Sometimes it is easier to measure the change in the amount of a reactant that has been used up; sometimes it is easier to measure the change in the amount of product that has been produced.

In the graph below, T1 is the standard temperature and T2 is the higher temperature.

As you can see, when the temperature is increased the number of particles with higher than the required activation energy is increased, therefore more reactions will likely occur.

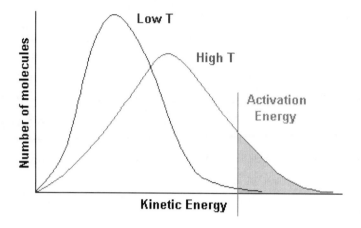

Required Practical 3:

Investigate how the rate of a reaction changes with temperature.

1.5.4 – Effect of concentration and pressure

Increasing the concentration of the reactants would mean there were more particles in the reaction chamber, and therefore collisions between the reactants would occur at a greater frequency.

If more collisions are occurring, then the likelihood of more collisions occurring with the required activation energy increases. Therefore, the rate of the reaction will increase.

The reaction rate would slow down as the reactants are used up.

Increasing the pressure on a reaction involving reacting gases increases the rate of reaction. Changing the pressure on a reaction which involves only solids or liquids has no effect on the rate.

An example

In the manufacture of ammonia by the Haber Process, the rate of reaction between the hydrogen and the nitrogen is increased by the use of very high pressures.

$$N_{2(g)} + 3H_{2(g)} \rightleftharpoons 2NH_{3(g)}$$

In fact, the main reason for using high pressures is to improve the percentage of ammonia in the equilibrium mixture, but there is a useful effect on rate of reaction as well.

1.5.5 - Catalysts

Catalysts increase the rate of a reaction, or cause a reaction to occur, without themselves being used up in the reaction.

A catalyst brings two other substances together, creates a reaction between them to form a new substance, and is not itself used in the reaction. A catalyst simply facilitates the reaction process.

Given that catalysts are not used in a reaction (they remain chemically unchanged) they can be recycled and used again and again on other reactions as catalysts.

Note that if a substance catalyses one reaction, it probably will not catalyse a different reaction between different chemicals. There is not a universal catalyst that will catalyse every reaction; they are very specific in their actions.

An example of a reaction that requires a catalyst is the hydrogenation of the double bond in ethene:

$$C_2H_4 + H_2 \rightarrow C_2H_6$$

In this case, nickel is used as a catalyst. You will note that the nickel (or indeed any other catalyst) never appears in the equation; this is because it is not chemically altered in any way.

If the catalyst used in the above reaction were in the form of a solid lump of nickel, the reaction would be less efficiently catalysed.

If it was in small chips, however, then the surface area of the catalyst would be increased, more collisions could occur, and the reaction rate would be increased because the catalyst would be more efficient in catalysing the reaction.

How Do Catalysts Work?

You will remember that in collision theory we said that reactions could only occur if two substances collide with each other.

We also noted that not all collisions result in reactions; sometimes a collision requires a catalyst in order to allow the reaction to occur.

The reactants begin at a given energy level (as in the illustration below). They require an input of energy (activation energy) for the reaction to begin.

Once that energy is there, the reaction will progress, and more energy may be evolved during the process than was required initially.

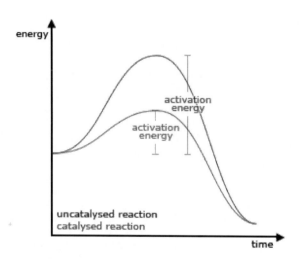

The presence of a catalyst in a reaction gives an alternative and easier route for the reaction to occur involving a lower activation energy level.

Given that the activation energy is lower, more collisions will result in reactions. The reaction occurs at a faster rate because the alternative catalysed route requires less energy.

Catalysts provide an alternative route with a lower activation level.

Consider the railway tracks below:

The railway line on the right is straight and therefore a shorter route to your destination. The track on the left is circuitous and it would require a lot more effort to reach the goal.

Catalysed reactions are much like the track on the right. They provide an alternative route to reach the same goal, one that requires less activation energy.

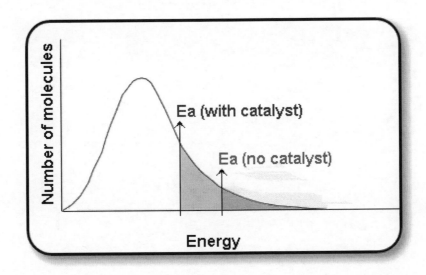

1.6 – Chemical equilibria, Le Chatelier's principle and Kc

In contrast with kinetics, which is a study of how quickly reactions occur, a study of equilibria indicates how far reactions will go. Le Chatelier's principle can be used to predict the effects of changes in temperature, pressure and concentration on the yield of a reversible reaction. This has important consequences for many indistrial processes. The further study of the equilibrium constant Kc, considers how the mathematical expression for the equilibrium constant enables us to calculate how an equilibrium yield will be influences by the concentration of reactants and products.

1.6.1 – Chemical equilibria and Le Chatelier's principle.

Many chemical reactions are reversible, which is to say they can progress in both the forwards and backwards directions, and are symbolised by a reversible arrow. In reversible reactions:

- Forward and reverse reactions proceed at equal rates
- The concentrations of reactants and products remain constant

With equations that can achieve equilibrium, then if they are in a closed system, we would have both reactants and products together. This may be sometimes desirable, but most often we would want to change the equilibrium. For example, in an industrial process we would want to increase the amount of products produced by the reaction.

It is possible to change the position of the equilibrium:

- If the proportion of the products in the equilibrium mixture is increased, we can say that the equilibrium is moved to the right
- If the proportion of the products in the equilibrium mixture is decreased, we can say that the equilibrium is moved to the left

Le Chatelier's Principle

Le Chatelier's principle tells us whether the equilibrium moves to the right or to the left when the conditions of a reaction change.

Le Chatelier's principle states:

If a system at equilibrium is disturbed, the equilibrium moves in the direction that tends to reduce the disturbance

That is to say that if any factor is changed which affects the equilibrium mixture, the equilibrium position will shift to oppose the change.

Note that this principle cannot be used to calculate quantities as it cannot tell us how far the position of the equilibrium will change, just that it will change and in which direction.

Effect of a Change in Concentration

Le Chatelier's principle tells us that if we increase the concentration of one of the reactants in a given reaction, the equilibrium will move in the direction that tends to reduce that reactant.

Consider again:

$$A + B \rightleftharpoons C + D$$

If we add more of substance B to the reaction, we effectively increase its concentration in the reaction chamber. The only way the system can regain equilibrium is if some of B reacts with some A to produce more C and D. This would move the equilibrium to the right.

The same would happen, of course, if we added more of substance A.

If we removed either C or D from the reaction chamber, the equilibrium would again move to the right, with more C and D being produced, using up some A and B in the process.

If we added some of substance D to the reaction chamber, then the equilibrium would move to the left, with more A and B being formed.

Activity 51 – What effect do you think changing pressure would have?

Effect of a Change in Pressure

A change in pressure will only have an effect if both the reactants and products are gases.

A change in pressure will change the equilibrium if there are a different number of molecules on either side of the reaction.

Consider the simple reaction:

$$N_2O_4(g) \rightleftharpoons 2NO_2(g)$$

A system will be under greater pressure if there are more molecules present.

If the pressure on a reaction is increased, therefore, Le Chatelier's principle tells us that the equilibrium will move to reduce that pressure, i.e. to reduce the number of molecules present.

Activity 52 – Which direction would the equilibrium move in, therefore?

Answer to Activity 52:

In the case of the above reaction, the equilibrium would move to the left.

Note that if there are the same number of molecules on either side of the equation, then increasing the pressure will have no effect.

Effect of a Change in Temperature

A reversible reaction can be exothermic in one direction and endothermic in the other.

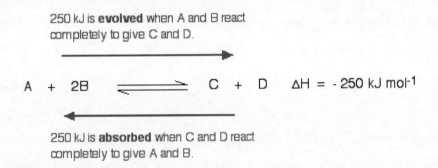

The negative ΔH symbol indicates that heat is given out in the reaction that moves from left to right, i.e. that the reaction is exothermic when A and B react to form C and D.

Le Chatelier's principle tells us that if we increase the heat in the reaction chamber the equilibrium will move in the direction required to cool down the system.

Activity 53 – Which direction will the equilibrium move in the above reaction if it is heated?

Answer to Activity 53:

The equilibrium will move to the left as this reaction is endothermic, thus absorbing heat and cooling down the system.

Effect of a Catalyst

A catalyst will have no impact on the *position* of the equilibrium, and therefore catalysts do not affect the composition in the reaction chamber.

They do, however, allow the equilibrium position to be reached more quickly, and are economically valuable in industry.

Importance of Equilibria in Industrial Processes

There are a number of industrial processes that involve the use of reversible reactions, and applying Le Chatelier's principle can help determine the reaction conditions required to produce the optimum results.

Ammonia NH_3

Ammonia is a vitally important commercial chemical with world production around 140 million tonnes per year. The majority of this is used in fertilisers, but it is also an important chemical in the production of synthetic fibres, plastics and explosives. The reaction for the production of ammonia is:

$$N_2(g) \ + \ 3H_2(g) \ \rightleftharpoons \ 2NH_3(g) \quad \Delta H \ -92 \ kJ \ mol^{-1}$$

The majority of ammonia is manufactured using the Haber process. This is a process that occurs in stages:

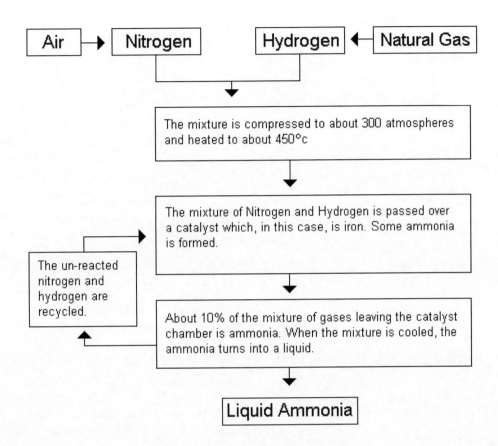

Le Chatelier's principle predicts the following:

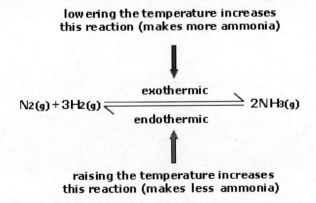

In the industrial Haber process, it has been observed that the following conditions produce the following results:

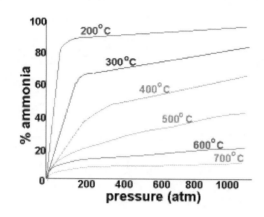

You can see, broadly speaking, that yield increases as temperature decreases, exactly as Le Chatelier's principle predicts.

In reality, some compromise is needed between temperature and pressure to ensure the optimum output. Yield may be high, but the rate slow!

Ethanol (C_2H_5OH)

Ethanol is the most commercially important of all of the alcohols, as it is the alcohol in alcoholic drinks.

Ethanol is used more broadly than this though. It is used in the production of cosmetics, drugs, detergents and some fuels. UK production is around 330,000 tonnes per year.

The main source of industrial ethanol is from the fractional distillation of crude oil, followed by cracking.

The final stage of ethanol manufacture is achieved by adding water to ethene (hydrating ethene) in the following reaction:

$$C_2H_4(g) + H_2O(g) \rightleftharpoons C_2H_5OH(g) \quad \Delta H\ \text{-46 kJ mol}^{-1}$$

The reaction can be speeded up by the use of a catalyst of phosphoric acid absorbed on silica.

Le Chatelier's principle predicts that a maximum yield will be produced if:

- the pressure is high (the reaction would be forced to the right as there are fewer molecules on the right hand side)
- the temperature is low (the reaction to the right is exothermic so reducing the temperature will force more heat out and move the equilibrium to the right)
- excess water present (this will force the equilibrium to the right to reduce the steam concentration)

The practical problems with this process could include:

- Low reaction temperatures will slow down the rate of reaction
- High temperatures cause the ethene to polymerise (more on this later in the course)
- High pressure increases the cost of the plant and process
- The catalyst can be diluted by too much excess steam

Methanol CH_3OH

Methanol is another commercially important chemical, although it is valuable almost entirely because it can be used as the raw material in the production of many other materials, for example:

- Methanal (formaldehyde)
- Plastics
- Motor fuel (often as a replacement to petrol)

Worldwide production is around 33 million tonnes per year. It is most often produced by the reversible reaction of hydrogen and carbon monoxide using a copper catalyst:

$CO(g) + 3H_2(g) \rightleftharpoons CH_3OH(g)$ ΔH -91 kJ mol^{-1}

Activity 54 – What does Le Chatelier's principle tell us about this reaction?

Answer to Activity 54:

Le Chatelier's principle tells us a number of things:

- The highest yield will be at low temperatures (because the reaction is exothermic)
- The highest yield will be at high pressures (because of the no. of molecules on either side of the equation: 4 on the left hand side, 1 on the right hand side)

In industry, compromise conditions are used, and the highest yields (5-10%) are produced at 500K and 10,000kPa.

1.6.2 – Equilibrium constant Kc for homogenous systems

As you know, many chemical reactions are reversible when the conditions are right. These reactions tend not to run to completion, but will simultaneously progress in both directions.

<u>Equilibrium Reactions</u>

Given enough time, a reversible reaction will reach equilibrium. This is the state where the reactions progressing to the right are balanced out by the reactions progressing to the left. Although reactions are still occurring, the relative proportions of the materials on either side of the equation remain constant and therefore the amount of each material will remain constant.

An example is:

$$2SO_{2(g)} \; + \; O_{2(g)} \; \rightleftharpoons \; 2SO_{2(g)}$$

<u>The Equilibrium Constant</u>

The general formula for *any* reaction at equilibrium is:

$$aA \; + \; bB \; + \; cC \; \rightleftharpoons \; xX \; + \; yY \; + \; zZ$$

Note that the upper case letter refers to the chemical and the lower case letter to the number of atoms or molecules of that chemical present in the reaction.

For the above generic reaction, we can say that the following expression will be a constant:

$$\frac{[X]eqm^x \ [Y]eqm^y \ [Z]eqm^z}{[A]eqm^a \ [B]eqm^b \ [C]eqm^c}$$

Eqm in the equation simply means that the reactants are at equilibrium.

This expression will be constant provided that the temperature is constant. Changing the temperature will change the position of equilibrium of the reaction. The expression will give a constant, called the **equilibrium constant, Kc.** This expression can be applied to any reversible reaction that has reached a state of equilibrium. Note that the equilibrium constant will be different for every reaction. The units of the Kc value also change with every reaction. Consider:

$$2A \ + \ B \ \rightarrow \ 2C$$

The units for the Kc of this reaction would be:

$$Kc \ = \ \frac{[C]^2}{[A]^2 \ + \ [B]}$$

$$\frac{(mol \ dm^{-3})^2}{(mol \ dm^{-3})^2 \ (mol \ dm^{-3})}$$

cancelling out =

$$\frac{1}{(mol \ dm^{-3})}$$

Units for this reaction would be:

$$\mathbf{mol^{-1} \ dm^3}$$

Calculating the Value of Kc

Let us look at the reaction:

$$C_2H_5OH(l) + CH_3CO_2H(l) \rightleftharpoons CH_3CO_2C_2H_5(l) + H_2O(l)$$

Ethanol + Ethanoic acid $\rightleftharpoons$ Ethyl ethanoate + Water

From experimentation, we know that the number of moles of the four substances are:

0.033 mol + 0.033 mol $\rightleftharpoons$ 0.067 mol + 0.067 mol

The concentration of each substance is (assuming a total volume of $0.035dm^3$):

$$C_2H_5OH(l) + CH_3CO_2H(l) \rightleftharpoons CH_3CO_2C_2H_5(l) + H_2O(l)$$

$\dfrac{0.033 \text{ mol dm}^{-3}}{0.035}$ $\dfrac{0.033 \text{ mol dm}^{-3}}{0.035}$ $\dfrac{0.067 \text{ mol dm}^{-3}}{0.035}$ $\dfrac{0.067 \text{ mol dm}^{-3}}{0.035}$

If we now enter the concentrations into the equilibrium equation:

$$K_c = \frac{[CH_3CO_2C_2H_5]\ [H_2O]}{[C_2H_5OH]\ [CH_3CO_2H]}$$

$$K_c = \frac{[0.067/0.035 \text{ mol dm}^{-3}]\ [0.067/0.035 \text{ mol dm}^{-3}]}{[0.033/0.035 \text{ mol dm}^{-3}]\ [0.033/0.035 \text{ mol dm}^{-3}]}$$

$K_c = 4.12$

In this case the equilibrium constant has no units as they all cancel each other out.

Calculations using Kc

We can use the equilibrium expression to calculate the composition of a mixture at equilibrium for a given constant temperature.

Let us look at the same reaction again:

$$C_2H_5OH(l) + CH_3CO_2H(l) \rightleftharpoons CH_3CO_2C_2H_5(l) + H_2O(l)$$

We know that at equilibrium the following is true:

$$Kc = \frac{[CH_3CO_2C_2H_5]\ [H_2O]}{[C_2H_5OH]\ [CH_3CO_2H]}$$

If we assume that the equilibrium constant (Kc) is 4 at our given constant temperature, then we need to calculate how much ethyl ethanoate would be produced by reacting 1 mol of ethanol and 1 mol of ethanoic acid.

Equation:	$C_2H_5OH(l)$	+ $CH_3CO_2H(l)$	$\rightleftharpoons$ $CH_3CO_2C_2H_5(l)$	+ $H_2O(l)$
Start of reaction:	(a) 1 mol	(b) 1 mol	0 mol	0 mol
Equilibrium	$(1 - x)$ mol	$(1 - x)$ mol	x mol	x mol

So we have the moles in the system, but we need the concentrations in order to use the equilibrium expression.

If we assume that the volume in the system is V dm^{-3} then we know that:

$$[C_2H_5OH]eqm \; = \; \frac{(1-x)}{V} \; mol \; dm^{-3}$$

$$[CH_3CO_2H]eqm \; = \; \frac{(1-x)}{V} \; mol \; dm^{-3}$$

$$[CH_3CO_2C_2H_5]eqm \; = \; \frac{x}{V} \; mol \; dm^{-3}$$

$$[H_2O]eqm \; = \; \frac{x}{V} \; mol \; dm^{-3}$$

We can now substitute these figures into the equilibrium expression as follows:

$$K_c \quad = \quad \frac{(x/V) \; x \; (x/V)}{((1-x)/V) \; x \; ((1-x)/V)}$$

cancelling out:

$$4 \quad = \quad \frac{x \; x \; x}{(1-x) \; x \; (1-x)}$$

$$4 \quad = \quad \frac{x^2}{(1-x)^2}$$

Take the square root of each side:

$$2 = \frac{x}{(1-x)}$$

$$2(1-x) = x$$

$$2 - 2x = x$$

$$2 = 3x$$

$$x = \frac{2}{3}$$

Therefore 2/3 mole of ethyl ethanoate and 2/3 mole of water will be produced at equilibrium. The equilibrium mixture would, therefore, also contain 1/3 mole of ethanol and 1/3 mole of ethanoic acid.

<u>Qualitative Effects of Changes of Temperature and Concentration</u>

We already know from Le Chatelier's principle that if a system is disturbed, the equilibrium position will move, either to the left or to the right. The move will occur in the direction that will act to reduce the disturbance.

We can use Le Chatelier's principle to predict the qualitative effect of changing the temperature or pressure on the position of equilibrium in a reversible reaction.

We know from Le Chatelier's principle that if we increase the pressure in a system, the equilibrium will move in the direction with the fewest molecules. We also know that if we increase the temperature of the reaction, the equilibrium will move in the endothermic direction to try and balance out the change in conditions.

Effect of Changes in Temperature on Kc

Changes in temperature also affect the equilibrium constant. Kc can either increase or decrease and this depends on whether the reaction is exothermic or endothermic.[2]

Reaction Type	Temperature Change	Effect on Kc	Effect on Products	Effect on Reactants	Direction of Change of Equilibrium
Endothermic	Decrease	Decrease	Decrease	Increase	Moves Left
Endothermic	Increase	Increase	Increase	Decrease	Moves Right
Exothermic	Increase	Decrease	Decrease	Increase	Moves Left
Exothermic	Decrease	Increase	Increase	Decrease	Moves Right

If the equilibrium constant increases in value then the equilibrium will move to the right. If the equilibrium constant decreases in value then the equilibrium will move to the left.

Effect of Changes in Concentration on the Position of Equilibrium

The equilibrium constant only changes with a change in temperature. The concentration of any of the species in the reaction does not affect the value of Kc. If more of one of the reactants is added to a reaction at equilibrium, more of the products will be produced and the reaction will act to regain its equilibrium position. In this way, the equilibrium constant will remain unchanged from the initial reaction to the new reaction, after it has regained its equilibrium position.

Effects of a Catalyst on Kc

Catalysts affect the rate of reaction in the forwards and backwards direction equally, and therefore have no effect at all on the equilibrium constant.

---

[2] Table taken from Lister & Renshaw, 2009, 25.

1.7 – Oxidation, reduction and redox equations

Redox reactions involve a transfer of electrons from the reducing agent to the oxidising agent. The change in the oxidation state of an element in a compound or ion is used to identify the element that has been oxidised or reduced in a given reaction. Separate half-equations are written for the oxidation or reduction processes. These half-equations can then be combined to give an overall equation for any redox reaction.

Oxidation and Reduction

Redox stands for reduction/oxidation. A substance is considered to be oxidised when it loses electrons. A substance is considered to be reduced when it gains electrons (although this may seem counter intuitive). There is more to redox reactions than this, but that is enough for now.

- Oxidation = loss of electrons (or the gain of oxygen)
- Reduction = gain of electrons (or the loss of oxygen)

You can remember this using the mnemonic OiLRiG – **O**xidation is **L**oss, **R**eduction is **G**ain (of electrons)

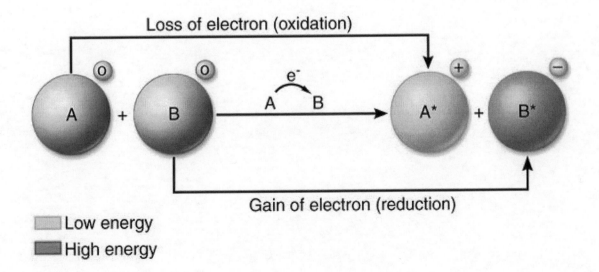

The formation of sodium chloride from its atomic components is an excellent example of such a reaction.

Activity 55 – Think about the reaction forming sodium chloride and the nature of the ionic bond, and state which substance is reduced and which is oxidised.

Answer to Activity 55:

I hope that you can see from the illustration below that the sodium loses an electron and is therefore oxidised. Chlorine gains an electron and is therefore reduced.

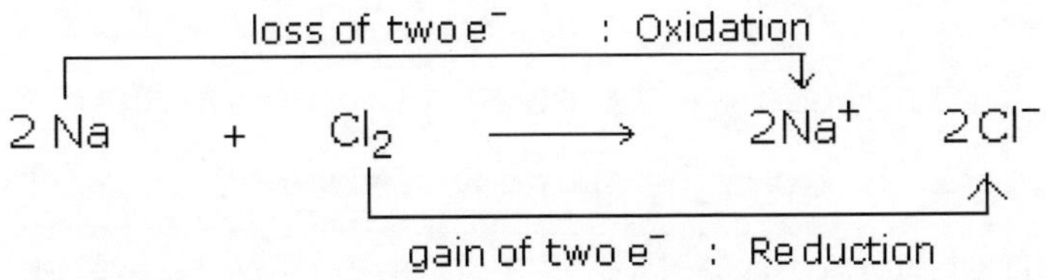

$$\overbrace{2\,Na \quad + \quad Cl_2 \quad \longrightarrow \quad 2Na^+ \quad 2Cl^-}$$

loss of two e⁻ : Oxidation

gain of two e⁻ : Reduction

You should have been able to predict this from the periodic table too. Sodium is in group 1 and therefore has 1 electron in its outer shell. Chlorine is in group 7 and therefore has 7 electrons in its outer shell.

Sodium therefore needs to lose 1 electron and chlorine needs to gain 1. From the periodic table, therefore, you can predict redox reactions and which substance will be oxidised and which will be reduced.

The chlorine acts as the oxidising agent because it caused the redox reaction to occur by taking the electron.

- Oxidising agents are electron acceptors
- Reducing agents are electron donors

Oxidation States

Oxidation states can be used to determine which materials have been oxidised and which have been reduced in a redox reaction. Oxidation states are also called oxidation numbers.

Every element in a compound can be given an oxidation state. In ionic compounds this tells us how many electrons the element has gained or lost. In a molecule it tells us the distribution of electrons between elements of different electronegativity. The most electronegative elements have a negative oxidation state.

Some notes on oxidation states:

- An element always has an oxidation state of 0
- A positive number means the element has lost electron(s) and been oxidised
- A negative number means the element has gained electron(s) and been reduced
- The higher the number, the more electrons have been gained or lost

element	usual oxidation state	exceptions
Group 1 metals	always +1	
Group 2 metals	always +2	
Oxygen	usually -2	except in peroxides and F_2O (see below)
Hydrogen	usually +1	except in metal hydrides where it is -1 (see below)
Fluorine	always -1	
Chlorine	usually -1	except in compounds with O or F (see below)

Rules for calculating oxidation state:

- An atom in an element has an oxidation state of 0
- Some elements always have the same oxidation state; with others it occasionally changes (see the table above)
- The total oxidation state of a compound is 0 since they are always electrically neutral
- The total oxidation state of an ion is equal to the electrical charge of the ion (e.g. NH_4^+)
- In compounds, the most electronegative element always has a negative oxidation state

Calculating Oxidation States

Consider the following:

- Phosphorous pentachloride (PCl_5)
- Ammonia (NH_3)
- Sulphuric acid (H_2SO_4)
- Ammonium (NH_4^+)
- Copper II oxide (CuO)
- Sulphate ions (SO_4^{2-})

Phosphorous Pentachloride (PCl_5)

We know the following:

- that chlorine has an oxidation state of -1 (from the table above)
- the overall charge of the compound is 0

Therefore, we can deduce that phosphorous must have an oxidation state of +5 (as there are 5 x Cl atoms at -1 each and 0 charge overall).

Ammonia (NH_3)

We know the following:

- that hydrogen has an oxidation state of +1 (from the table above)
- the overall charge of the compound is 0

Therefore, we can deduce that nitrogen must have an oxidation state of -3 (as there are 3 x H atoms at +1 each).

Sulphuric Acid (H_2SO_4)

We know the following:

- that each oxygen has an oxidation state of -2 (from the table above) giving a total of -8 (as there are 4 oxygen atoms)
- Hydrogen has an oxidation state of +1, giving a total of +2
- the overall charge of the compound is 0

Therefore, we can deduce that sulphur must have an oxidation state of +6 ((overall) Hydrogen = +2, Oxygen = -8: 0 overall charge means sulphur must be -6).

Ammonium (NH_4^+)

We know the following:

- that each hydrogen has an oxidation state of +1
- the overall charge of the compound is +1

Therefore, we can deduce that nitrogen must have an oxidation state of -3 ((overall) Hydrogen = +4, nitrogen must have an oxidation state of -3 in order for the overall charge to be +1).

Activity 56 – Calculate the oxidation states of the remaining two examples:

- **Copper II oxide (CuO)**
- **Sulphate ions (SO_4^{2-})**

Answer to Activity 56:

Copper II Oxide (CuO)

We know the following:

- that each oxygen has an oxidation state of -2
- the overall charge of the compound is 0

Therefore, we can deduce that copper must have an oxidation state of +2.

Sulphate Ions (SO_4^{2-})

We know the following:

- that each oxygen has an oxidation state of -2
- the overall charge of the compound is -2

Therefore, we can deduce that sulphur has an oxidation state of +6.

Redox Equations

You should know by now that:

- Oxidation = loss of electrons (or the gain of oxygen)
- Reduction = gain of electrons (or the loss of oxygen)

We can also use the oxidation state to determine which elements in a redox reaction have been oxidised and which have been reduced.

Oxidation state	+3	-1	+2	0
Reaction		Fe^{3+} + I^- →	Fe^{2+} +	$\frac{1}{2} I_2$

We can say from the oxidation states that:

- Iron has been reduced because its oxidation state has gone down from +3 to +2
- Iodide has been oxidised because its oxidation state has gone up from -1 to 0

We can also use oxidation states to help balance equations. For equations to balance, the following must be true:

- The number of atoms of each element must be the same on each side of the equation
- The total charge on each side of the equation must be the same

Let us consider the reaction between iron III oxide and aluminium:

Oxidation state	+3 -2	0	0	+3 -2
Reaction	$Fe_2O_3(s)$ +	$Al(s)$ →	$Fe(l)$ +	$Al_2O_3(s)$

Here the iron is reduced (+3 down to 0), the aluminium is oxidised (0 up to +3) and the oxygen remains unchanged.

Looking at the ionic half equations (i.e. just one part of the equation), they would be:

$$Fe^{3+} + 3e^- \rightarrow Fe$$

$$Al \rightarrow Al^{3+} + 3e^-$$

1.8 - Thermodynamics

The further study of thermodynamics builds on the Energetics section and is important in understanding the stability of compounds and why chemical reactions occur. Enthalpy change is linked with entropy change enabling the free-energy change to be calculated.

1.8.1 – Born-Haber cycles

Born-Haber cycles are used to calculate lattice enthalpies using the following data:

Enthalpy Change (ΔH)

We must start this section by defining some basic terms that you must be aware of (some of which you have already met):

Enthalpy of formation – (ΔH_f) is the energy change when one mole of a compound is formed from its constituent elements under standard conditions, all reactants and products in their standard states.

Ionisation enthalpy – the first ionisation energy (IE) is the standard enthalpy change when one mole of gaseous atoms is converted into one mole of gaseous ions, each with a single positive charge.

Enthalpy of atomisation of an element – (ΔH_{at}) is the enthalpy change which accompanies the formation of one mole of gaseous atoms from the element in its standard state under standard conditions.

Enthalpy of atomisation of a compound – (ΔH_{at}) is the enthalpy change which accompanies the formation of one mole of gaseous atoms from the compound in its standard state under standard conditions. All the bonds in the compound are broken in atomisation, so the value is always positive.

Bond dissociation enthalpy – this is the standard enthalpy change that accompanies the breaking of a covalent bond in a gaseous molecule to form two radicals also in the gaseous phase.

Electron affinity – (ΔH_{ea}) is the standard enthalpy change when an electron is added to an isolated atom in the gas phase.

Lattice enthalpy – the lattice energy of an ionic solid is a measure of the strength of the bonds in that ionic compound. It is usually defined as the enthalpy of formation of the ionic compound from gaseous ions, and as such is invariably exothermic.

Enthalpy of hydration – (ΔH_{hyd}) is the standard enthalpy change when water molecules surround one mole of gaseous ions.

Enthalpy of solution – is the standard enthalpy change for the process in which one mole of an ionic solid dissolves in an amount of water large enough to ensure that the dissolved ions are well separated and do not interact with one another.

Born-Haber Cycles

A Born-Haber cycle is a thermo-chemical cycle that includes all of the enthalpy changes involved in the formation of an ionic compound. Their construction starts from the constituent elements in their standard states, as these have zero enthalpy by definition.

Let us consider the formation of sodium chloride (NaCl), a simple ionic compound.

There are a number of steps in the formation of the sodium chloride compound.

Basic reaction:

$$Na(s) \ + \ \tfrac{1}{2} \, Cl_2(g) \ \rightarrow \ NaCl(s)$$

Stages (enthalpies will be slightly different in other sources):

$$Na(s) \rightarrow Na(g) \qquad \Delta H_{at} = +109 \text{ kJ mol}^{-1}$$

$$\tfrac{1}{2} Cl_2(g) \rightarrow Cl(g) \qquad \Delta H_{at} = +121 \text{ kJ mol}^{-1}$$

$$Na(g) \rightarrow Na+(g) + e^- \qquad 1^{st} \text{ IE } = +494 \text{ kJ mol}^{-1}$$

$$Cl(g) + e^- \rightarrow Cl^-(g) \qquad 1^{st} \text{ EA } = -364 \text{ kJ mol}^{-1}$$

$$Na(s) + \tfrac{1}{2} Cl_2(g) \rightarrow NaCl(s) \qquad \Delta H_f = -411 \text{ kJ mol}^{-1}$$

Below is an illustration of the Born-Haber cycle for the production of sodium chloride:

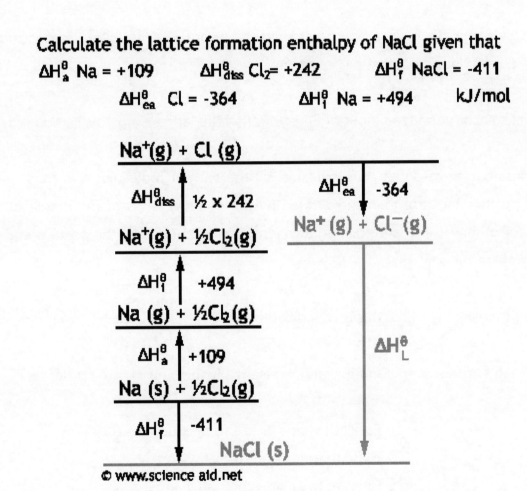

The enthalpy we are looking for is ΔH_L in the illustration above.

Once you have constructed the cycle, calculating the enthalpy is a simple case of following the alternative route for the reaction. Remember that if you go in the opposite direction to the arrows in the diagram, the sign of the enthalpy is reversed (i.e. +109 becomes -109 and vice versa).

$$\Delta H_L = \Delta H_f - \text{steps 1-4}$$

$$\Delta H_L = -411 - 109 - 494 - (\tfrac{1}{2} \times 242) - (-364)$$

$$\Delta H_L = -771 \text{ kJ mol}^{-1}$$

Enthalpies of Solution

Ionic solids only dissolve well in polar solvents. In order for the ionic compound to dissolve, the lattice must first be broken up.

In order to achieve this, an input of energy, called the lattice enthalpy, is required.

The ions that are produced are solvated by the solvent molecules, typically water. These positive ions are then surrounded by the negative ends of the dipole of the water (or other solvent) and the negative ions are surrounded by the positive ends of the dipole of the solvent.

When the solvent is water, this is called hydration.

Dissolving an ionic compound in water is essentially the sum of three processes:

1) Break the ionic lattice to produce gaseous ions
2) Hydrate the cations (positive ions)
3) Hydrate the anions (negative ions)

For ionic compounds, the enthalpy change of hydration is small, and can be either positive or negative.

Consider the enthalpy of hydration (ΔH_{hyd}) for sodium chloride:

Equation:

$$NaCl(s) + solvent \rightarrow Na^+(aq) + Cl^-(aq)$$

The stages needed for the calculation are:

Enthalpy change for lattice dissociation:

$$NaCl(s) \rightarrow Na^+(g) + Cl^-(g) \quad \mathbf{\Delta H_L = +771 \ kJ \ mol^{-1}}$$

Enthalpy change for the hydration of the sodium ion:

$$Na^+(g) + Solvent + Cl^-(g) \rightarrow Na^+(aq) + Cl^-(g) \quad \mathbf{\Delta H_{hyd} = -406 \ kJ \ mol^{-1}}$$

Enthalpy change for the hydration of the chloride ion:

$$Na^+(aq) + Cl^-(aq) + Solvent \rightarrow Na^+(aq) + Cl^-(aq) \quad \mathbf{\Delta H_{hyd} = -363 \ kJ \ mol^{-1}}$$

Therefore:

$$\Delta H_{solution} (NaCl) = \Delta H_L (NaCl) + \Delta H_{hyd} (Na^+) + \Delta H_{hyd} (Cl^-)$$

So:

$$\Delta H_{solution} (NaCl) = +771 + -406 + -363$$

$$\mathbf{\Delta H_{hyd} (NaCl) = +2 \ kJ \ mol^{-1}}$$

Lattice Enthalpies and Bonding

We can calculate the theoretical value for the enthalpy of formation of an ionic compound if we have some key data:

- The charge of the ions
- The distance apart
- The geometry of the structure

In many ionic compounds, the lattice formation enthalpy calculated experimentally (using a Born-Haber cycle) agrees very closely with the theoretical value.

There are some compounds where a large discrepancy exists between the theoretical value and the experimental value, however.

This occurs because the bond in question has some covalent characteristics.

All ionic and covalent bonds are part of a continuum from purely ionic at one end of the spectrum to purely covalent at the other. We can say that those in the middle have some of the properties of each, which is why the theoretical and experimental values differ.

Calculating Enthalpy Changes using Mean Bond Enthalpies

Hess's Law states that the enthalpy change for a reaction that is carried out in a series of steps is equal to the sum of the enthalpy changes for the individual steps.

We can use this law to help us calculate the mean bond enthalpies of a compound.

The standard enthalpy of bond dissociation is the enthalpy change when a mole of gaseous molecules each breaks a covalent bond to form two free radicals.

Bond enthalpies are specific to a bond in a particular compound. For example, a C–Cl bond will have slightly different bond enthalpies in different compounds.

The mean bond dissociation enthalpy can be calculated by averaging the differences over several compounds. We call this the mean bond dissociation enthalpy. These are often called bond energies, and they can be used in calculations.

Note that different sources are likely to give slightly different values for these bond energies.

We can compare the bond energy (essentially the strength of bonds) in a compound and use this information to speculate as to which bond will break first.

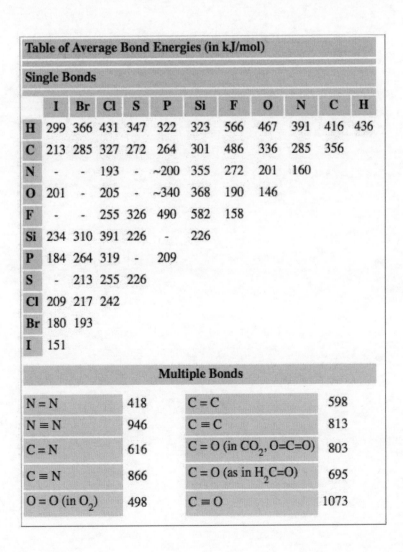

Table of Average Bond Energies (in kJ/mol)										
Single Bonds										
	I	**Br**	**Cl**	**S**	**P**	**Si**	**F**	**O**	**N**	**C**	**H**
H	299	366	431	347	322	323	566	467	391	416	436
C	213	285	327	272	264	301	486	336	285	356	
N	-	-	193	-	~200	355	272	201	160		
O	201	-	205	-	~340	368	190	146			
F	-	-	255	326	490	582	158				
Si	234	310	391	226	-	226					
P	184	264	319	-	209						
S	-	213	255	226							
Cl	209	217	242								
Br	180	193									
I	151										

Multiple Bonds			
N = N	418	C = C	598
N ≡ N	946	C ≡ C	813
C = N	616	C = O (in CO_2, O=C=O)	803
C ≡ N	866	C = O (as in $H_2C=O$)	695
O = O (in O_2)	498	C ≡ O	1073

Activity 98 – Consider bromoethene. Draw the bonds that exist in that substance and their bond energies using data from the table above.

Answer to Activity 98:

The structure of bromoethene is:

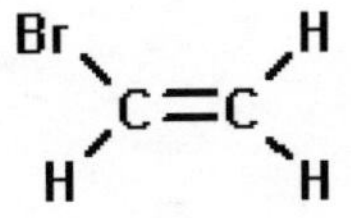

The bonds and bond energies are:

- C–H = 416 kJ mol^{-1}
- C=C = 598 kJ mol^{-1}
- C–Br = 285 kJ mol^{-1}

We can see that the weakest bond, the one with the lowest bond energy, is the C–Br bond. We could infer that this is the bond that will break first, and typically this is the case.

Be wary of this approach, however, as there may be other factors that influence which bond breaks first, such as the presence of a catalyst, for example.

1.8.2 – Gibbs free-energy change, ΔG, and entropy change, ΔS

The term "spontaneous" is typically used in chemistry to describe reactions that can occur of their own accord. Some of these reactions are very fast, and some are so slow as to be virtually undetectable.

Many (but not all) spontaneous reactions are exothermic (ΔH is negative). Some, however, are endothermic (ΔH is positive), for example ammonium nitrate reacting to produce aqueous ammonium nitrate.

Many spontaneous processes involve the molecules spreading out. Think about what happens when a solid becomes a gas, for example.

You should be aware of the tendency of particles towards randomness (or disorganisation); this is an important factor in chemical reactions. Because of the arrangement of particles, we can say:

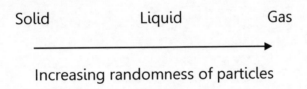

Solid   Liquid   Gas

Increasing randomness of particles

Endothermic reactions can therefore be spontaneous if they involve the particles spreading out or becoming more disordered.

Consider the reaction that changes ammonium nitrate from a solid to an aqueous solution.

The equation is:

$$NH_4NO_3(s) + Solvent \rightarrow NH_4NO_3(aq)$$

The ammonium nitrate starts out as a solid and forms a liquid. We know that the molecules in a liquid are more spread out and disordered than those in a solid. The randomness of a system is called entropy and is given the symbol S. Reactions where the randomness of the molecules increases will have a positive value for ΔS.

Entropies have been calculated for a huge range of substances and are available in tables and databases. They are typically quoted for standard conditions:

- 298K
- 100KPa

Calculating Entropy Change

The entropy of a reaction can be calculated theoretically fairly easily. Add all of the entropies of the products, and subtract all of the entropies of the reactants.

Consider the following reaction:

$$CaCO_3(s) \rightarrow CaO(s) + CO_2(g)$$

Using standard entropy values, we can calculate:

Entropy of products = $40 + 214 = 254$ JK^{-1} mol^{-1}
Entropy of reactants = 93 JK^{-1} mol^{-1}

Therefore:

$$\Delta S = \Sigma S \text{ PRODUCTS} - \Sigma S \text{ REACTANTS}$$
$$254 \quad - \quad 93$$

$\Delta S = 161$ JK^{-1} mol^{-1}

This value is positive and it is fairly large because a gas is formed from a solid.

Gibbs Free Energy Change (ΔG)

Two factors govern the feasibility of a chemical reaction:

- Enthalpy change
- Entropy change

These two factors can be combined into a concept called:

- Gibbs free energy (ΔG)

If the change in Gibbs free energy, ΔG, is negative, then the reaction is feasible. If it is positive, then the reaction is not feasible.

$$\Delta G = \Delta H - T\Delta S$$

We can see from the above statement that ΔG depends on temperature (the T in ΔS).

The implication of this is that some reactions are not feasible at one temperature, but might become feasible at another.

An endothermic reaction, therefore, can become increasingly feasible when the temperature of the reaction is increased, if there is a large enough positive entropy change.

Note that a positive entropy change will make the ΔG more negative because of the -$T\Delta S$ term in the equation.

Let us look again at the reaction:

$$CaCO_3(s) \rightarrow CaO(s) + CO_2(g)$$

We have already calculated that ΔS is $+161$ JK^{-1} mol^{-1} (equal to 0.161 kJK^{-1} mol^{-1})

NB. Entropy units are converted by dividing by 1000 because enthalpy is measured in kilojoules per mole, and entropy in joules per Kelvin per mole.

At room temperature (298K):

$$\Delta G = \Delta H - T\Delta S$$

$$\Delta G = 178 - (298 \times 0.161)$$

$$\mathbf{\Delta G = 130 \text{ kJ mol}^{-1}}$$

Activity 99 – Is this reaction feasible?

Answer to Activity 99:

The Gibbs free energy value is positive, so the reaction is not feasible at room temperature. Changing the temperature will make the reaction feasible, however.

Try this calculation again at different temperatures to see at what point the reaction becomes feasible.

<u>Calculating Entropy Change</u>

We can use the temperature at which the ΔG value will be zero to calculate an entropy change for a reaction.

For example, ice at its melting point will exist partly as the solid form and partly as a liquid. An equilibrium will exist between the solid and liquid.

ΔG for the melting process is 0 and therefore:

$$0 \quad = \Delta H - T\Delta S$$

Considering water again, the melting point is 273K, and the enthalpy change for melting is 6 kJ mol^{-1}.

Therefore:

$$0 = 6 - 273 \times \Delta S$$

$$\Delta S = \frac{6}{273}$$

$$\mathbf{\Delta S = 0.022 \text{ kJ mol}^{-1} \text{ (or 22 JK}^{-1}\text{ mol}^{-1}\text{)}}$$

1.9 – Rate equations

In rate equations, the mathematical relationship between rate of reaction and concentraction gives information about the mechanism of a reaction that may occur in several steps.

1.9.1 – Rate equations

The rate of a reaction is not fixed and can be affected by a number of factors. We will start by looking at these.

Activity 73 – List the issues that you think can affect the rate of a chemical reaction.

Answer to Activity 73:

The factors that can affect the rate of reaction are: temperature, pressure, concentration of the reactants, the presence of a catalyst and the surface area of the reactants/catalyst.

Chemical reactions involve reactants and products. The rate of reaction is defined as the rate at which the reactants are used, or the rate at which the products are produced.

Generally speaking, a reaction will begin with a large amount of the reactants, and a small amount of product.

As the reaction proceeds, the volume of reactants decreases as the volume of the products increases.

In a reversible reaction, this occurs until the equilibrium position is reached.

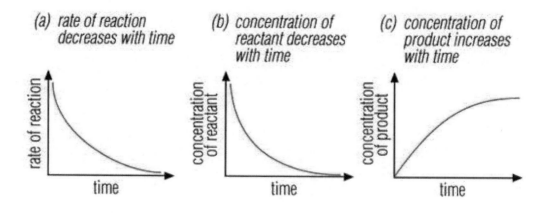

In a normal reaction, the rate of reaction decreases steadily over time. The rate of reaction at any given instant can be measured by looking at the gradient on the graph of the whole reaction.

Measuring a Rate of Reaction

In order to measure the reaction rate, we need a method of measuring the concentration of at least one of the reactants or products over time; a calorimeter can often be used for this. If the reaction is a relatively slow one, then a calorimeter is a perfect tool, as a reading can be taken every 15 or 30 seconds and plotted on a graph. The rate of reaction is typically defined as the change in concentration over the time in which that change occurred.

$$\text{Reaction rate} = \frac{\text{Change in concentration}}{\text{Time period}}$$

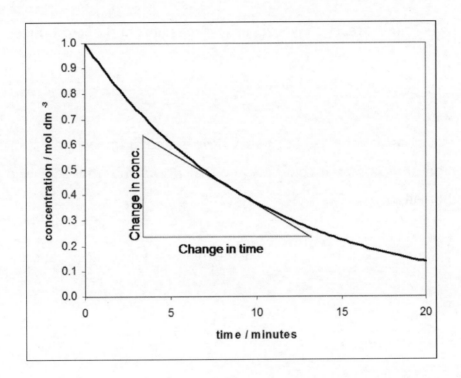

When the graph is of the change in concentration of reactants, the gradient is always negative. This is the case because the reactants are being used up in the reaction and their concentration therefore decreases. When the graph is of the change in concentration of products, the gradient is always positive. This is because the products are being formed gradually in the reaction, and their concentration therefore increases.

The Rate Expression

The rate of reaction depends on a number of factors, including:

- The concentration of the reactants
- The concentration of the products
- The presence of catalysts

They do not, however, all make exactly the same contribution to the rate at which the reaction progresses. The rate equation tells us about the contributions of the species (chemicals) that do affect the rate.

Consider a very simple reaction which has two reactants and one product:

$$A + B \rightarrow C$$

The concentrations of either [A] or [B] may have a greater impact on the rate than the concentration of the other. It could also be that [A] has no impact on the rate at all and only [B] matters.

Note that square brackets are used in chemistry to denote concentration:

- [A] = The concentration of A
- [B] = The concentration of B
- [C] = The concentration of C

The rate expression is the equation that describes how the rate of reaction at a given temperature depends on the concentration of the chemicals in the reaction. It is possible that one or more of the chemicals in the reaction may not appear in the rate expression.

The reaction:

$$A + B \rightarrow C$$

might have the rate expression:

$$Rate \propto [A]\,[B]$$

Note that $\propto$ means proportional to in equations.

The above equation would mean that both [A] and [B] have an equal impact upon the rate of reaction. Doubling the concentration of both will quadruple the rate of the reaction.

In many reactions, however, the concentration of one reactant has a greater impact than the concentration of another. This can be illustrated as follows:

$$Rate \propto [A]^2\,[B]$$

This would mean that doubling [B] would double the rate of reaction, but doubling [A] would quadruple the rate of reaction.

The Rate Constant

If we introduce a constant to the above expression, we can eliminate the proportionality sign. The original expression was:

$$Rate \propto [A]^2 [B]$$

Introducing a constant would change this to:

$$Rate = k[A]^2 [B]$$

Note that k is the rate constant.

The rate constant is not like other constants you have encountered in chemistry, as it changes for every reaction. It also depends on the temperature of the reaction. For this reason, the temperature at which the rate constant was measured needs to be stated.

If the concentrations of all of the species (chemicals) in the rate equation are 1 mol dm^{-1}, then the rate equation is equal to the value of the rate constant.

Order of Reaction

Look again at the equation:

$$Rate = k[A]^2 [B]$$

In this equation [A] is raised to the power of 2. It has double the effect on the rate of reaction as does [B].

The order of reaction with respect to one of the chemicals in the equation is the power to which it is raised.
In the equation:

Rate = $k[A]^2[B]$

- The order of reaction with respect to [A] = 2
- The order of reaction with respect to [B] = 1

The overall order of reaction is the total of the individual orders of reaction for all of the chemicals (sometimes called species) in the rate equation.

In the equation:

Rate = $k[A]^2[B]$

The overall order of reaction = 2 + 1

$$= 3$$

For this reaction, three statements can be made:

- This is a *first order* reaction with respect to B
- This is a *second order* reaction with respect to A
- This is a *third order* reaction overall

If the rate equation were:

Rate = $k[A]^m[B]^n$

the overall order of reaction for this equation would be = m + n

Determination of the Rate Equation

The rate expression tells us of the relationship between the concentration of the reactants and the rate of reaction.

- If the rate of a reaction will not be altered by the substance, then the reaction is zero order with respect to that substance
- If the rate is proportional to the concentration of a substance, then the rate will be first order with respect to that substance
- If the rate is proportional to the concentration of a substance squared, then the reaction is second order with respect to that substance

You can determine the order of a reaction from a graph of the rate against concentration of a reaction (the graph on the left below). The line that is produced on the graph will determine the order of reaction with respect to the substance whose concentration you measured.

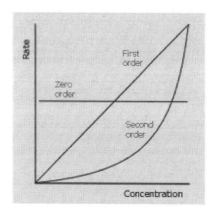
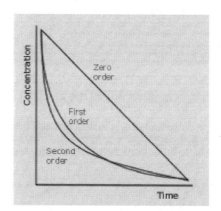

The chart can also be plotted slightly differently (as on the right). If you plot concentration against time for a given material, then you can also determine the order of reaction with respect to that substance from the graph that results.

The Initial Rate Method of Determining the Order of Reaction

With this method, a series of experiments are conducted at a constant temperature, which must be recorded.

Each experiment should be conducted by changing only one variable from the previous experiment; for example, changing the concentration of ONE of the reactants. The concentration of one of the reactants is measured and recorded each time, but it must be the same reactant each time.

The results should be plotted on a graph which would look something like the one below.

On this graph a tangent should be drawn at time = 0, as indicated. The gradient of this tangent is the initial rate of the reaction.

It is important to use the initial rate each time because we can know with certainty what the concentration of the substance in question was.

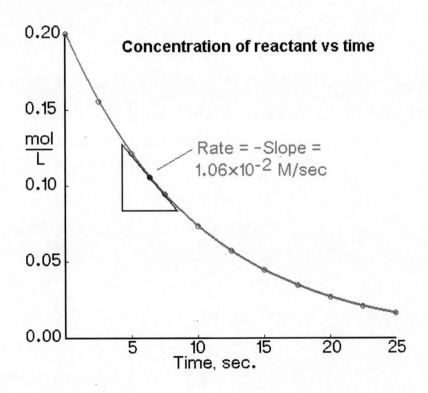

Comparing the initial concentration and initial rates of reaction for the different experiments will allow us to discover the order of reaction with regard to each reactant.

Consider the reaction and the experimental results:

$$2NO(g) + 2H_2(g) \rightarrow N_2(g) + 2H_2O(g)$$

Experiment	Initial concentration (mol/l)		Initial rate of formation of N2 (mol/l)
	[NO]	[H_2]	
1	0.006	0.001	1.8×10^{-4}
2	0.006	0.002	3.6×10^{-4}
3	0.001	0.006	0.3×10^{-4}
4	0.002	0.006	1.2×10^{-4}

Compare experiment 1 with experiment 2. The concentration of NO remains the same, but the concentration of H_2 doubles. This causes a doubling of the rate. This suggests that:

$$Rate \propto [H]$$

Now consider experiment 3 compared to experiment 4. This time [NO] doubles while [H_2] remains the same. This has a quadrupling effect on the rate of the reaction. This suggests that:

$$Rate \propto [NO]^2$$

Providing the data is correct, and there are no other reactants that impact upon the rate, we can conclude:

The overall order of reaction is $= 3$
The rate expression is:

$$\text{Rate} = k[NO]^2[H_2]$$

Finding the Rate Constant k

We can find the rate constant k by substituting values for concentration and rate into the equation:

$$\text{Rate} = k[NO]^2[H_2]$$

Look at the values for experiment 1 above:

$$\text{Rate} = k[NO]^2[H_2]$$

Therefore:

$$1.8 \times 10^{-4} = k\,(0.006)^2 \times 0.001$$

$$k = \frac{1.8 \times 10^{-4}}{(0.006)^2 \times 0.001}$$

$$k = \frac{1.8 \times 10^{-4}}{3.6 \times 10^{-8}}$$

$$\textbf{\textit{k} = 5000}$$

The Effect of Temperature on k

As a general rule (although it is not always the case), if the temperature of a reaction is increased by 10K, then the rate of reaction doubles. Looking at the equation above, we can say that the concentration of the reactant does not change in the equation with an increase in temperature, so the rate constant k must change.

The larger the value of k, then the faster the reaction progresses, and given that increasing the temperature increases the rate of reaction, then increasing the temperature must increase the value of k.

The rate constant k varies with temperature as shown by the equation:

$$k = Ae^{-E_a/RT}$$

Where A is a constant, known as the Arrhenlus constant, E_a is the activation energy and T is the temperature in K.

1.9.2 – Determination of the rate equation

The Rate Determining Step

Many chemical reactions take place in several stages. These stages collectively are called the reaction mechanism.

Consider the following reaction:

$$A + 6B + 2C \rightarrow 4D + 3E$$

The actual reactants are not relevant, but this type of reaction must take place in stages because there are 9 ions on the reactant side of the equation (left of the arrow) and it is extremely unlikely that all 9 will react together at the same time.

Where there are several stages to a reaction, the products of the first stage are the reactants of the second stage. The products of the second stage will then be the reactants of the third stage and so on.

The rate of the slowest stage of the process may, therefore, define the overall rate of the reaction. The slowest stage of the reaction is called the **rate determining stage** or the **rate determining step.**

Any stage that occurs *after* the rate determining stage will not affect the overall rate of the reaction as long as it occurs at the same rate or faster than the rate determining stage.

The species that are involved in the reaction mechanism after the rate determining stage do not appear in the rate expression.

Consider the reaction:

$$A + B + C \rightarrow Y + Z$$

The following stages could occur in this reaction:

1) A + B → M (1st intermediate stage)

2) M → K (2nd intermediate stage)

3) K + C → Y + Z

Stage 2 may be the slowest reaction and therefore determines the overall rate of the reaction. As soon as any K is produced, it will react with C to produce the products Y and Z.

Stage 1 might affect the overall rate because the concentration of M (the product of reaction 1) is critical to stage 2, and therefore may affect the rate determining stage.

The Order of Reaction and the Rate Determining Stage

Consider the following reaction:

$$C_4H_9Br + OH^- \rightarrow C_4H_9OH + Br^-$$

Two reaction mechanisms are possible for this reaction.

Mechanism 1:

Stage 1 (slow) $C_4H_9Br \rightarrow C_4H_9^+ + Br^-$

Stage 2 (fast) $C_4H_9^+ + OH^- \rightarrow C_4H_9OH$

The slow stage involves the breaking of the C – Br bond and the formation of two ions. Ions are charged and therefore highly reactive. Stage two involves the reaction of two ions, which occurs at a much faster rate.

Mechanism 2:

$$C_4H_9Br + OH^- \rightarrow C_4H_9OH + Br^-$$

This is a single stage mechanism where the C – Br bond breaks at the same time as the C – OH bond is forming. This reaction is slow as it depends on the breaking of the C – Br bond, which is itself a slow process.

Activity 74 – Draw the three structural isomers of bromobutane (C_4H_9Br).

Answer to Activity 74:

Bromobutane has three structural isomers:

1-bromobutane:

2-bromobutane:

2-bromo,2-methylpropane

Experimentation would show that 1-bromobutane reacts via a second order mechanism:

$$Rate = k[C_4H_9Br][OH^-]$$

The rate is determined by the concentration of *both* bromobutane and hydroxide ions, suggesting a single stage reaction or mechanism 2.

Experimentation also shows that 2-bromo 2-methylpropane reacts via a first order mechanism:

$$Rate = k[C_4H_9Br]$$

This implies that mechanism 1 is the process here, as the slow step of breaking the C – Br bond is followed by the very rapid step of the ions reacting together. So the breaking of the C – Br bond is the rate determining stage.

Required Practical 7:

Measuring the rate of reaction:
- **By an initial rate method**
- **By a continuous monitoring method**

1.10 – Equilibrium constant Kp for homogeneous systems

The further study of equilibria considers how the mathematical expression for the equilibrium constant Kp enables us to calculate how an equillibrium yield will be influenced by the partial pressures of reactants and products. This has important consequences for many industrial processes.

A homogeneous equilibrium is one in which everything in the equilibrium mixture is present in the same phase. In this case, to use K_p, **everything must be a gas**.

A good example of a gaseous homogeneous equilibrium is the conversion of sulphur dioxide to sulphur trioxide at the heart of the Contact Process:

$$2SO_{2(g)} + O_{2(g)} \rightleftharpoons 2SO_{3(g)}$$

Writing an expression for K_p

We are going to start by looking at a general case with the equation:

$$aA_{(g)} + bB_{(g)} \rightleftharpoons cC_{(g)} + dD_{(g)}$$

If you allow this reaction to reach equilibrium and then measure (or work out) the equilibrium partial pressures of everything, you can combine these into the equilibrium constant, K_p. Just like K_c, K_p always has the same value (provided you don't change the temperature), irrespective of the amounts of A, B, C and D you started with.

$$K_p = \frac{P_C{}^c \times P_D{}^d}{P_A{}^a \times P_B{}^b}$$

K_p has exactly the same format as K_c, except that partial pressures are used instead of concentrations. The gases on the right-hand side of the chemical equation are at the top of the expression, and those on the left at the bottom.

The Contact Process equilibrium

You will remember that the equation for this is:

$$2SO_{2(g)} + O_{2(g)} \rightleftharpoons 2SO_{3(g)}$$

K_p is given by:

$$K_p = \frac{P_{SO_3}{}^2}{P_{SO_2}{}^2 \times P_{O_2}}$$

The Haber Process equilibrium

The equation for this is:

$$N_{2(g)} + 3H_{2(g)} \rightleftharpoons 2NH_{3(g)}$$

. . . and the K_p expression is:

$$K_p = \frac{P_{NH_3}{}^2}{P_{N_2} \times P_{H_2}{}^3}$$

K_p in heterogeneous equilibria

A typical example of a heterogeneous equilibrium will involve gases in contact with solids.

Writing an expression for K_p for a heterogeneous equilibrium

Exactly as happens with K_c, you *don't include any term for a solid in the equilibrium expression.* The next two examples have already appeared on the K_c page.

The equilibrium produced on heating carbon with steam

$$H_2O_{(g)} + C_{(s)} \rightleftharpoons H_{2(g)} + CO_{(g)}$$

Everything is exactly the same as before in the expression for K_p, except that you leave out the solid carbon.

$$K_p = \frac{P_{H_2} \times P_{CO}}{P_{H_2O}}$$

The equilibrium produced on heating calcium carbonate

This equilibrium is only established if the calcium carbonate is heated in a closed system, preventing the carbon dioxide from escaping.

$$CaCO_{3(s)} \rightleftharpoons CaO_{(s)} + CO_{2(g)}$$

The only thing in this equilibrium which isn't a solid is the carbon dioxide. That is all that is left in the equilibrium constant expression.

$$K_p = P_{CO_2}$$

Calculations involving K_p

On the K_c page, I've already discussed the fact that the internet isn't a good medium for learning how to do calculations.

If you want lots of worked examples and problems to do yourself centred around K_p, you might be interested in my book on chemistry calculations.[3]

---

[3] http://www.chemguide.co.uk/physical/equilibria/kp.html

1.11 – Electrode potentials and electromechanical cells

Redox reactions take place in electrochemical cells where electrons are transferred from the reducing agent to the oxidising agent indirectly via an external circuit. A potential difference is created that can drive an electric current to do work. Electrochemical cells have very important commercial applications as a portable supply of electricity to power electric devices such as mobile phones, tablets and laptops. On a larger scale, they can provide energy to power a vehicle.

1.11.1 - Electrode potentials and electromechanical cells

If we were to take two metal rods, one made from a more reactive metal, and one from a less reactive metal, and then place these rods into a salt solution and connect them together, an electric current will flow from the more reactive metal to the less reactive metal. This is the fundamental process that occurs in a battery.

<u>Half Cells</u>

If we take a rod of metal and suspend it in a solution of ions of that metal, an equilibrium will form. For example:

$$Zn(s) \rightleftharpoons Zn^{2+}(aq) + 2e^-$$

The experiment that establishes the equilibrium

We can measure the electrical potential difference between two different electrodes (half cells) by using a voltmeter. This can only occur if there is a salt bridge between the two solutions:

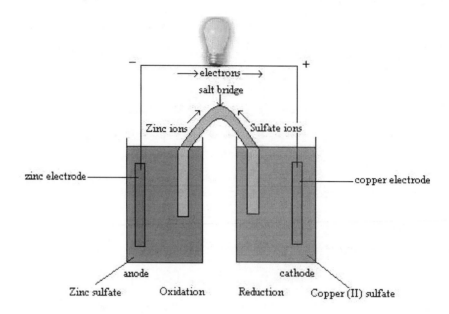

The resulting cell and the flow of electrons

The following changes would occur in the system:

1. Zinc would dissolve to form Zn^{2+}(aq), increasing the concentration of these ions in the solution.
2. The electrons would flow through the wire to the copper rod where they would combine with Cu^{2+}(aq) ions from the copper sulphate solution, depositing copper onto the copper rod, decreasing the concentration of Cu^{2+} ions in solution.

The following half reactions would be occurring:

$$Zn(s) \rightarrow Zn^{2+}(aq)\ 2e^-$$

$$Cu^{2+}(aq)\ +\ 2e^-\ \rightarrow Cu(s)$$

Overall, the system is:

$$Zn(s) + Cu^{2+}(aq) \rightarrow Zn^{2+}(aq) + Cu(s)$$

The Hydrogen Electrode

We can compare the tendency of different metals to release electrons by adding a constant to the system. This constant would be in the form of a hydrogen electrode.

In this system, we bubble hydrogen gas into an acid solution (H^+ ions) at 1 mol dm³. Since hydrogen does not conduct, the electrical contact is made using a wire of unreactive platinum metal coated with finely divided platinum to increase the surface area of the wire.

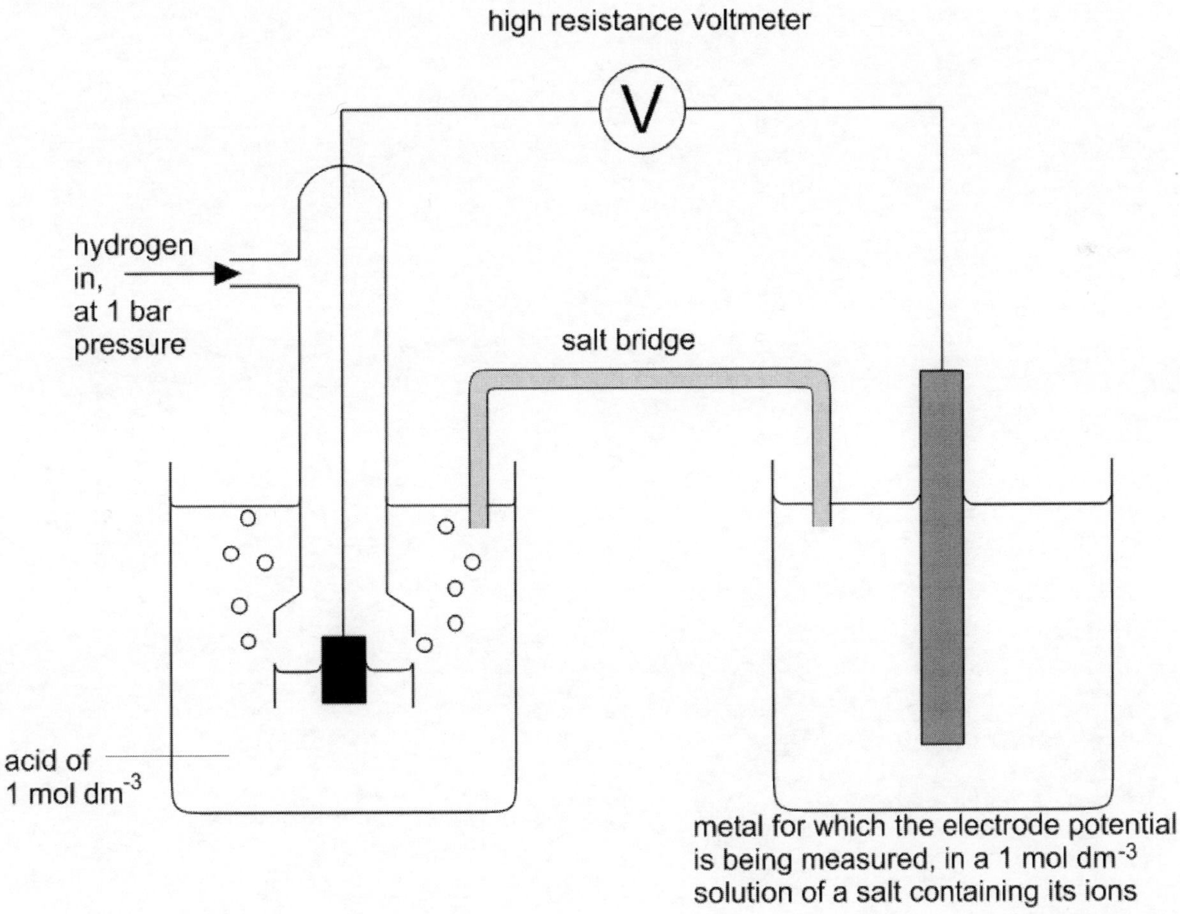

high resistance voltmeter

hydrogen in, at 1 bar pressure

salt bridge

acid of 1 mol dm⁻³

metal for which the electrode potential is being measured, in a 1 mol dm⁻³ solution of a salt containing its ions

The electrode must be under standard conditions:

- 298K
- 100KPa
- $[H^+(aq)] = 1.00$ mol dm^{-3}

We define the potential of the hydrogen electrode as zero. If we therefore connect the hydrogen electrode to another electrode, as in the illustration above, the measured voltage is the electrode potential of that second cell.

This electrode potential is called electromotive force (emf), or more commonly E.

If the second electrode is under standard conditions (detailed above), then the emf is given the symbol E$^\circ$ or E standard.

The Electrochemical Series

As noted in the table below, the electrons are written to the left of the arrow, which is to say, as a reduction. These are called electrode potentials, or reduction potentials.

The electrochemical series

equilibrium	E° (volts)
$Li^+_{(aq)} + e^- \rightleftharpoons Li_{(s)}$	-3.03
$K^+_{(aq)} + e^- \rightleftharpoons K_{(s)}$	-2.92
$Ca^{2+}_{(aq)} + 2e^- \rightleftharpoons Ca_{(s)}$	-2.87
$Na^+_{(aq)} + e^- \rightleftharpoons Na_{(s)}$	-2.71
$Mg^{2+}_{(aq)} + 2e^- \rightleftharpoons Mg_{(s)}$	-2.37
$Al^{3+}_{(aq)} + 3e^- \rightleftharpoons Al_{(s)}$	-1.66
$Zn^{2+}_{(aq)} + 2e^- \rightleftharpoons Zn_{(s)}$	-0.76
$Fe^{2+}_{(aq)} + 2e^- \rightleftharpoons Fe_{(s)}$	-0.44
$Pb^{2+}_{(aq)} + 2e^- \rightleftharpoons Pb_{(s)}$	-0.13
$2H^+_{(aq)} + 2e^- \rightleftharpoons H_{2(g)}$	0
$Cu^{2+}_{(aq)} + 2e^- \rightleftharpoons Cu_{(s)}$	+0.34
$Ag^+_{(aq)} + e^- \rightleftharpoons Ag_{(s)}$	+0.80
$Au^{3+}_{(aq)} + 3e^- \rightleftharpoons Au_{(s)}$	+1.50

The normal organisation for such a list is to have the most negative values at the top of the list, increasing as you move down. This is called an electrochemical series.

We can calculate the voltage that would be obtained by connecting two standard electrodes together by calculating the difference between the E^o values for each electrode.

For example, if we connect an Al^{3+} electrode to an Ag^+ electrode, we would have:

Al^{3+} = -1.66V

Ag^+ = $^+$0.80V

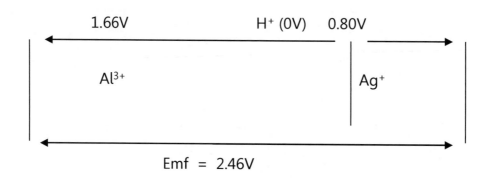

$E^o{}_{cell}$ = $E^o{}_{right}$ - $E^o{}_{left}$

So: 0.80 - ⁻1.66 = 2.46V

The total emf for the system is 2.46V

Activity 111 – Calculate the emf for a system consisting of a potassium and copper electrode.

Answer to Activity 111:

$K^+ = -2.92V$

$Cu^{2+} = +0.34V$

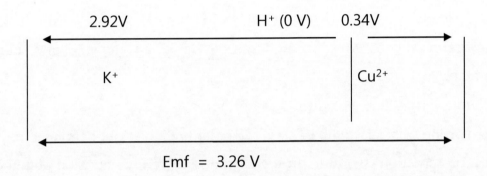

$= 0.34 - ^-2.92$

The emf for this system would be 3.26V.

Let us look at one final example. Consider cells of magnesium and zinc

$Mg^{2+} = -2.37V$

$Zn^{2+} = -0.76V$

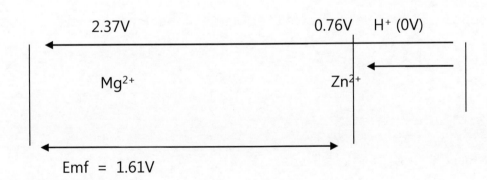

The emf for this system would be 1.61V.

Cell Representations

You must understand the convention for writing down the cell formation (i.e. the shorthand). These are the IUPAC conventions.

The conventions are:

- A vertical solid line represents a phase boundary (between solid and solution, for example).
- A double vertical line illustrates a salt bridge.
- When giving values for emf we state the polarity of the right hand electrode, as the cell representation is written. In the case of a system comprising aluminium and copper cells, the copper cell is positive and electrons would flow from aluminium to copper.

$$Al(s) \mid Al^{3+}(aq) \mid\mid Cu^{2+}(aq) \mid Cu(s) \quad E^{0}_{cell} = +2.00\,V$$

We could have written the cell in reverse (also reversing the emf symbol) as:

$$Cu(s) \mid Cu^{2+}(aq) \mid\mid Al^{3+}(aq) \mid Al(s) \quad E^{0}_{cell} = -2.00\,V$$

This second representation still tells us that electrons will flow from the aluminium cell to the copper cell, as we always give the polarity of the right hand electrode (as noted above).

We can say that:

$$emf = E^{o}(R) - E^{o}(L)$$

With $E^{o}(R)$ representing the emf of the right hand electrode, and $E^{o}(L)$ representing the emf of the left hand electrode.

Electrochemical Cells

Batteries are ubiquitous in the modern world; indeed, it is difficult to imagine a world without them. They power everything from mobile telephones to cars and from laptops to power tools. You need to understand the operation of cells, but not the construction of batteries. We will look at three types of cells, non-rechargeable, rechargeable and fuel cells.

Non-rechargeable Cells

These can be made from a number of combinations of cells. For example:

Zinc/copper – Like the Daniell Cell developed in the 1830s. These were large and not overly portable.

Zinc/carbon – Electrodes can sometimes be made from materials other than metals, like carbon, for example. In the Leclanché cell, the positive electrode is made from carbon.

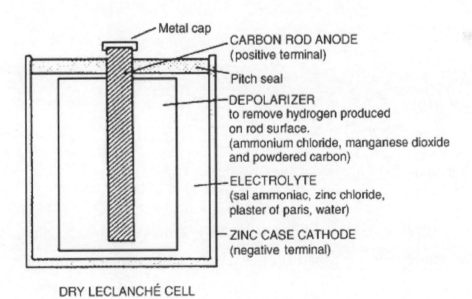

DRY LECLANCHÉ CELL

Here, the carbon acts in the same way as does the inert platinum in the hydrogen electrode. This type of cell is the basis for most commercial batteries.

The commercial versions of these cells consist of a zinc canister filled with ammonium chloride paste and water (the electrolyte). The carbon rod is in the centre as illustrated. The half equations are:

$$Zn(s) + 2e \rightleftharpoons Zn^{2+}(aq) \qquad E \approx -0.8V$$

$$2NH_4^+(aq) + 2e \rightleftharpoons 2NH_3(g) + H_2(g) \qquad E \approx +0.7V$$

Note that these are not E^o values, as the conditions are not standard.

The reaction taking place at the zinc electrode is:

$$Zn(s) \rightarrow Zn^{2+}(aq) + 2e-$$

(Note that this is the reverse of the above half equation.)

And at the carbon rod:

$$2NH_4^+(aq) + 2e^- \rightarrow 2NH_3(g) + H_2(g)$$

Overall, the reaction is:

$$2NH_4^+(aq) + Zn(s) \rightarrow 2NH_3(g) + Zn^{2+}(aq)$$

emf $\approx$ 1.5V with Zn as the negative terminal.

As the cell is used, the zinc canister is depleted, and the risk of leakage increases. Long-life zinc chloride cells are based on the same system, but with zinc chloride as the electrolyte.

Required practical 8:

Measuring the EMF of an electrochemical cell
1.11.2 – Commercial applications of electrochemical cells

<u>Rechargeable Batteries</u>

Rechargeable batteries can be recharged by reversing the cell reactions. This is done by applying a voltage that forces the electrons to travel in the opposite direction to their normal flow.

<u>Lead-Acid Batteries</u>

These are the types of batteries that are used in cars. There are six 2V cells in series, each of which consists of two lead plates dipped into a sulphuric acid solution. The positive plate is coated with lead (IV) oxide. The negative plate is pure lead.

The reaction at the lead plate is:

$$Pb(s) \; + \; SO_4^{2-}(aq) \; \rightarrow \; PbSO_4(s) \; + \; 2e^-$$

The reaction at the lead (IV) oxide plate is:

$$PbO_2(s) \; + \; 4H^+(aq) \; + \; SO_4^{2-}(aq) \; + \; 2e^- \; \rightarrow \; PbSO_4(s) \; + \; 2H_2O(l)$$

The combined reaction is:

$$PbO_2(s) \; + \; 4H^+(aq) \; + \; SO_4^{2-}(aq) \; + \; Pb(s) \; \rightarrow \; 2PbSO_4(s) \; + \; 2H_2O(l)$$

Many rechargeable batteries are portable and consist of nickel/cadmium or lithium ion cells. These are of tremendous commercial importance.

The Lithium Cell

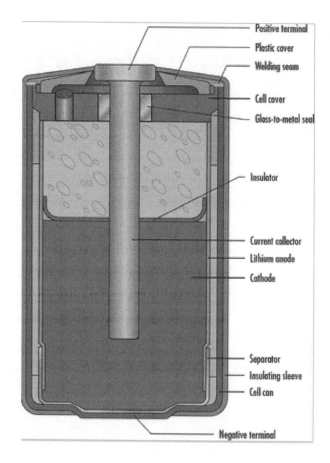

The simplified electrode reactions in a lithium cell are:

Positive electrode:

$$Li^+ + CoO_2 + e^- \rightarrow Li^+[CoO_2]^-$$

Negative Electrode:

$$Li \rightarrow Li^+ + e^-$$

The Fuel Cell

Hydrogen is widely believed to be a fuel source that could potentially replace fossil fuels in combustion engines. Hydrogen can be burnt directly, as with fossil fuels, or it could be used in a fuel cell.

A fuel cell consists of two platinum based electrodes in a polymer electrolyte. The electrolyte allows ions to pass through it.

The half equations are:

$$2H^+(aq) + 2e^- \rightleftharpoons H_2(g) \qquad E \approx 0.0 \text{ V}$$

$$4H^+(aq) + O_2(g) + 4e^- \rightleftharpoons 2H_2O(l) \qquad E \approx 1.2 \text{ V}$$

Overall:

$$H_2(g) \rightarrow 2H^+(aq) + 2e^-$$

In a fuel cell, the electrons flow through an electrical circuit where they power a motor. The H^+ ions flow through the electrolyte to a second electrode. At this second electrode, they react with oxygen and electrons to form water, which is the only emission from the unit.

The half equations are (second electrode first):

$$4H^+(aq) + O_2(g) + 4e^- \rightleftharpoons 2H_2O(l)$$

$$2H_2(g) \rightleftharpoons 4H^+(aq) + 4e^-$$

Overall:

$$2H_2(g) + O_2(g) \rightarrow 2H_2O(l)$$

Hydrogen Fuel Cell

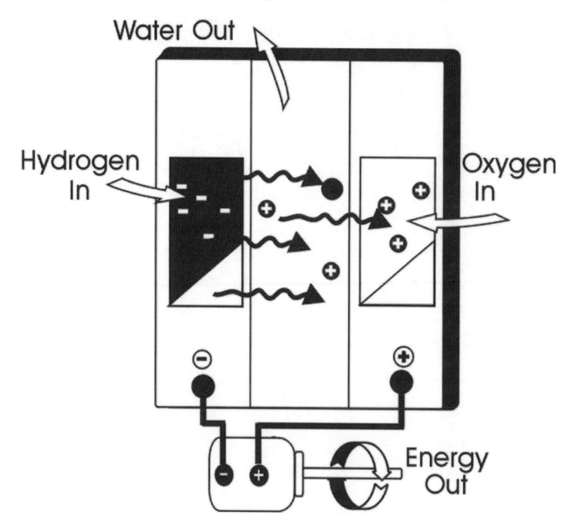

Hydrogen is not without its dangers. It is flammable (see the Hindenburg, for example), difficult to transport, and water is one of the worst greenhouse gases; the by-product of the cell would need to be harvested rather than released.

1.12 – Acids and Bases

Acids and bases are important in domestic, environmental and industrial contexts. Acidity in aqueous solutions is caused by hydrogen ions, and a logarithmic scale, pH, has been devised to measure acidity. Buffer solutions, which can be made from partially neutralised weak acids, resist changes in pH and find many important industrial and biological applications.

1.12.1 – Brønsted-Lowry acid-base equilibria in aqueous solution

The Brønsted-Lowry definition of acids and bases was developed in 1923, but is still relevant:

An Acid is a substance that can donate protons (H^+ ion) – Proton donor
A Base is a substance that can accept protons – Proton acceptor

Consider the following reaction:

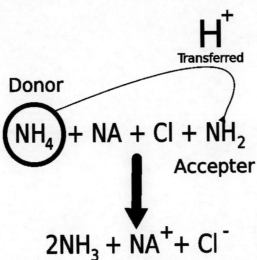

In this reaction the NH_4 will give an H^+ ion to the NH_2 molecule. The NH_4, therefore, is acting as a proton donor and is a Brønsted-Lowry acid. The NH_2 is acting as a proton acceptor and is therefore a Brønsted-Lowry base. Note that this reaction produces two ions of opposite charges. These can then react together, making this reaction reversible. When the reaction is reversed, the roles are also reversed. Acid-base equilibria involve the transfer of protons.

1.12.2 – Definition and determination of pH

pH is a measure of the acidity or alkalinity of a substance. This is achieved by measuring the concentration of [H^+(aq)] ions and is defined as follows:

$$pH = -\log_{10}[H^+(aq)]$$

The concentration of H^+ ions in this definition is measured in mol dm^{-3}.

On the pH scale:

- The lower the pH, the greater the concentration of H^+ ions
- pH is a logarithmic scale, which is to say a 1 point difference in pH means a tenfold increase (or decrease) in the concentration of H^+ ions

The scale runs from 0 to 14 with 7 being neutral.

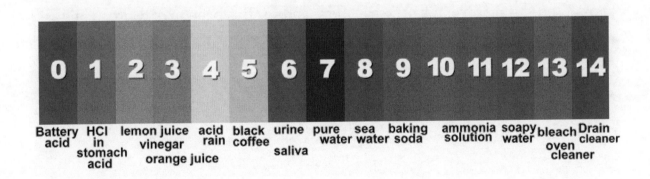

Calculating the pH of a Strong Acid

Hydrochloric acid, HCl, dissociates completely as per the following reaction:

$$HCl(aq) \rightarrow H^+(aq) + Cl^-(aq)$$

This reaction will go to completion, which means that all of the HCl will dissociate and there will be none left in the reaction chamber at the end. Acids that dissociate completely like this are called strong acids.

Assume a 0.17 mol dm^{-3} solution of HCl(aq):

$$pH = -\log_{10}[H^+(aq)]$$

$$pH = -\log_{10}[0.17]$$

$$\mathbf{pH = 0.77}$$

Look at the illustration of the pH scale above and see the location of hydrochloric acid at around pH 1.

Activity 75 – Calculate the pH of HCl at the following concentrations:

- **0.157**
- **0.26**

Answer to Activity 75:

$0.157 \text{ mol dm}^{-3}$ solution of HCl(aq):

$$pH = -\log_{10}[H^+(aq)]$$

$$pH = -\log_{10}[0.157]$$

$$\mathbf{pH = 0.804}$$

0.26 mol dm^{-3} solution of HCl(aq):

$$pH = -\log_{10}[H^+(aq)]$$

$$pH = -\log_{10}[0.26]$$

$$\mathbf{pH = 0.585}$$

Converting pH into Concentration

If we know the concentration, we can calculate the pH, as demonstrated above, but we can also calculate the concentration if we know the pH by using the anti-logarithm.

Assume a recorded pH of 2.

$$pH = -\log_{10}[H^+(aq)]$$

$$2 = -\log_{10}[H^+(aq)]$$

$$-2 = \log_{10}[H^+(aq)]$$

Now take the anti-log of each side (press invert on your scientific calculator, then log):

$$-2 = \log_{10}[H^+(aq)]$$

Or simply 10^{-2}

$$\mathbf{0.01 = [H^+(aq)]}$$

1.12.3 – The ionic product of water, K_w

In its normal state, water is slightly ionised (or weakly dissociated) in the following reversible reaction:

$$H_2O(l) \rightleftharpoons H^+(aq) + OH^-(aq)$$

This equilibrium situation will be established in every sample of water and every aqueous solution. We can use a modified version of the equilibrium expression to calculate the concentration of either ion:

$$K_w = [H^+(aq)]eqm \ [OH^-(aq)]eqm$$

K_w is the ionic product of water, and at 298K it is equal to:

$$K_w = 1.0 \times 10^{-14} mol^2 dm^{-6}$$

Each H_2O molecule that dissociates produces one H^+ and one OH^- (in pure water, at 298K).

Therefore:

$$[OH^-(aq)] = [H^+(aq)]$$

so:

$$1.0 \times 10^{-14} = [H^+(aq)]^2$$

Taking the square root of each side (to get the square root of a power, divide by 2):

$[H^+(aq)] = 1.0 \times 10^{-7} \text{ mol dm}^{-3} = [OH^-(aq)]$

$pH = -\log_{10} 10^{-7} = 7.$

So the pH of pure water at 298 K is 7

Calculating Concentration of a Base from pH

This is similar to calculating the concentration of an acid from its known pH value, the difference being that with bases there are two steps. Assume the pH of a substance we wish to know the base concentration of is 10.

$$pH = -\log_{10}[H^+(aq)]$$

$$10 = -\log_{10}[H^+(aq)]$$

$$-10 = \log_{10}[H^+(aq)]$$

Now take the anti-log of either side:

$$1.0 \times 10^{-10} = [H^+(aq)]$$

We know that:

$$Kw = [OH^-(aq)]\ [H^+(aq)]$$

which is:

$$1.0 \times 10^{-14} mol^2 dm^{-6} = [OH^-(aq)]\ [H^+(aq)]$$

If we now substitute our value for $[H^+(aq)]$ into the above equation we get:

$$1.0 \times 10^{-14} mol^2 dm^{-6} = [OH^-(aq)] \times 1.0 \times 10^{-10}$$

Rearranging that equation we get:

$$[OH^-(aq)] = \frac{1.0 \times 10^{-14}}{1.0 \times 10^{-10}}$$

Therefore: $$\mathbf{[OH^-(aq)] = 1.0 \times 10^{-4}\ mol\ dm^{-3}}$$

1.12.4 – Weak acids and bases K_a for weak acids

You know by now that acids which dissociate completely are referred to as strong acids.

The same terminology applies to bases. When a base dissociates completely it is called a strong base. For example, sodium hydroxide is a strong base, as in the reaction:

$$NaOH(aq) \rightarrow Na^+(aq) + OH^-(aq)$$

Sodium hydroxide completely dissociates and is therefore a strong base.

The opposite of this is also true: if a substance only dissociates partly, then it is called either a weak acid or a weak base.

We encountered the following equation earlier:

$$NH_3(aq) + H_2O(l) \rightleftharpoons NH_4^+(aq) + OH^-(aq)$$

In this equation, the equilibrium lies well to the left, and in reality very little of the ammonia dissociates. The solution is certainly alkaline, but it is weak.

Activity 76 – Name the reactants and products in the above equation.

Dissociation of Weak Acids and Bases

Consider the following generic equation for the dissociation of a weak acid:

$$HA(aq) \rightleftharpoons H^+(aq) + A^-(aq)$$

The equilibrium constant for this reaction would be:

$$Kc = \frac{[H^+(aq)]eqm \ [A^-(aq)]eqm}{[HA(aq)]eqm}$$

When we are calculating this for a weak acid, the symbol Kc is substituted for **Ka** and is called the **acid dissociation constant.**

Therefore:

$$Ka = \frac{[H^+(aq)]eqm \ [A^-(aq)]eqm}{[HA(aq)]eqm}$$

We can say a number of things from the Ka value:

- The larger the value, the further the equilibrium is to the right
- The more acid that is dissociated, the stronger the acid
- The units of Ka need to be stated

The units can be determined by a simple substitution. Consider the above expression again:

$$Ka = \frac{[H^+(aq)]eqm \ [A^-(aq)]eqm}{[HA(aq)]eqm}$$

Therefore:

$$Ka = \frac{mol\ dm^{-3}\ x\ mol\ dm^{-3}}{mol\ dm^{-3}}$$

Cancelling out, therefore:

$$\mathbf{Ka = mol\ dm^{-3}}$$

Calculating the pH of Solutions of Weak Acids

When we calculated the pH of strong acids earlier, we were able to assume that they were fully dissociated because otherwise they would not have been strong acids. By definition, with weak acids we cannot assume this.

First, we must use the acid dissociation expression to determine $[H^+]$.

Consider the following hypothetical reaction where we are looking to calculate the pH of 1 mole of a substance called XY:

$$XY(aq) \rightleftharpoons X^+(aq) + Y^-(aq)$$

(moles) Before dissociation	1	0	0
(moles) At equilibrium	$1 - [XY^-]$	$[X^+]$	$[Y^-]$

$$Ka = \frac{[Y^-]\ [X^+]}{[XY]}$$

We also know, from the equation, that for every XY molecule that dissociates, $1\ x\ X^+$ and $1\ x\ Y^-$ are produced.

If we assume that XY is a weak acid, the dissociation will be very small and therefore $[X^+]$ will be very small.

As an approximation, we can say:

$$1.00 - [X^+(aq)] \approx 1.00$$

Therefore:

$$K_a = \frac{[X^+]^2}{1.00}$$

In the equation, it is $[X^+]$ squared, because the concentrations of X^+ and Y^- are the same; when 1 XY dissociates, 1 of each ion is produced (look at the chemical equation to check this). From experimentation, we know the K_a value for XY:

$$K_a = 1.9 \times 10^{-5}$$

Therefore:

$$1.9 \times 10^{-5} = [X^+(aq)]^2$$

$$[X^+(aq)] = \sqrt{1.9 \times 10^{-5}}$$

$$[X^+(aq)] = 4.36 \times 10^{-3} \text{ mol dm}^{-3}$$

Taking the logarithm:

$$\log [X^+(aq)] = -2.36$$

In this example, we have used a hypothetical weak acid. This method can also be used to calculate the dissociation of a real weak acid.

pKa

You now know that Ka is the acid dissociation constant.

pKa is a measure of how strong a weak acid is: the smaller the number of pKa, the stronger the acid.

pKa is calculated as follows:

$$pKa = -\log_{10}Ka$$

1.12.5 – pH curves, titrations and indicators

Acid-Base Titrations

Titrations are very common laboratory scale experiments and are used to determine the concentration of a solution by dripping a second solution into a flask containing the first solution in the presence of an indicator solution. The two substances will react together and the results can be measured.

It is imperative that you know the equation for the reaction that is occurring.

The apparatus will look something like the following:

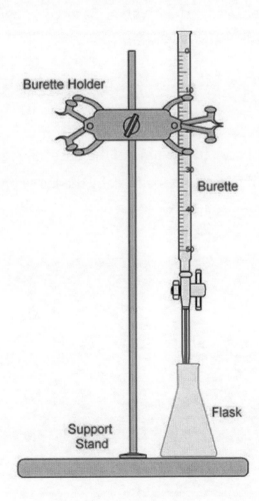

Titrations often involve acids and bases.

In an acid-base titration, an acid of known concentration is dripped into a beaker containing a base and an indicator solution (or an electronic pH meter).

When the indicator solution changes colour, the stopper on the burette is turned to prevent any more acid entering the beaker.

The change in colour of the indicator solution occurs when the alkali has been neutralised. The concentration of the alkali can be calculated by using the measured volume of acid used.

Note that the reverse can also occur, with a base of known concentration being dripped into an acid of unknown concentration.

Titration Curves

If a base is dripped into an acid, the volume of the base can be measured periodically, as can the change in pH of the acid in the flask by means of an electronic pH meter. A graph can be plotted of the results.

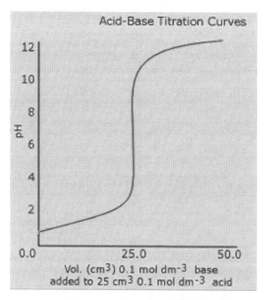

Strong acid & strong base

The pH starts at a low level and gradually rises until the equivalence point is met. (This is the vertical part of the line on the graph above).

This is the point at which sufficient base has been added to neutralise the acid. The equivalence point is reached at 25cm^3 of base in the above experiment (from the graph).

The equivalence point is very long in the case of a strong acid and a strong base. You will also note that the pH rises slowly until the equivalence point is reached, and it rises slowly again once the pH is above around 10.

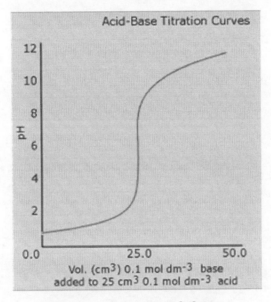

Strong acid & weak base

This graph is similar to the strong acid and strong base graph, but differs as the line leaves the equivalence point at a lower level. The highest pH achieved is also slightly lower.

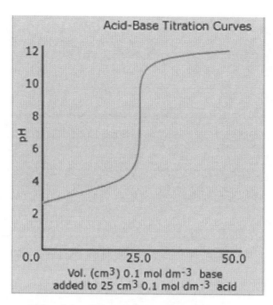

Weak acid and strong base

In the weak acid and strong base graph, the pH starts at a higher level. The top of the graph is the same as the strong acid & strong base graph.

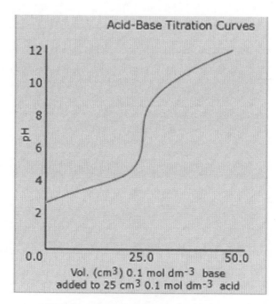

Weak acid & weak base

In this titration of a weak acid and weak base, the start point is fairly high and the equivalence point is minimal. The highest pH is also quite low.

<u>Choice of Indicator</u>

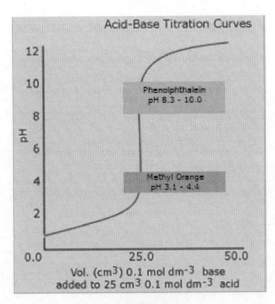

Indicators

We noted earlier that an electronic pH meter can be used to determine the pH of a solution at any given moment. Indicator solutions can also be used, however, and the illustration above shows which are best at given pH ranges.

A suitable indicator must be chosen; it must change colour in the right pH range.

The colour change must also be sharp rather than gradual.

The end point of the titration must be the same as the equivalence point (the point at which the acid or base is neutralised).

If the equivalence point is reached at a pH of 5 for a given reaction, and the indicator chosen changes colour at a pH of 10, then a colour change may occur, but only long after the equivalence point had been passed.

Titration Calculations

We can use the equivalence point (look again at the graphs above) to help us calculate the concentration of an unknown acid or base.

For example:

We will look first at a **monoprotic acid**. By experimentation, we find that the equivalence point is reached when 30cm³ of 0.0190 mol dm⁻³ sodium hydroxide is neutralised by 20.5cm³ of hydrochloric acid.

Activity 77 – Write out the reaction that is occurring.

Answer to Activity 77:

$HCl(aq) + NaOH(aq) \rightarrow NaCl(aq) + H_2O(l)$

The equivalence point (remember this is when the substance in the flask is neutralised) tells us that 20.5cm³ of hydrochloric acid of unknown concentration contains the same number of moles as 30cm³ of sodium hydroxide at a concentration of 0.0190 mol dm⁻³ (from the equation above).

$$\text{No. moles in a solution} = M \times \frac{V}{1000}$$

(M = concentration in moles, V = volume in cm³)

We know from the equation for the reaction that is occurring that the no. moles of HCl = no. moles of NaOH.

Therefore:

$$30.0 \times \frac{0.0190}{1000} = 20.5 \times \frac{x}{1000}$$

so:

$$5.70 \times 10^{-4} = 20.5 \times \frac{x}{1000}$$

Therefore:

$$x = \frac{(5.70 \times 10^{-4}) \times 1000}{20.5}$$

$$x = 0.0278 \text{ mol dm}^{-3}$$

We will now look at a **diprotic acid**. By experimentation, we find that the equivalence point is reached when 25cm^3 of 0.0153 mol dm^{-3} sodium hydroxide is neutralised by 12.2cm^3 of sulphuric acid.

Activity 78 – Write out the reaction that is occurring.

Answer to Activity 78:

$$H_2SO_4(aq) \ + \ 2NaOH(aq) \ \rightarrow \ Na_2SO_4(aq) \ + \ 2H_2O(l)$$

$$\text{No. moles in a solution} \ = \ M \ \times \ \frac{V}{1000}$$

(M = concentration in moles, V = volume in cm^3)

We know from the equation for the reaction that 1 mol of H_2SO_4 will neutralise 2 moles of NaOH.

Therefore:

$$\text{No. moles NaOH} \ = \ 25.0 \ \times \ \frac{0.0153}{1000}$$

so:

$$\text{No. moles NaOH} \ = \ 3.825 \times 10^{-4}$$

From the equation, no. of moles H_2SO_4 = ½ no. moles of NaOH

Therefore:

$$\text{No. moles } H_2SO_4 \ = \ \frac{3.825 \times 10{-4}}{2}$$

$$= \ 0.191 \times 10^{-4}$$

so:

$$0.191 \times 10^{-4} = 12.2 \times \frac{x}{1000}$$

Therefore:

$$x = \frac{(0.191 \times 10^{-4})}{12.2} \times 1000$$

$$x = 0.0157 \text{ mol dm}^{-3}$$

Required practical 9:

Investigate how pH changes when a weak acid reacts with a strong base and a strong acid reacts with a weak base.

1.12.6 – Buffer action

Buffer solutions are ones which act to resist a change in pH; their pH remains almost constant.

Buffers act to essentially absorb either H^+ or OH^- ions in order to keep the total number of those ions almost unchanged.

They work by means of an equilibrium reaction where the equilibrium will move in the direction required to remove an excess of either of those ions.

Acidic Buffers

Acid buffers are made from weak acids. They work because the dissociation of ions in weak acids is incomplete and is a reversible reaction of the generic formula:

$$HA(aq) \rightleftharpoons H^+(aq) + A^-(aq)$$

If we add some alkali to this reaction at equilibrium, the OH^- ions will react with the HA as follows:

$$HA(aq) + OH^-(aq) \rightarrow H_2O(aq) + A^-(aq)$$

This buffer solution reaction will act to remove the additional OH^- ions and therefore maintain the pH of the solution.

If we add some acid to the solution, the additional H^+ ions will react with the A^- ions already present and produce more HA; that is to say, the equilibrium will move to the left.

Remember, however, that weak acids are not well dissociated and the A^- will quickly be used up. At that point the solution will no longer act as a buffer.

We can improve the situation, however, by adding a soluble salt to the solution. This will more fully ionise, providing more A^- for the H^+ ions to react with, and making the solution a much better acidic buffer.

Acid buffers are made of a weak acid and a soluble salt of that acid, and will maintain the pH of a solution below 7.

Note that different buffers can be manufactured that will maintain the pH at different levels.

Commercial Value

Buffer solutions have a certain degree of commercial value and are used in a number of everyday products such as:

- Detergents
- Washing powders
- Shampoo

With any of these products, if they became too acidic or too alkaline they could cause considerable damage to either clothes or to the skin. Buffer solutions ensure that their pH remains at the desired safe level.

Activity 79 – Try to think of some other products that may use buffer solutions.

Calculating the pH of Acidic Buffer Solutions

We have already looked at the generic equation for the dissociation of a weak acid:

$$HA(aq) \rightleftharpoons H^+(aq) + A^-(aq)$$

We can use this reaction to write the following expression:

$$Ka = \frac{[H^+(aq)]\ [A^-(aq)]}{[HA(aq)]}$$

Remember Ka is the dissociation constant.

We can use this dissociation expression to calculate the pH of a buffer solution.

Consider a solution that contains:

- 0.25 mol dm^{-3} ethanoic acid
- 0.25 mol dm^{-3} sodium ethanoate

Ka for ethanoic acid $= 1.65 \times 10^{-5}$

Therefore:

$$Ka = \frac{[H^+(aq)]\ [A^-(aq)]}{[HA(aq)]}$$

In this equation sodium ethanoate is fully dissociated, therefore [A$^-$] = 0.25 mol dm^{-3}. Ethanoic acid is almost un-dissociated (because it is a weak acid), therefore [HA] = 0.25 mol dm^{-3}.

From the equation:

$$1.65 \times 10^{-5} = [H^+(aq)] \times \frac{0.25}{0.25}$$

Therefore:

$$1.65 \times 10^{-5} = [H^+(aq)] \text{ and pH} = -\log_{10}[H^+(aq)]$$

$$\mathbf{pH = 4.78}$$

Activity 80 – Try a calculation yourself using:

0.4 mol dm-3 ethanoic acid

0.2 mol dm-3 sodium ethanoate

Answer to Activity 80:

$$Ka = \frac{[H^+(aq)]\ [A^-(aq)]}{[HA(aq)]}$$

Therefore:

$$1.7 \times 10^{-5} = [H^+(aq)] \times \frac{0.2}{0.4}$$

So:

$$1.7 \times 10^{-5} = [H^+(aq)] \times 0.5$$

Therefore:

$$\frac{1.7 \times 10^{-5}}{0.5} = [H^+(aq)] \quad \text{and} \quad pH = -\log_{10}[H^+(aq)]$$

Therefore:

pH = 4.47

Topic 2

Inorganic Chemistry

Topic 2

2.1 - Periodicity

The Periodic Table provides chemists with a structured organisation of the known chemical elements from which they can make sense of their physical and chemical properties. The historical development of the Periodic Table and models of atomic structure provide good examples of how scientific ideas and explanations develop over time.

2.1.1 - Classification

The periodic table can be divided up in several ways. For now, we will look at the four "blocks":

- s block
- p block
- d block
- f block

In the A-Level, you only need to know about s, p and d blocks.

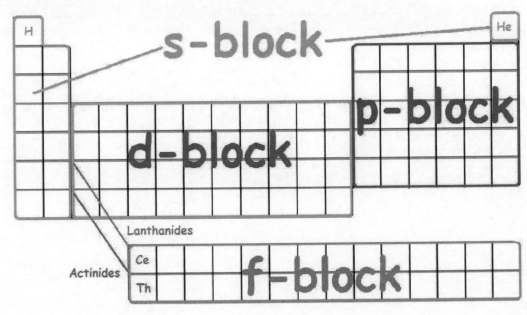

- All of the atoms that have their highest energy electron in s orbitals are in the s block

- All of the atoms that have their highest energy electron in p orbitals are in the p block

- All of the atoms that have their highest energy electron in d orbitals are in the d block

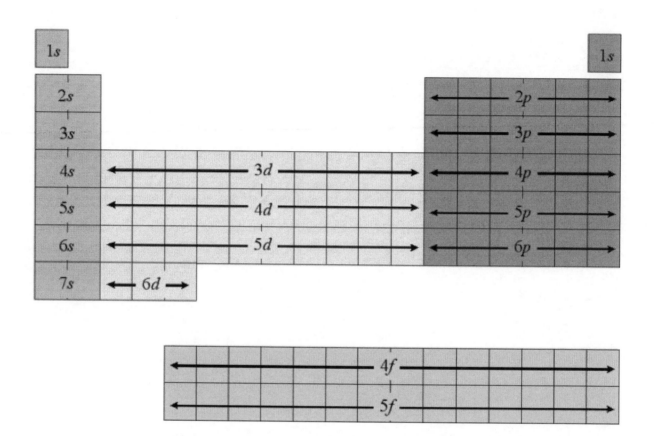

Activity 30 – Look at the position of Caesium (Cs) in the periodic table and use that position to predict the outermost shell of electrons.

Answer to Activity 30:

Caesium is in group 1, on the extreme left of the periodic table. It is therefore located in the s block. It is also in the 6s position, so even without looking at the electron configuration, you know that its outermost electrons are in the 6s orbital.

Periodic Table Background

Groups run in vertical columns and are typically numbered 1-7 with 0 (or sometimes 8) used to denote the noble gases; the transition metals are often ignored.

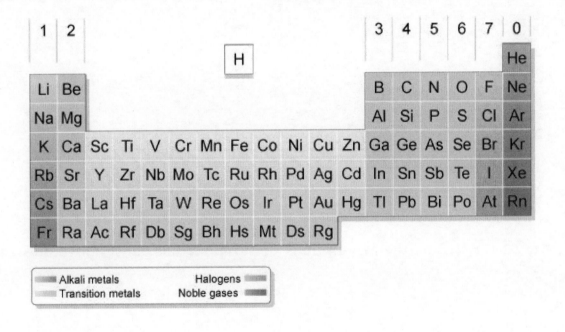

It is sometimes the case that 1-8 will be used (8 being the noble gases) and occasionally 1-18, with each group of the transition metals also included. Roman numerals are also often used.

In this course, we will use the 1-7 (and group 0) numbering system predominantly, but you need to be aware of others in case you encounter them.

The importance of the organisation is that all of the elements in the same group have the same number of electrons in their outer shells.

Reactivity:

- s block elements (alkali metals) become more reactive as we move down a group
- p block elements, especially the non-metals (groups 3-6), tend to become more reactive as we move up a group
- d block transition elements are relatively unreactive

Horizontal rows in the periodic table are called periods. The periods are numbered 1-7. Period 1 contains only hydrogen and helium. Period 2 contains lithium to neon, etc.

There are trends in the properties of elements in a period, which is what we will be looking at next.

On the periodic table:

- Groups are vertical
- Periods are horizontal

Activity 31 – What are the assumptions of atomic radius as we move down a group?

Answer to Activity 31:

We know that as we move down a group (taking group 1 as an example here), each atom has its outermost electrons in the s orbital. We also know that the orbital increases with every period. Li is in the 2s location, Na in the 3s location etc. down the group. We also know that the second s orbital is further away from the nucleus than the first s orbital, therefore the atomic radius increases down the group. This trend exists down every group.

The illustration below shows the relative atomic radius for the elements, excluding the transition metals.

Trends in Atomic Radius (Å)

1A	2A	3A	4A	5A	6A	7A	8A
H 0.37							He 0.5
Li 1.52	Be 1.11	B 0.88	C 0.77	N 0.70	O 0.66	F 0.64	Ne 0.70
Na 1.86	Mg 1.60	Al 1.43	Si 1.17	P 1.10	S 1.04	Cl 0.99	Ar 0.94
K 2.31	Ca 1.97	Ga 1.22	Ge 1.22	As 1.21	Se 1.17	Br 1.14	Kr 1.09
Rb 2.44	Sr 2.15	In 1.62	Sn 1.40	Sb 1.41	Te 1.37	I 1.33	Xe 1.30
Cs 2.62	Ba 2.17	Ti 1.71	Pb 1.75	Bi 1.46	Po 1.5	At 1.4	Rn 1.4

2.1.2 – Physical properties of Period 3 elements

What about trends in atomic radius across a period?

There are trends across a period just as there are down a group. Thinking specifically about period 3:

- Groups 1, 2 and 3 of period 3 are sodium, magnesium and aluminium. These three are metals with giant structures and lose their outermost electrons to form ionic compounds.
- The group 4 element, silicon, has 4 electrons in its outer shell and will form 4 covalent bonds. Silicon has some metallic properties and is classed as a semi-metal.
- The group 4, 5 and 6 elements, phosphorus, sulphur and chlorine, are non-metals. They will either accept electrons to form ionic compounds or share their outer electrons to form covalent compounds.
- Argon is a noble gas, as are all of group 0, and has a full outer shell; it is therefore unreactive.

Look at the illustration below on the trends in melting and boiling points for period 3 elements:

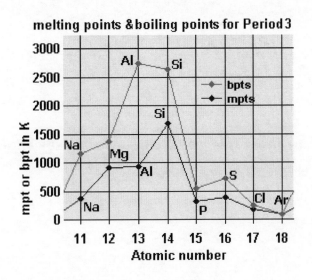

The trend is that they have a lower mpt (melting point) and bpt (boiling point) on the right and higher on the left, sodium being the main exception. This is due to their structures.

- Giant structures (on the left) tend to have higher mpt and bpt
- Molecular or atomic structures (on the right) tend to have lower mpt and bpt

The mpt and bpt increase (for group 1 to 3 elements) in period 3 is because of the strength of metallic bonding. Group 3 (aluminium) will have a greater ion charge and therefore release more electrons into the sea of delocalised electrons that forms, therefore holding the metallic lattice together more strongly.

The mpt of non-metals with molecular structures depends on the size of the intermolecular forces that act upon them. This depends on the number of electrons in the molecule and how closely they can be packed together.

The trend in atomic radius is also interesting across period 3.

The atomic radius of the elements declines across the period:

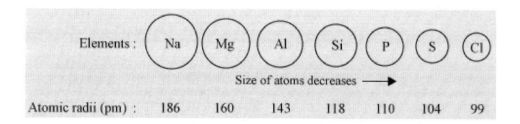

Activity 32 – Thinking about this trend, what can you say about the atomic radius of argon, the final element in period 3?

Answer to Activity 32:

Argon should (and does) have a lower atomic radius than chlorine.

The decline in atomic radius across a period can be explained by looking at the atomic structure.

Atom	Na	Mg	Al	Si	P	S	Cl
No. of Electrons	11	12	13	14	15	16	17
Electron Arrangement	2,8,1	2,8,2	2,8,3	2,8,4	2,8,5	2,8,6	2,8,7
Nuclear Charge No. of Protons	11^+	12^+	13^+	14^+	15^+	16^+	17^+

For a period, moving from group 1 to group 7, there are no additional main shells to provide shielding for the outer electrons from the nucleus. Coupled with this, there are an increasing number of protons in the nucleus, and therefore an increasing electrostatic attraction exerted by the nucleus on the outermost electrons, drawing them closer to the nucleus. When this happens the atomic radius decreases.

Activity 33 – Draw out the electron arrangements for another period and see if the same applies there.

There is also a trend in the first ionisation energies across period 3.

Remember that the first ionisation energy is the energy required to remove the outermost electron.

The trend is for the 1st IE to increase across a period and to decrease down a group.

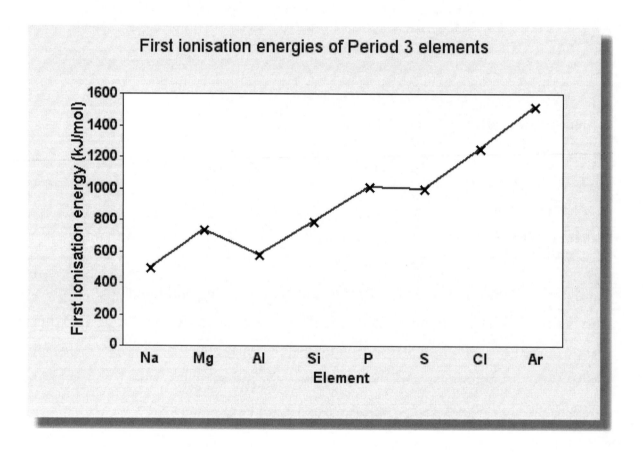

The increase is generally because of the increase in the number of protons in the nucleus and the increase in nuclear charge which that brings.

A greater attraction to the nucleus makes it harder to remove the first electron (it is closer to the nucleus and held with a stronger force of attraction).

If we now look at the trend in the 1st IE across a group (group 2 in the illustration) we will see something different.

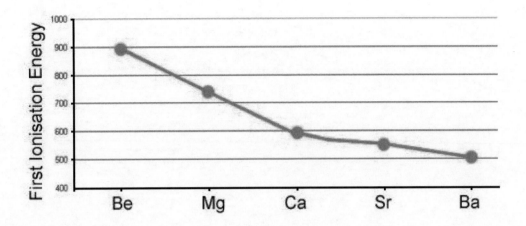

The 1st IE decreases down a group because the outermost electrons are further away from the nucleus; thus it exerts a lower attractive force, and also because the number of shells increases down a group, meaning more shielding from inner electrons. Therefore, it takes less energy to remove the outermost electrons as you move down a group.

Activity 34 – In your own words, explain:

Why does atomic radius decrease across a period?
Why does atomic radius increase down a group?
Why do noble gases have the highest 1st IE?

2.2 – Group 2, the alkaline earth metals

The elements in Group 2 are called the alkaline earth metals. The trends in the solubilities of the hydroxides and the sulphates of these elements are linked to their use. Barium sulphate, magnesium hydroxide and magnesium sulphate have applications in medicines whilst calcium hydroxide is used in agriculture to change soil pH, which is essential for good crop production and maintaining the food supply.

Trends in Physical Properties (Mg-Ba)

We will now look at group 2 - the alkaline earth metals.

1	2												13	14	15	16	17	18
H Hydrogen 1.00794																		**He** Helium 4.003
Li Lithium 6.941	**Be** Beryllium 9.012182												**B** Boron 10.811	**C** Carbon 12.0107	**N** Nitrogen 14.00674	**O** Oxygen 15.9994	**F** Fluorine 18.9984032	**Ne** Neon 20.1797
Na Sodium 22.989770	**Mg** Magnesium 24.3050												**Al** Aluminium 26.981538	**Si** Silicon 28.0855	**P** Phosphorus 30.973761	**S** Sulfur 32.066	**Cl** Chlorine 35.4527	**Ar** Argon 39.948
K Potassium 39.0983	**Ca** Calcium 40.078	**Sc** Scandium 44.955910	**Ti** Titanium 47.867	**V** Vanadium 50.9415	**Cr** Chromium 51.9961	**Mn** Manganese 54.938049	**Fe** Iron 55.845	**Co** Cobalt 58.933200	**Ni** Nickel 58.6934	**Cu** Copper 63.546	**Zn** Zinc 65.39		**Ga** Gallium 69.723	**Ge** Germanium 72.61	**As** Arsenic 74.92160	**Se** Selenium 78.96	**Br** Bromine 79.904	**Kr** Krypton 83.80
Rb Rubidium 85.4678	**Sr** Strontium 87.62	**Y** Yttrium 88.90585	**Zr** Zirconium 91.224	**Nb** Niobium 92.90638	**Mo** Molybdenum 95.94	**Tc** Technetium (98)	**Ru** Ruthenium 101.07	**Rh** Rhodium 102.90550	**Pd** Palladium 106.42	**Ag** Silver 107.8682	**Cd** Cadmium 112.411		**In** Indium 114.818	**Sn** Tin 118.710	**Sb** Antimony 121.760	**Te** Tellurium 127.60	**I** Iodine 126.90447	**Xe** Xenon 131.29
Cs Cesium 132.90545	**Ba** Barium 137.327	**La** Lanthanum 138.9055	**Hf** Hafnium 178.49	**Ta** Tantalum 180.9479	**W** Tungsten 183.84	**Re** Rhenium 186.207	**Os** Osmium 190.23	**Ir** Iridium 192.217	**Pt** Platinum 195.078	**Au** Gold 196.96655	**Hg** Mercury 200.59		**Tl** Thallium 204.3833	**Pb** Lead 207.2	**Bi** Bismuth 208.98038	**Po** Polonium (209)	**At** Astatine (210)	**Rn** Radon (222)
Fr Francium (223)	**Ra** Radium (226)	**Ac** Actinium (227)	**Rf** Rutherfordium (261)	**Db** Dubnium (262)	**Sg** Seaborgium (263)	**Bh** Bohrium (262)	**Hs** Hassium (265)	**Mt** Meitnerium (266)	110 (269)	111 (272)	112 (277)		113	114				

58	59	60	61	62	63	64	65	66	67	68	69	70	71
Ce Cerium 140.116	**Pr** Praseodymium 140.90765	**Nd** Neodymium 144.24	**Pm** Promethium (145)	**Sm** Samarium 150.36	**Eu** Europium 151.964	**Gd** Gadolinium 157.25	**Tb** Terbium 158.92534	**Dy** Dysprosium 162.50	**Ho** Holmium 164.93032	**Er** Erbium 167.26	**Tm** Thulium 168.93421	**Yb** Ytterbium 173.04	**Lu** Lutetium 174.967
90	91	92	93	94	95	96	97	98	99	100	101	102	103
Th Thorium 232.0381	**Pa** Protactinium 231.03588	**U** Uranium 238.0289	**Np** Neptunium (237)	**Pu** Plutonium (244)	**Am** Americium (243)	**Cm** Curium (247)	**Bk** Berkelium (247)	**Cf** Californium (251)	**Es** Einsteinium (252)	**Fm** Fermium (257)	**Md** Mendelevium (258)	**No** Nobelium (259)	**Lr** Lawrencium (262)

Activity 60 – What do you think the trends in atomic radius and melting point will be down the group?

Atomic Radius

Looking at the physical properties, from Beryllium to Barium, we can see that the atomic radius increases down the group, as it does down every group.

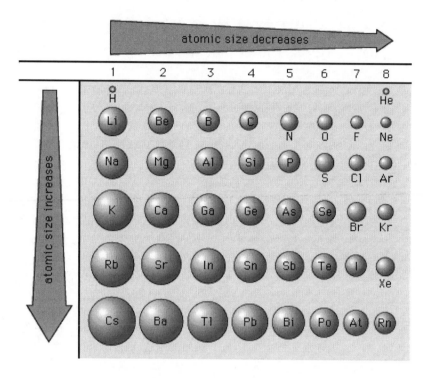

Group 2 elements have 2 electrons in their outermost s orbital. As we move down the group, there are progressively more electrons and the outermost ones are further away from the nucleus at every stage down the group.

Melting Point

Group 2 elements are metals that have high melting points and typically exist in giant metallic structures.

As we move down the group, the sea of delocalised electrons is generally further away from the influence of the nucleus, and therefore the strength of the metallic bonds decreases down the group. The trend in melting points, therefore, is to decrease down the group from calcium to barium.

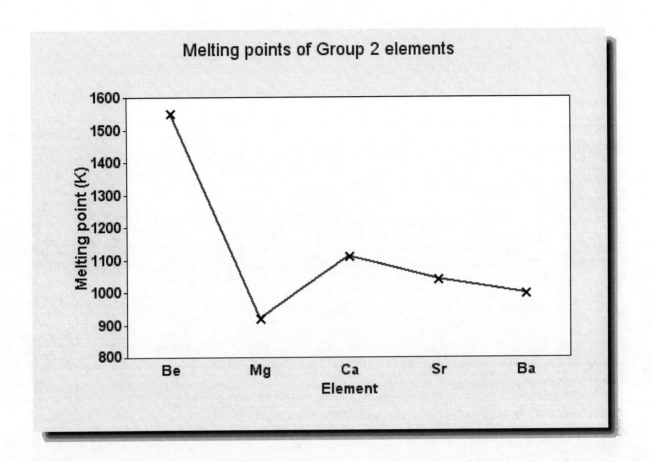

Magnesium has a lower melting point because it has a different lattice structure that makes the separation of electrons easier than in the next three elements.

1st Ionisation Energies

Group 2 elements always react to lose their outer 2 electrons and form ions with a 2+ charge.

$$Mg \rightarrow Mg^{2+} + 2e^-$$

Remember, however, that the 1st IE reaction is to remove the 1st outer electron, and is:

$$Mg \rightarrow Mg^+ + e^-$$

The reaction for the 2nd IE is to remove the second electron as follows:

$$Mg^+ \rightarrow Mg^{2+} + e^-$$

The trend in 1st IE is to decline down the group, as illustrated below:

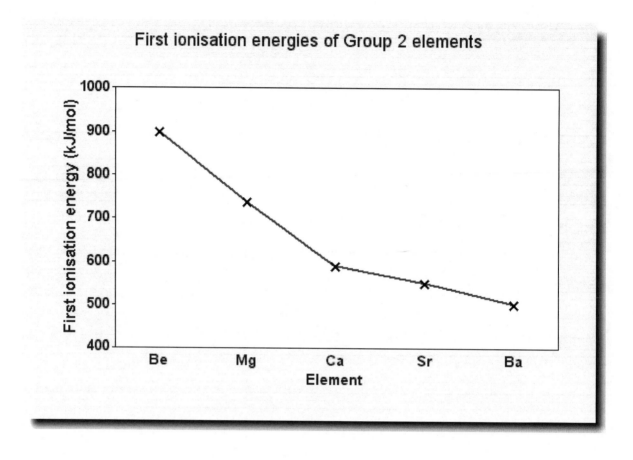

Note that the trend in 2nd ionisation energies is the same as we move down the group.

Trends in Chemical Properties (Mg-Ba)

Group 2 elements are always oxidised during their reactions as they always lose their outer 2 electrons. Their oxidation state changes as follows:

Oxidation state $\qquad\qquad$ 0 $\qquad$ +2

$$Mg \rightarrow Mg^{2+} + 2e^-$$

Example reaction:

Oxidation state $\qquad$ 0 $\qquad\qquad\qquad$ +2

$$Ca(s) + 2H_2O(l) \rightarrow Ca(OH)_2(aq) + H_2(g)$$

Group 2 metals react very slowly with water, but the reaction rate increases considerably if the reaction occurs with steam rather than cold water. The products are also different:

$$Ca(s) + H_2O(g) \rightarrow CaO(s) + H_2(g)$$

Steam causes the production of calcium oxide and hydrogen gas. The same applies to any other member of group 2; an alkaline oxide is produced along with hydrogen gas.

The reaction between the alkaline metal and water becomes more vigorous as we move down the group.

Group 2 hydroxides can have commercial uses. For example, $Mg(OH)_2$ can be used to settle a stomach upset (its other name is "milk of magnesia"). Calcium hydroxide $Ca(OH)_2$ can be used in agriculture to give the soil a pH of 6. This is valuable with crops such as wheat, barley, oats and corn, which thrive in these slightly acidic conditions.

Solubility of Hydroxides and Sulphates

As we move down the group, there is a clear trend in the solubility of the hydroxides; they become increasingly soluble. The sulphates, on the other hand, decrease in solubility down the group.

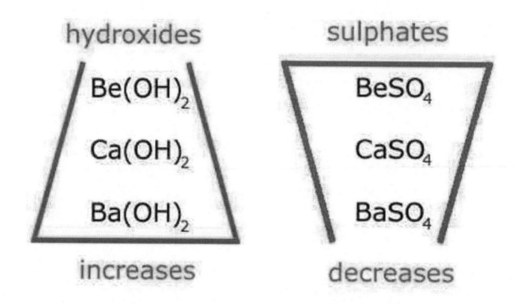

- Magnesium hydroxide is only slightly soluble. It is a suspension in water rather than a true solution
- Calcium hydroxide is sparingly soluble
- Strontium hydroxide is more soluble
- Barium hydroxide dissolves readily to form a solution

The insolubility of barium sulphate can be used as a test for sulphate ions. A test solution can be acidified with nitric acid solution. Barium chloride solution can then be added. If a sulphate is present, a white precipitate of barium sulphate is formed as follows:

$$Ba^{2+}(s) + SO_4^{2-}(aq) \rightarrow BaSO_4(s)$$

Barium sulphate is virtually insoluble and can be used, if ingested, to outline the gut on a medical X-ray.

Titanium Extraction

Titanium is an excellent construction material because it is strong, low density and corrosion resistant.

Titanium cannot be reduced by carbon because the temperatures required for the reaction would result in the formation of titanium carbide, which makes the metal brittle.

It is produced by reduction with more reactive metals, such as sodium and magnesium.

The process involves two stages:

- Conversion of oxide into chloride
- Reduction of the chloride

First, the titanium is converted to titanium chloride:

$$TiO_2(s) + 2C(s) + 2Cl_2(g) \rightarrow TiCl_4(l) + 2CO(g)$$

The liquid titanium chloride can be purified by distillation.

The titanium chloride is then reduced with molten sodium in an inert argon atmosphere at 1300K:

$$TiCl_4(l) + 4Na(l) \rightarrow Ti(l) + 4NaCl(l)$$

Magnesium can also be used in place of sodium.

2.3 – The Halogens

The halogens in Group 7 are very reactive non-metals. Trends in their physical properties are examined and explained. Fluorine is too dangerous to be used in a school laboratory but the reactions of chlorine are studied. Challenges in studying the properties of elements in their group include explaining the trends in ability of the halogens to behave as oxidising agents and the halide ions to behave as reducing agent.

2.3.1 – Trends in properties

As with all of the other groups of the periodic table, group 7 contains a range of elements with an almost unique set of characteristics.

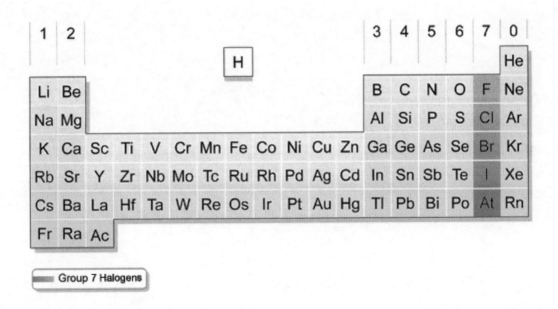

Halogens are generally very reactive substances and often react with metals to form salts, the most famous (probably) being sodium chloride (common table salt). There are many others too, however.

Their position on the periodic table tells you they are non-metals. You will also be able to determine that they typically exist in a diatomic form, because of their reactivity.

Activity 57 – What does "diatomic" mean?

Answer to Activity 57:

Diatomic means that they exist as a molecule containing two atoms of the same element. For example: Cl_2, Br_2 and so on.

As you would expect, the melting and boiling point of each member of the series increases as you move down the group.

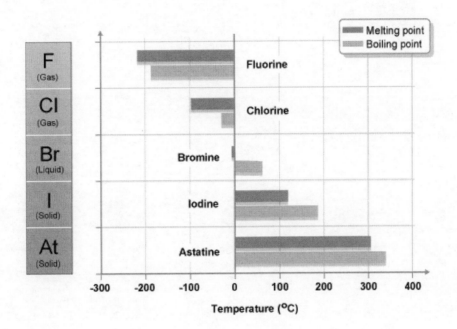

Fluorine and chlorine are both gasses at RTP, bromine is a liquid (but easily turns to its gaseous form), whilst iodine and astatine are both solids.

As with group 0 and group 1 elements, the final element in the sequence, astatine (At), is radioactive.

Other properties that you can probably deduce by now include:

- Given they are non-metals, the halogens do not conduct heat or electricity very well
- They are also brittle when in solid form, and are certainly unlike most metals in this regard

A summary of the trends in the properties of the halogens can be seen below:

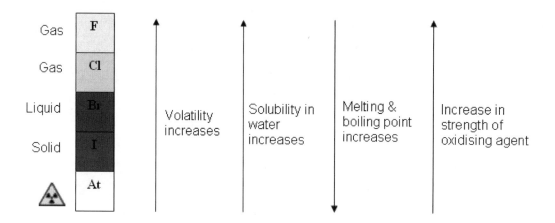

Their atomic radius increases down the group, as you would expect:

You may find it odd, but the reactivity of the halogens actually decreases as you move down the group, fluorine being the most reactive of all. That is not to say, of course, that astatine is not dangerous (particularly given that it is radioactive).

Fluorine is the most dangerous of the halogens; it is extremely reactive and should only be used in experiments under strictly controlled conditions. Chlorine is only slightly less dangerous than fluorine, and neither should be experimented with lightly.

Every member of group 7 produces toxic vapours and should only ever be used in a fume cupboard. The exhaust gases of the cupboard also need to be strictly controlled.

The trend in electronegativity is for it to decrease as you move down the group:

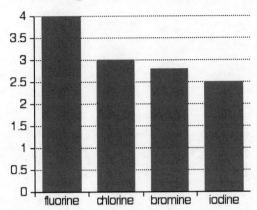

Electronegativity of the Group 7 elements

Trends in the Oxidising Abilities of the Halogens

The halogens require a single electron to fill their outer shells and usually react with other substances in order to gain that single electron, resulting in the outer shell being filled. These reactions are therefore redox reactions with the halogens acting as oxidising agents (electron acceptors) and themselves being reduced:

$$Cl_2 + 2e^- \rightarrow 2Cl^-$$

The oxidising ability of the halogens is highest at the top of the group, and declines as you move down the group.

This is because the atomic radius increases down the group and therefore the outer shell is further away from the nucleus. Fluorine is one of the most powerful oxidising agents known.

Fluorine, F   Chlorine, Cl   Bromine, Br   Iodine, I   Astatine, At

Displacement Reactions

In these reactions, more reactive substances will displace less reactive substances in compounds, and the halogens give us a good opportunity to study this phenomenon.

Take a solution of potassium bromide and add a chlorine solution:

$$2KBr(aq) + Cl_2(aq) \rightarrow 2KCl(aq) + Br_2(aq)$$

In this case, the more reactive chlorine has displaced the less reactive bromine in the potassium bromide molecule.

Activity 58 – Predict what will now happen if you:

   i.   Add fluorine to potassium chloride

  ii.   Add iodine to potassium chloride

Answer to Activity 58:

In the case of adding fluorine, another displacement reaction will occur as fluorine is the most reactive of the halogens, and certainly more reactive than chlorine.

$$2KCl(aq) + F_2(aq) \rightarrow 2KF(aq) + Cl_2(aq)$$

In the case of iodine, it is less reactive than chlorine, so a displacement reaction will not occur, and no reaction will take place.

Trends in the Reducing Abilities of the Halide Ions

Halide ions can act as reducing agents (electron donors). In this case halide ions will lose an electron and become a halogen molecule.

There is a trend in the reducing ability that is linked to the atomic radius of the ions. The larger the atomic radius, the easier it is to lose the outermost electron as it is further away from the "pull" of the nucleus.

	F-	Cl-	Br-	I-
Ionic Radius	0.133nm	0.180nm	0.195nm	0.215nm

→

Increasing Reducing Power

You also need to know the reactions between the halides of sodium and sulphuric acid:

NaF

$$NaF(s) + H_2SO_4(l) \rightarrow NaHSO_4(s) + HF(g)$$

NaCl

$$NaCl(s) + H_2SO_4(l) \rightarrow NaHSO_4(s) + HCl(g)$$

NaBr

$$NaBr(s) + H_2SO_4(l) \rightarrow NaHSO_4(s) + HBr(g)$$

NaI

$$NaI(s) + H_2SO_4(l) \rightarrow NaHSO_4(s) + HI(g)$$

Identification of Halide Ions using Silver Nitrate

First, we will look at a test to demonstrate the presence of four halide ions:

- Fluoride (F^-)
- Chloride (Cl^-)
- Bromide (Br^-)
- Iodide (I^-)

This test must be conducted in solution. If the sample you are starting with is a solid, then it must first be dissolved in pure water or the test will be unsuccessful.

To the solution under test should be added dilute nitric acid solution and silver nitrate solution. The nitric acid reacts with any impurities in the sample to remove them, and the silver nitrate reacts with the sample to provide the required precipitate. The precipitates are as follows:

Ion present	Observation
F^-	no precipitate
Cl^-	white precipitate
Br^-	very pale cream precipitate
I^-	very pale yellow precipitate

The precipitates are insoluble silver halides and the reactions are as follows:

$$AgNO_3(aq) + NaCl(aq) \rightarrow AgCl(s) + NaNO_3(aq)$$

$$AgNO_3(aq) + NaBr(aq) \rightarrow AgBr(s) + NaNO_3(aq)$$

$$AgNO_3(aq) + NaI(aq) \rightarrow AgI(s) + NaNO_3(aq)$$

If we take these precipitates and add a few drops of concentrated ammonia solution, the following reactions occur:

- Silver chloride dissolves in dilute ammonia
- Silver bromide dissolves in concentrated ammonia
- Silver iodide does not dissolve in ammonia

Halide	AgF	AgCl	AgBr	AgI
Colour	No precipitate	White precipitate	Cream precipitate	Pale yellow precipitate
Reaction with conc. ammonia solution		Dissolves in dilute ammonia	Dissolves in concentrated ammonia	Insoluble in concentrated ammonia

In dilute ammonia solution, only the silver chloride precipitate dissolves.

2.3.2 - Uses of Chlorine and Chlorate I

You know that chlorine is a poisonous gas, but despite this it does have some commercial uses.

<u>Reaction with Water</u>

Chlorine reacts with water to form chloric(I) acid (HClO) and hydrochloric acid (HCl). This reaction is reversible as follows:

$$Cl_2(g) + H_2O(l) \rightleftharpoons HClO(aq) + HCl(aq)$$

The oxidation state of chlorine in this reaction is interesting. There are 2 chlorine atoms on the left of the equation; these are split and form a component part of two different molecules on the right. One of these chlorine atoms is oxidised and one is reduced as follows:

Oxidation number of Cl	0	+1	-1
Reaction	$Cl_2(g) + H_2O(l) \rightleftharpoons$	$HClO(aq) +$	$HCl(aq)$

This kind of redox reaction is called **disproportionation**, because chlorine is both oxidised and reduced.

This reaction is used to purify water for both drinking and for swimming pools. Chloric(I) acid is an oxidising agent and will kill harmful bacteria in the water. It can also be used as bleach when in higher concentrations.

When we react chlorine with water in the presence of sunlight, however, a different reaction occurs:

$$Cl_2(g) + H_2O(l) \rightarrow 4HCl(aq) + O_2(g)$$

Activity 59 – Why is this reaction relevant to humans?

Answer to Activity 59:

Swimming pools in particular are exposed to a great deal of sunlight, and the chlorine is rapidly lost from the pool water in the presence of sunlight. Shallow pools, therefore, need more frequent additions of chlorine.

Obviously, given that chlorine is a toxic gas, it needs to be added to water in small enough quantities that it is not harmful to humans. Its benefits in water treatment, if used properly, outweigh its toxic effects.

Reaction with Sodium Hydroxide (NaOH$_{(aq)}$)

Chlorine reacts with cold sodium hydroxide (dilute solution) to form sodium chlorate(I) (NaClO). This is another oxidising agent and the active ingredient in household bleach.

The reaction is:

Oxidation no.   0   +1   -1
Reaction $Cl_2(g) + 2NaOH(aq) \rightarrow NaClO(aq) + NaCl(aq) + H_2O(l)$

As you can see from the oxidation number of the chlorine atoms, this is another example of a disproportionation reaction.

Required Practical 4:

Carry out simple test-tube reactions to identify:
- **Cations – Group 2, NH^{4+}**
- **Anions – Group 7 (halide ions), OH^-, CO_3^{2-}, SO_4^{2-}**

2.4 – Properties of Period 3 elements and their oxides

In this section, we will be looking at the period 3 elements, sodium to argon, of the periodic table.

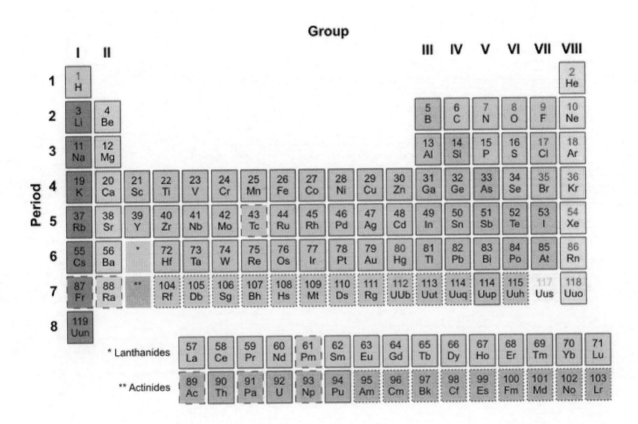

As we move across the period from left to right, we see some basic trends which by now you will be able to predict.

First of all, we see a general increase in the electronegativity of the elements across the period.

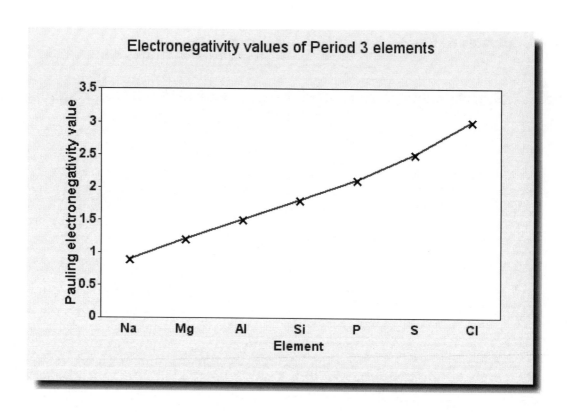

Electronegativity values of Period 3 elements

The trend in first ionisation energies also shows a general increase.

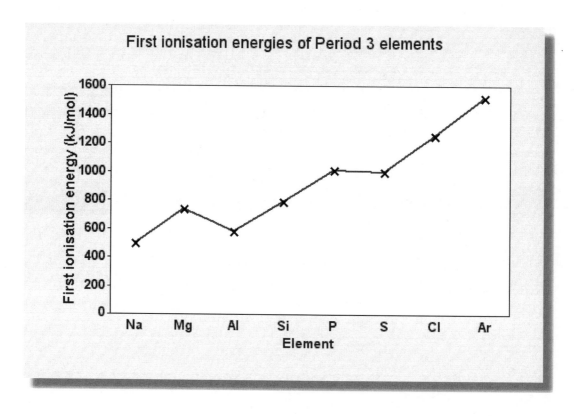

First ionisation energies of Period 3 elements

The elements of period three all undergo redox reactions. The oxidation state of all of these elements starts at zero, and always ends up either positive or negative.

Reactions with Water

Sodium and magnesium are metals in period three, and they both react with water in the following ways:

Sodium reacts vigorously with water; it fizzes and melts because of the exothermic nature of the reaction. The result is a strongly alkaline solution of sodium hydroxide.

The reaction is:

$$2Na(s) \; + \; 2H_2O(l) \; \rightarrow \; 2NaOH(aq) \; + \; H_2(g)$$

Oxidation states: 0   +1 -2   +1 -2 +1   0

Magnesium reacts rather less vigorously with water at room temperature. The reaction is so slow that it will take several days for a few bubbles of hydrogen to appear.

The resulting solution is less alkaline than sodium hydroxide because the magnesium hydroxide product is only partially soluble.

The reaction is:

$$Mg(s) \; + \; 2H_2O(l) \; \rightarrow \; Mg(OH)_2(aq) \; + \; H_2(g)$$

Oxidation states: 0   +1 -2   +2 -2 +1   0

Activity 100 – Write a paragraph explaining what oxidation states are.

Reactions with Oxygen

Argon is a noble gas, and is therefore unreactive. Other than argon, however, the period three elements react with oxygen. The specification notes that you need to be aware of these reactions from Na to S.

Sodium

Sodium burns with a bright yellow flame in air, forming white sodium oxide:

$$2Na(s) \ + \ \tfrac{1}{2} O_2(g) \ \rightarrow \ Na_2O(s)$$

Oxidation states: 0   0   +1 -2

Magnesium

Magnesium burns with a bright white flame in air, producing a white powder of magnesium oxide:

$$2Mg(s) \ + \ O_2(g) \ \rightarrow \ 2MgO(s)$$

Oxidation states: 0   0   +2 -2

Aluminium

Aluminium powder will burn brightly in pure oxygen, producing a white powder of aluminium oxide:

$$4Al(s) \ + \ 3O_2(g) \ \rightarrow \ 2Al_2O_3(s)$$

Oxidation states: 0   0   +3 -2

Silicon

Silicon needs to be heated strongly in oxygen to produce silicon dioxide:

$$Si(s) + O_2(g) \rightarrow SiO_2(s)$$

Oxidation states: 0   0   +4 -2

Phosphorus

Red phosphorus must first be heated before it will react with oxygen. White phosphorus, on the other hand, ignites in air and produces a white smoke of phosphorus pentoxide.

White and red phosphorus are allotropes of phosphorous. They are the same element with the atoms arranged differently.

$$4P(s) + 5O_2(g) \rightarrow P_4O_{10}(s)$$

Oxidation states: 0   0   +5 -2

NB. If the supply of oxygen is limited, then phosphorus trioxide will also be formed (P_2O_3).

Sulphur

If sulphur power is heated and then reacted with pure oxygen, it will burn with a blue flame forming sulphur dioxide, a colourless gas:

$$S(s) + O_2(g) \rightarrow SO_2(s)$$

Oxidation states: 0   0   +4 -2

Acid Base Properties of the Oxides of Period 3 Elements

Background to Period 3 Oxides

Three good examples of metals bonded to non-metals are:

- Sodium oxide
- Magnesium oxide
- Aluminium oxide

They form large ionic lattices with the bonds extending throughout the lattice, and have a high melting point as a result.

The bonding in aluminium oxide, for example, is ionic but with some covalent properties.

The aluminium ion is very small with a large positive charge. This means that it can get close to an O^{2-} ion and distort the oxygen electron cloud, giving some properties of a covalent bond.

Silicon dioxide has a giant covalent structure. As with aluminium oxide, the bonds extend throughout the structure, but this time are entirely covalent in nature.

Activity 101 – Draw a representation of a "large iconic lattice" as occurs in these metal oxides.

Reaction of Oxides with Water

Basic Oxides

Sodium and magnesium oxide are both bases. Sodium reacts with water to give sodium hydroxide. Magnesium oxide reacts with water to give magnesium hydroxide, a less soluble material and a weaker alkali.

$$Na_2O(s) + H_2O(l) \rightarrow 2Na^+(aq) + 2OH^-(aq)$$

The pH of the resulting solution in the above reaction is around 14 (strongly alkaline).

$$MgO(s) + H_2O(l) \rightarrow Mg(OH)_2(s) \rightleftharpoons Mg^{2+}(aq) + 2OH^-(aq)$$

The pH of the resulting solution in the above reaction is around 9-10 (weakly alkaline).

Insoluble Oxides

Aluminium oxide and Silicone dioxide are insoluble in water.

Acidic Oxides

Phosphorus pentoxide is acidic.

The non-metals to the right of the periodic table typically form acidic oxides.

Phosphorus pentoxide reacts violently with water to form phosphoric (v) acid:

$$P_4H_{10}(s) + 6H_2O(l) \rightarrow 4H_3PO_4(aq)$$

$H_3PO_4(aq)$ ionises in stages, beginning with:

$$4H_3PO_4(aq) \rightleftharpoons H^+(aq) + H_2PO_4^-(aq)$$

Sulphur Dioxide

Sulphur dioxide is soluble in water and reacts to give an acidic, aqueous solution of sulphuric acid:

$$SO_2(s) + H_2O(l) \rightarrow H_2SO_4(aq)$$

$$H_2SO_4(aq) \rightleftharpoons H^+(aq) + HSO_3^-(aq)$$

Sulphur Trioxide

Sulphur trioxide reacts violently with water to produce sulphuric acid:

$$SO_3(g) + H_2O(l) \rightarrow H_2SO_4(aq) \rightarrow H^+(aq) + HSO_4^-(aq)$$

Oxide	Bonding	Acidity / Alkalinity	pH
Na_2O	Ionic	Strongly alkaline	14
MgO	Ionic	Somewhat alkaline	9-10
Al_2O_3	Covalent/Ionic	NA	7
SiO_2	Covalent	NA	7
P_4O_{10}	Covalent	Strong acid	0-1
SO_2	Covalent	Weak acid	2-3
SO_3	Covalent	Strong acid	0-1

Period 3 as Acids and Bases

As we move from left to right across the period, there is a trend to move from alkalis to acids.

Sodium and Magnesium Oxides

Sodium oxide and magnesium oxide will react with acids to give a salt and water:

$$Na_2O(s) \; + \; H_2SO_4(aq) \; \rightarrow \; Na_2SO_4(aq) \; + \; H_2O(l)$$

$$MgO(s) \; + \; 2HCl(aq) \; \rightarrow \; MgCl_2(aq) \; + \; H_2O(l)$$

Aluminium Oxide

Aluminium oxide reacts with both acids and alkalis. It is therefore called an **amphoteric oxide**.

With an acid:

$$Al_2O_3(s) \; + \; 6HCl(aq) \; \rightarrow \; 2AlCl_3(aq) \; + \; 3H_2O(l)$$

With a hot alkali:

$$Al_2O_3(s) \; + \; 2NaOH(aq) \; + \; 3H_2O(l) \; \rightarrow \; 2NaAl(OH)_4(aq)$$

Silicon Dioxide

Silicon dioxide will act as a weak acid when reacting with a strong base:

$$SiO_2(s) + 2NaOH(aq) \rightarrow Na_2SiO_3(aq) + H_2O(l)$$

Phosphorus Pentoxide

Phosphorus pentoxide, when in aqueous solution, will form phosphoric (V) acid. This acid has three H groups, each of which can detach an acidic hydrogen atom. There are, therefore, three stages to the reaction with sodium, as each hydrogen reacts in turn:

$$H_3PO_4(aq) + NaOH(aq) \rightarrow NaH_2PO_4(aq) + H_2O(l)$$

$$NaH_2PO_4(aq) + NaOH(aq) \rightarrow Na_2HPO_4(aq) + H_2O(l)$$

$$Na_2HPO_4(aq) + NaOH(aq) \rightarrow Na_3PO_4(aq) + H_2O(l)$$

Sulphur Dioxide

If we react an aqueous solution of sulphur dioxide with sodium hydroxide, we get a two stage reaction:

$$SO_2(aq) + NaOH(aq) \rightarrow NaHSO_3(aq)$$

$$NaHSO_3(aq) + NaOH(aq) \rightarrow Na_2SO_3(aq) + H_2O(l)$$

2.5 – Transition metals

The 3d block contains 10 elements, all of which are metals. Unlike the metals in Group 1 and 2, the transition metals Ti and Cu form coloured compounds and compounds where the transition metal exists in different oxidation states. Some of these metals are familiar as catalysts. The properties of these elements are studied in this section with opportunities for a wide range of practical investigations.

2.5.1 – General properties of transition metals

In this section, we will examine the transition metals. Think back to AS-Level and you will remember that these elements are the d block elements.

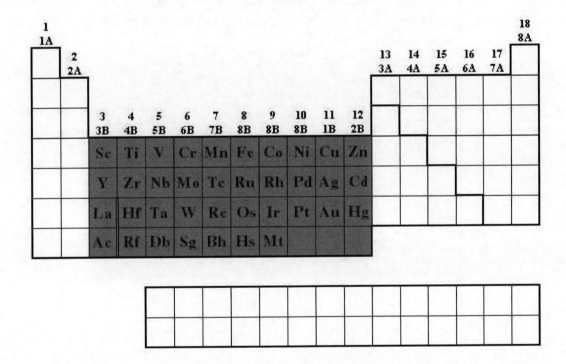

We will be looking at Sc – Cu specifically. The transition elements are:

- Metallic
- Good conductors of heat and electricity
- Hard and shiny

They have high melting and boiling points.

Looking at the illustration below, you can see that the transition elements generally have a full 4s shell, and the 3d shell is progressively filled along the period. Only copper and chromium do not fit this general pattern.

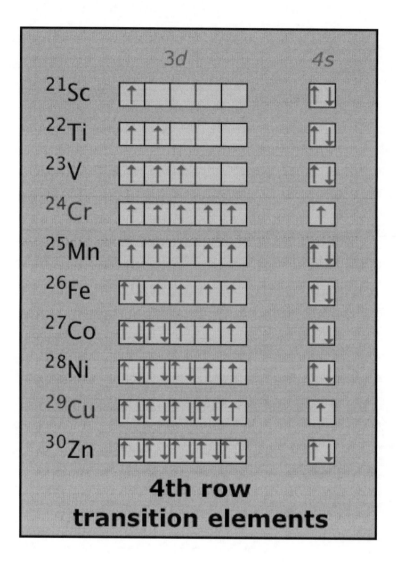

4th row transition elements

The strict definition of a transition element:

A transition element is an element having an incomplete d (or f) shell, either in the element or in one of its ions.

Zinc only forms Zn^{2+} which has $3d^{10}$. It does not have a part filled d shell and therefore is not, strictly speaking, one of the transition elements.

Chemical Properties of Transition Elements

There are four main shared characteristics of the transition elements:

- Variable oxidation states – They have more than one oxidation state in their compounds: Cu(I) and Cu(II); Fe(II) and Fe(III), for example. This means that they can take part in a range of redox reactions.
- Colour – The majority of the ions of these elements are coloured.
- Catalysts – Many transition elements will act as catalysts in some reactions.
- Complex formation – The transition elements form complex ions.

Activity 112 – Think back over the course and try to remember some of what you have learned in order to answer these two questions:

A – Give some examples of coloured ions of transition elements.

B – Think of some reactions we have seen that use a transition element as a catalyst.

Complex Formation

As noted above, all of the transition elements can form complex coordinate bonds by accepting pairs of electrons from other atoms or ions.

An ion with a lone pair of electrons that forms a coordinate bond with a transition element is called a **ligand**.

In some cases, four or six ligands bond with a transition element to form a transition metal ion; a complex ion.

The number of coordinate bonds to ligands in a transition metal ion is called the **coordination number**.

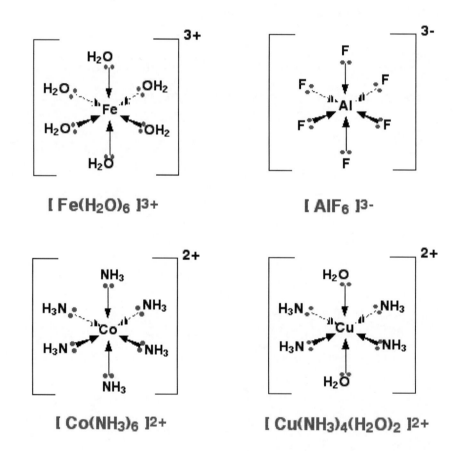

$[Fe(H_2O)_6]^{3+}$

$[AlF_6]^{3-}$

$[Co(NH_3)_6]^{2+}$

$[Cu(NH_3)_4(H_2O)_2]^{2+}$

The above structures are called complexes. A complex consists of a central metal ion surrounded by ligands.

Ligands can fall into three categories:

- Unidentate – These are ligands with one pair of electrons available for bonding (e.g. H_2O, NH_3, Cl^-)
- Bidentate – These are ligands with two donor sites (i.e. two pairs of electrons available for bonding (e.g. ethane-1,2-diamine, C_2O_4)
- Multidentate – These are ligands with multiple donor sites available for bonding (e.g. $EDTA^{4-}$)

Examples of bidentate ligands

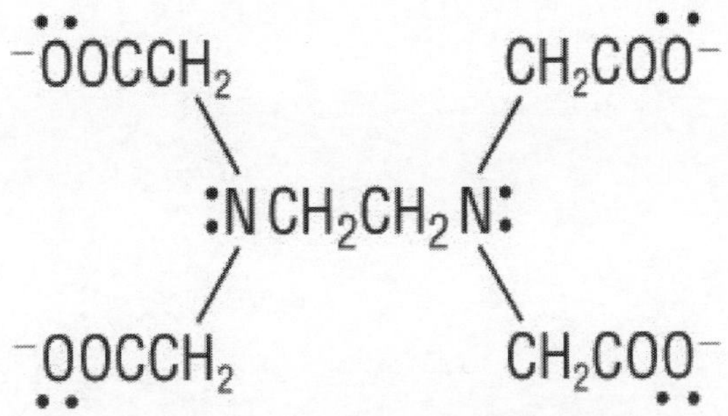

Example of a multidentate ligand

Haem (a constituent of haemoglobin) is an iron (II) complex with a multidentate ligand.

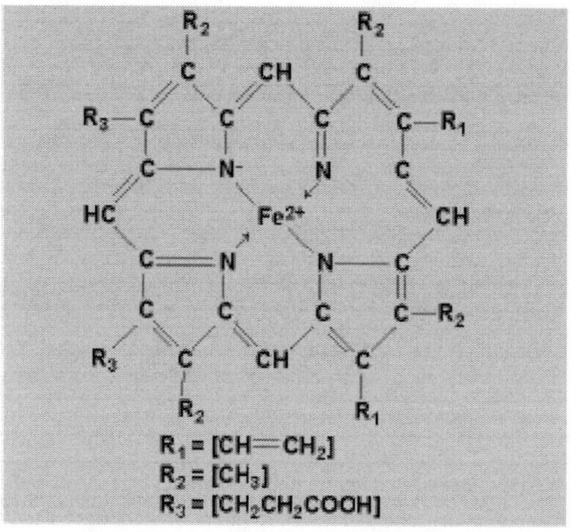

$R_1 = [CH=CH_2]$
$R_2 = [CH_3]$
$R_3 = [CH_2CH_2COOH]$

The structure of haem

Activity 113 – Do you think the nature of the ligand(s) will affect the shape of the resulting molecule? If so, why? If not, why not?

2.5.2 – Substitution reactions

Water molecules that act as ligands in complex transition metal aqua ions can be replaced with other ligands. This occurs either because the other ligands are better Lewis bases, and therefore form stronger coordinate bonds, or because they are present in the reaction in higher concentration and the equilibrium of the reaction is displaced as a result.

- Water molecules may be replaced by other neutral ligands like ammonia.
- Water molecules could be replaced by negatively charged ions, such as chloride ions.
- Water molecules may be replaced by bidentate or multidentate ligands. This process is called chelation.
- Water replacement may be either partial or complete.

Ammonia and water are of roughly the same size, so when substitution occurs for these, there is no change to the coordination number or the charge on the molecule. With ammonia, for example, the substitution of water does not have to be complete. It occurs in stages:

$$[M(H_2O)_6]^{2+} + NH_3 \rightleftharpoons [M(NH_3)(H_2O)_5]^{2+} + H_2O$$

$$[M(NH_3)(H_2O)_5]^{2+} + NH_3 \rightleftharpoons [M(NH_3)_2(H_2O)_4]^{2+} + H_2O$$

$$[M(NH_3)_2(H_2O)_4]^{2+} + NH_3 \rightleftharpoons [M(NH_3)_3(H_2O)_3]^{2+} + H_2O$$

$$[M(NH_3)_3(H_2O)_3]^{2+} + NH_3 \rightleftharpoons [M(NH_3)_4(H_2O)_2]^{2+} + H_2O$$

$$[M(NH_3)_4(H_2O)_2]^{2+} + NH_3 \rightleftharpoons [M(NH_3)_5(H_2O)]^{2+} + H_2O$$

$$[M(NH_3)_5(H_2O)]^{2+} + NH_3 \rightleftharpoons [M(NH_3)_6]^{2+} + H_2O$$

Cobalt (II)

When we take a complex of cobalt, the first stage is the formation of a blue precipitate (cobalt (II) hydroxide). This is produced by the loss of a proton from each of two of the six water molecules:

$$[Co(H_2O)_6]^{2+} + 2NH_3 \rightleftharpoons [Co(H_2O)_4(OH)_2] + 2NH_4^+$$
$$\text{pink} \qquad\qquad\qquad \text{blue-green precipitate}$$

If we continue to add ammonia (an excess), the following will happen:

$$[Co(H_2O)_4(OH)_2](s) + 6NH_3(aq) \rightleftharpoons [Co(NH_3)_6]^{2+}(aq) + 4H_2O(l) + 2OH^-(aq)$$
$$\text{Blue/green ppt} \qquad\qquad\qquad \text{Pale brown}$$

This substitution occurs because ammonia is a better ligand than water, so replaces it in the complex. The high concentration of ammonia also displaces the equilibria, thus displacing the H_2O and the OH^-. When left in air, the Cobalt $^{2+}$ is oxidised to Cobalt $^{3+}$:

$$[Co(NH_3)_6]^{2+}(aq) \rightarrow [Co(NH_3)_6]^{3+}(aq)$$
$$\text{pale brown} \qquad\qquad \text{brown/yellow}$$

Copper (II)

With copper (II) ions in solution, the ligand replacement (when reacting with ammonia) is only partial. Only four of the H_2O ligands will be replaced.

The overall reaction is:

$$[Cu(H_2O)_6]^{2+} + 2NH_3 \rightleftharpoons [Cu(NH_3)_4(OH)_2] + 2NH_4^+$$
$$\text{Blue solution} \qquad\qquad \text{pale blue precipitate}$$

$$[Cu(H_2O)_6]^{2+} + 4NH_3 \rightleftharpoons [Cu(NH_3)_4(H_2O)_2]^{2+} + 4H_2O$$
$$\text{Blue solution} \qquad\qquad\qquad \text{deep blue solution}$$

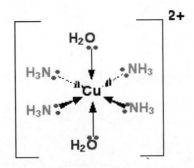

the tetraamminediaquacopper(II) ion

Structure of $[Cu(NH_3)_4(H_2O)_2]^{2+}$

Chelate Effect

Chelation is the formation of complexes with multidentate ligands. These are ligands with more than one lone pair. The result of this is that they can form more than one coordinate bond.

Note that the substitution of an unidentate ligand with a bidentate or a multidentate ligand leads to a more stable complex.

Let us look at one final example:

$$[Cu(H_2O)_6]^{2+}(aq) \; + \; EDTA^{4-}(aq) \; \rightarrow \; [CuEDTA]^{2-}(aq) \; + \; 6H_2O(l)$$

Looking at the equation, there are 2 entities (groups) on the left hand side of the equation, but 7 entities on the right.

The larger number of entities on the right means that there is a significant entropy increase as the reaction progresses from left to right.

This entropy change favours the formation of chelates (i.e. bidentate or multidentate ligands) over complexes with unidentate ligands.

Reactions of Metal (II) Ions with Bases

M(II) (aq)	OH$^-$ (little)	OH$^-$ (excess)	NH$_3$ (little)	NH$_3$ (excess)	CO$_3^{2-}$
Fe(II) green [Fe(H$_2$O)$_6$]$^{2+}$	Green ppt Fe(OH)$_2$	Does not dissolve	Green ppt Fe(OH)$_2$ Easily oxidised by air – turns brown	Green ppt. Dissolves to give pale brown solution – turns brown in air	Green ppt Carbonate FeCO$_3$
Co(II) pink [Co(H$_2$O)$_6$]$^{2+}$	Blue ppt Co(OH)$_2$ Easily oxidised by air – turns brown	Does not dissolve	Blue ppt Co(OH)$_2$ Easily oxidised by air – turns brown	Deep blue solution	Pink ppt Carbonate CoCO$_3$
Cu(II) Blue [Cu(H$_2$O)$_6$]$^{2+}$	Pale blue ppt Cu(OH)$_2$	Does not dissolve	Pale blue ppt Cu(OH)$_2$	Deep blue solution [Cu(NH$_3$)$_4$(H$_2$O)$_2$]$^{2+}$	Green-blue p Carbonate CuCO$_3$

Reactions of Metal (III) Ions with Bases

Fe(III) violet [Fe(H$_2$O)$_6$]$^{3+}$ Appears brown due to hydrolysis	Brown ppt [Fe(H$_2$O)$_3$(OH)$_3$]	Does not dissolve	Brown ppt [Fe(H$_2$O)$_3$(OH)$_3$]	Does not dissolve	Brown ppt hydroxide [Fe(H$_2$O)$_3$(OH CO$_2$ evolved
Cr(III) ruby [Cr(H$_2$O)$_6$]$^{3+}$	Green ppt [Cr(H$_2$O)$_3$(OH)$_3$]	Green solution [Cr(OH)$_6$]$^{3-}$	Green ppt [Cr(H$_2$O)$_3$(OH)$_3$]		Green ppt hydroxide [Cr(H$_2$O)$_3$(OH CO$_2$ evolved
Al(III) colourless	White ppt Al(OH)$_3$	Colourless solution [Al(OH)$_4$]$^-$	White ppt Al(OH)$_3$	Slightly soluble	White ppt hydroxide of Al(OH)$_3$ CO$_2$ evolved

ppt = precipitate – formation of an insoluble solid

2.5.3 – Shapes of complex ions

Complex ions are typically one of four basic shapes:

A. Linear

B. Square-planar

C. Tetrahedral

D. Octahedral

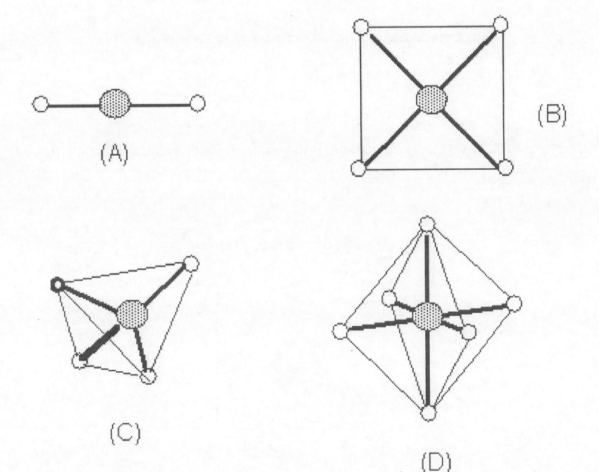

Complex ions that form from small ligands typically are of the octahedral shape, e.g. $[Co(H_2O)_6]^{2+}$.

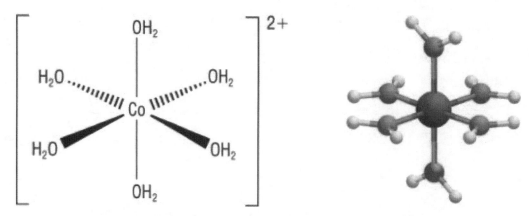

An octahedral shape is common with small ligands

When the ligands are larger, the shape of the complex ion is generally tetrahedral, e.g. $[CuCl_4]^{2-}$.

tetrachloro cuprate (II) ion

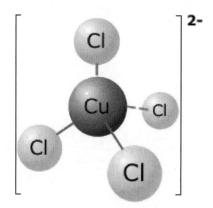

A tetrahedral structure

Square planar shapes are also formed. A good example of these is cisplatin, one of the most successful cancer drugs on the market.

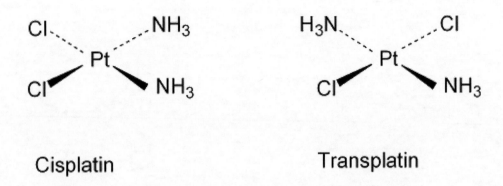

Cisplatin   Transplatin

Silver (Ag^+) commonly forms linear complexes, for example, in Tollens' reagent $[Ag(NH_3)_2].^+$

diammine silver (I) ion

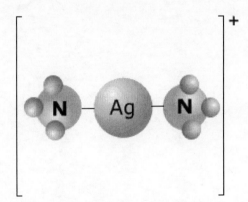

Octahedral complexes can display cis-trans isomerism with monodentate ligands[4] and optical isomerism with bidentate ligands[5].

Examples of a cis and trans isomer would be:

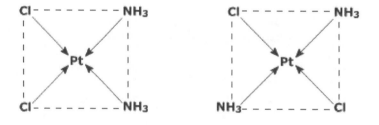

cis-2-butene   trans-2-butene

Square planar compounds can also display cis-trans properties:

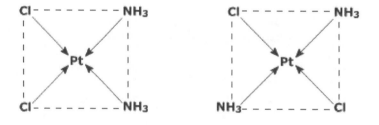

---

[4] Monodentate ligands are Lewis bases that donate a single pair ("mono") of electrons to a metal atom. Monodentate ligands can be either ions (usually anions) or neutral molecules.
[5] Bidentate ligands are Lewis bases that donate two pairs ("bi") of electrons to a metal atom. Bidentate ligands are often referred to as chelating ligands ("chelate" is derived from the Greek word for "claw") because they can "grab" a metal atom in two places.

2.5.4 – The formation of coloured ions

We noted earlier that one of the properties of the transition elements is that their compounds tend to be coloured. This colour is created by the compound absorbing light in a particular part of the visible spectrum.

We also saw earlier that the transition elements have part filled d shells. It is possible for these electrons to move from one d orbital to another if energy is applied (i.e. if they are excited).

In the atom of a transition element, all of the d shell electrons are of the same energy level, but this can change when they are in the form of a complex ion. The electrons have an ability to move from one d orbital to another. These different d orbitals can have slightly different energy levels.

When the electrons move from one energy level to another, they absorb energy in order to do this. This energy is in the visible spectrum, and different frequencies of energy relate to different energy levels. The frequency that is absorbed is then missing from what we see when we look at the solution; we essentially see the combination of the colours that are not absorbed.

The frequency of the visible light is related to the energy difference of the levels by the equation:

$$\Delta E \ = \ h v \ = \ hc/\lambda$$

E is the energy

v is the frequency

h is Planck's constant

c is the speed of light

λ is wavelength

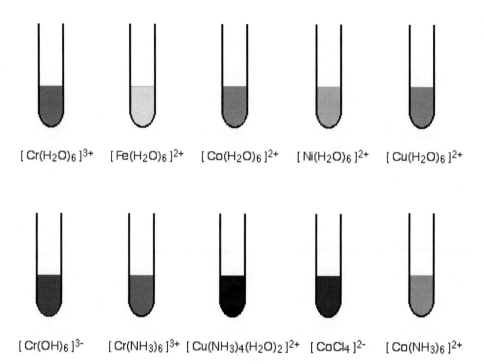

$[Cr(H_2O)_6]^{3+}$ $[Fe(H_2O)_6]^{2+}$ $[Co(H_2O)_6]^{2+}$ $[Ni(H_2O)_6]^{2+}$ $[Cu(H_2O)_6]^{2+}$

$[Cr(OH)_6]^{3-}$ $[Cr(NH_3)_6]^{3+}$ $[Cu(NH_3)_4(H_2O)_2]^{2+}$ $[CoCl_4]^{2-}$ $[Co(NH_3)_6]^{2+}$

Colours of transition metal compounds

The colour of a transition metal complex depends on the oxidation state of the metal and the ligands, as well as upon the shape of the ion and the coordination number. Different compounds of the same metal will have different colours (as illustrated above). The different colours occur because different metals, ligands, coordination numbers and shapes allow for different energy levels to be achieved when d orbital electrons are excited.

Colour, therefore, can be used to identify the transition metal ion.

Absorption of visible light can be used in spectroscopy to determine the concentration of coloured ions, and therefore the concentration of the solution.

2.5.5 – Variable oxidation states

You already know that group 1 elements lose their outer electron to form 1^+ ions and that group 2 elements lose both of their outer electrons to form 2^+ ions. Transition metals are a little more complex.

A typical transition metal can use either its 3d electrons or its 4s electrons in bonding; it can therefore have a variety of oxidation states in different compounds.

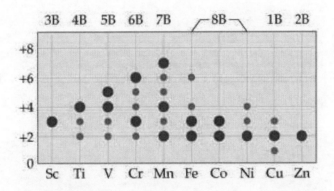

Oxidation states of transition metals

In the above diagram, the larger dots represent the most common oxidation states for the various transition metals.

Redox Reactions

Many of the reactions of the transition metal compounds are redox reactions in which the metals are either oxidised or reduced.

For example, iron (II) can be oxidised by chlorine:

$$2Fe^{2+}(aq) \ + \ Cl_2 \ \rightarrow \ 2Fe^{3+}(aq) \ + \ 2Cl^-(aq)$$

Oxidation state: +2   0   +3   -1

In terms of oxidation and reduction, remember the acronym:

OIL RIG

Oxidation
Is
Loss (of electrons)
Reduction
Is
Gain (of electrons)

You can see in the above reaction that chlorine acts as an oxidising agent as its oxidation number falls from 0 to -1 (i.e. it gains an electron).

Redox Titrations

We can use a redox titration to measure the concentration of an oxidising or a reducing agent. In principle this is the same as the acid-base titrations we studied earlier in the course.

An example of a redox titration is the reaction of Fe^{2+}(aq) ions with manganese (VII) ions (in potassium manganate (VII)).

Because of the colour change involved in the reaction, an indicator is not required as it would have been in an acid-base titration.

Using a burette, we gradually drip potassium manganate (VII) solution into a solution containing Fe^{2+}(aq) ions acidified with dilute sulphuric acid. The potassium manganate (VII) starts as an intense purple colour which disappears as the MnO_4^-(aq) are converted to the pale pink Mn^{2+}(aq) ions, leaving a virtually colourless solution.

Once we have added the correct amount of MnO_4^-(aq) to react with all of the Fe^{2+}(aq) ions, one more drop of MnO_4^-(aq) will turn the solution in the beaker purple. This is the end point of the titration.

Sulphuric acid must be used rather than hydrochloric acid because the chloride ions produced by the latter would interfere with the reaction and give a false result.

Consider the following calculation:

An iron supplement tablet states that it contains 0.220g of iron (II) sulphate. We can check this by a titration reaction.

Dissolve one of the tablets in dilute sulphuric acid and make the volume up to 250cm³.

25cm³ of this solution should then be transferred into a flask and titrated with 0.00100 mol dm⁻³ potassium manganate (VII) solution. This is done until the solution in the flask turns light pink. The amount of potassium manganate (VII) solution that was used can be measured and recorded. The experiment should be repeated several times and an average value taken.

If the average value was 28.50cm³ of potassium manganate (VII) solution used in the titration, then:

$$\text{No. moles potassium manganate (VII) solution} = M \times \frac{V}{1000}$$

M is the concentration of the solution in mol dm⁻³
V is the volume in cm³

Therefore:

$$\text{No. moles potassium manganate (VII) solution} = M \times \frac{V}{1000}$$

$$\text{No. moles potassium manganate (VII) solution} = 0.001 \times \frac{28.50}{1000}$$

$$= \mathbf{2.85 \times 10^{-5}}$$

The reaction is:

$$5Fe^{2+}(aq) + MnO_4^-(aq) + 8H^+(aq) \rightarrow 5Fe^{3+}(aq) + Mn^{2+}(aq) + 4H_2O(l)$$

Therefore we can say that 5 moles of $Fe^{2+}(aq)$ react with 1 mole of $MnO_4^-(aq)$.

$$\text{No. moles } Fe^{2+} = 5 \times 2.85 \times 10^{-5}$$

$$\textbf{No. moles } \mathbf{Fe^{2+}} = \mathbf{1.425 \times 10^{-4}}$$

We know that 25 cm³ of the solution contained 10% of the tablet (as it was dissolved in 250 cm³ acid). So:

$$\text{1 tablet contains } 1.425 \times 10^{-4} \times 10$$

$$= \mathbf{1.425 \times 10^{-3}}$$

1 mol of iron (II) sulphate contains 1 mol Fe^{2+}; each tablet therefore contains 1.425×10^{-3} mol $FeSO_4$.

The relative formula mass of $FeSO_4$ is 151.9

Each tablet, therefore, contains:

$\mathbf{1.425 \times 10^{-3} \times 151.9 = 0.215g}$ **iron (II) sulphate** (NB. the label was incorrect)

Potassium Dichromate (VI) Titrations

Acidified potassium dichromate (VI) can also be used in a titration experiment to measure the concentration of Fe^{2+} ions.

The half equations are:

$$Cr_2O_7^{2-}(aq) + 14H^+(aq) + 6e^- \rightarrow 2Cr^{3+}(aq) + 7H_2O(l)$$

$$Fe^{2+}(aq) \rightarrow Fe^{3+}(aq) + e^-$$

This is obviously not balanced; the second equation must be multiplied by 6 to balance the electrons, which then cancel out. The half equations then combine to form:

$$Cr_2O_7^{2-}(aq) + 14H^+(aq) + 6Fe^{2+}(aq) \rightarrow 6Fe^{3+}(aq) + 2Cr^{3+}(aq) + 7H_2O(l)$$

In this case, the colour change is not stark and an indicator must therefore be used – sodium diphenylaminesulphonate – which turns from colourless to purple.

Oxidation in Alkaline Solutions

In both of the examples above, a metal with a high oxidation number is reduced in an acid solution (Mn(VII) and Cr(VI)).

Oxidation of transition metals with low oxidation numbers tends to happen in alkaline solutions. This is because of the tendency to form negative ions.

Typical species (where M = a typical transition metal):

Acid solution – $M(H_2O)_6^{2+}$
Neutral solution – $M(H_2O)_4(OH)_2$
Alkaline solution – $M(H_2O)_2(OH)_4^{2-}$

Chromium example:

The most important oxidation states of chromium are: Cr(II), which is blue; Cr(III), which is green; and Cr(VI) which is yellow/orange.

In an aqueous solution, Cr(VI) exists as either:

Chromate (VI) ion – CrO_4^{2-} (Yellow)
Dichromate (VI) ion – $Cr_2O_7^{2-}$ (Orange)

The dichromate ion is stable in acid solutions and the chromate is stable in alkalis, as shown below:

$$2CrO_4^{2-}(aq) \ + \ H^+(aq) \ \rightleftharpoons \ Cr_2O_7^{2-}(aq) \ + \ H_2O(l)$$

Chromium (II) is easily oxidised to chromium (III) by oxygen, and can only be prepared in the absence of air. Chromium (III) is the most stable oxidation state of chromium.

Chromium (II) is prepared by reducing chromate (VI) by zinc in acid solution. The half equations are:

$$Cr_2O_7^{2-}(aq) \ + \ 14H^+(aq) \ + \ 6e^- \ \rightarrow \ 2Cr^{3+}(aq) \ + \ 7H_2O(l)$$

$$Zn(s) \ \rightarrow \ Zn^{2+}(aq) \ + \ 2e^-$$

The second equation needs to be multiplied by 3 to balance the electrons, and then we can combine the equations:

$$Cr_2O_7^{2-}(aq) \ + \ 14H^+(aq) \ + \ 3Zn(s) \ \rightarrow \ 2Cr^{3+}(aq) \ + \ 7H_2O(l) \ + \ 3Zn^{2+}(aq)$$

The half equation for the further reduction of chromium (III) to chromium (II) is:

$$Cr^{3+}(aq) + e^- \rightarrow Cr^{2+}(aq)$$

Ultimately, therefore, we have:

$$Zn(s) + 2Cr^{3+}(aq) \rightarrow Zn^{2+}(aq) + 2Cr^{2+}(aq)$$

If sodium hydroxide is added to a solution of chromium (III) salt, a green precipitate is first formed:

$$[Cr(H_2O)_6]^{3+}(aq) + 3OH^-(aq) \rightarrow [Cr(OH)_3(H_2O)_3](s) + 3H_2O(l)$$

This precipitate dissolves in excess sodium hydroxide to produce a green solution containing chromate (III):

$$[Cr(OH)_3(H_2O)_3](s) + 3OH^-(aq) \rightarrow [Cr(OH)_6]^{3-}(aq) + 3H_2O(l)$$

This solution can then be oxidised using hydrogen peroxide (H_2O_2). The solution turns yellow as chromate (VI) ions are formed:

$$[Cr(OH)_6]^{3-}(aq) + 3H_2O_2(aq) \rightarrow CrO_4^{2-}(aq) + OH^-(aq) + 8H_2O(l)$$

Cobalt example:

A number of M^{2+} ions will be oxidised to M^{3+} in alkaline solutions. Cobalt is a good example of this:

$$2[Co(OH)_6]^{4-}(aq) + H_2O_2(aq) \rightarrow 2[Co(OH)_6]^{3-}(aq) + 2OH^-(aq)$$

In ammoniacal solution, Co^{2+} ions can be oxidised by the air.

If we were to add an excess of ammonium solution to cobalt (II) in aqueous solution, a brown complex ion would be formed $[Co(NH_3)_6]^{2+}$.

In the first stage of the reaction, the precipitate is formed:

$$[Co(H_2O)_6]^{3+}(aq) + 2OH^-(aq) \rightarrow Co(H_2O)_4(OH)_2(s)$$

The second stage sees the precipitate dissolve in excess ammonia:

$$Co(H_2O)_4(OH)_2(s) + 6NH_3(aq) \rightarrow [Co(NH_3)_6]^{2+} + 2OH^-(aq) + 4H_2O(l)$$

The $[Co(NH_3)_6]^{2+}$ ion is then oxidised rapidly in air to $[Co(NH_3)_6]^{3+}$.

2.5.6 - Catalysts

You should already know what a catalyst is from your studies earlier in this course, but by way of revision:

Catalysts increase the rate of a reaction, or cause a reaction to occur, without themselves being used up in the reaction.

Many of the transition elements or their compounds can be used as catalysts in various reactions of industrial and commercial importance.

Catalysts can be divided into two groups, each will be examined separately:

- Heterogeneous
- Homogeneous

Heterogeneous Catalysts

These are catalysts that are present in the reaction chamber, but in a different phase than the actual reactants. For example, they could be solid pellets of metal in liquid reactants.

The catalytic reaction occurs at the surface of the solid catalyst (in this example).

Catalysts are very often expensive, and therefore the efficiency at which they operate is of critical commercial importance. You can increase the efficiency of a catalyst by a number of mechanisms:

- Increase the surface area (since that is where the reaction occurs).
- Spread the catalyst onto an inert support medium. This increases the surface area to mass ratio, making a small amount of the catalyst essentially go further. The catalytic converter in a car, for example, has rhodium and platinum finely spread on a ceramic surface.

Despite the basic definition that a catalyst is not used up in the reaction, they do not last indefinitely.

Over time, the surfaces may become clogged with impurities, or it may be lost from the support medium. Either way, the catalyst becomes less effective. This is called **poisoning**.

Examples of Heterogeneous Catalysts

The Haber Process

We encountered the Haber process in the AS part of the course, and I'm sure you will remember that it is the industrial process that is used to convert nitrogen and hydrogen to ammonia.

The Haber process uses iron pellets as a catalyst; they are in pellet form to increase the surface area of the catalyst.

The iron catalyst lasts around 5 years in this process before it becomes poisoned by sulphur and needs replacing.

The Contact Process

The Contact process is another process of considerable industrial and commercial importance. It reacts sulphur dioxide and oxygen to produce sulphuric acid. Just looking at the catalyst, the reaction is catalysed by vanadium (V) oxide (V_2O_5) in a two stage process:

Stage 1 – The vanadium (V) oxide oxidises the sulphur dioxide and is itself reduced:

$$SO_2 \ + \ V_2O_5 \ \rightarrow \ SO_3 \ + \ V_2O_4$$
$$ +5 +4$$

Stage 2 – The vanadium (IV) oxide is then regenerated into vanadium (V) oxide:

$$2V_2O_4 \ + \ O_2 \ \rightarrow \ 2V_2O_5$$
$$ +4 +5$$

Methanol Production

Methanol is produced from carbon monoxide and hydrogen. This reaction can employ a chromium oxide catalyst (Cr_2O_3). The reaction is again in two stages:

Stage 1 – The carbon monoxide and hydrogen are produced:

$$CH_4(g) \ + \ H_2O(g) \ \rightarrow \ CO(g) \ + \ 3H_2(g)$$

Stage 2 – The methanol is produced:

$$CO(g) \ + \ 3H_2(g) \ \rightarrow \ CH_3OH(g)$$

Homogeneous Catalysts

This occurs when the catalyst is in the same phase as the reactants, and an intermediate species is formed.

For example, peroxodisulphate ions oxidise iodide ions to iodine:

$$S_2O_8^{2-}(aq) + 2I^-(aq) \rightarrow 2SO_4^{2-}(aq) + I_2(aq)$$

The above reaction occurs in two stages.

Stage 1 – The peroxodisulphate ions oxidise iron (II) to iron (III):

$$S_2O_8^{2-}(aq) + 2Fe^{2+}(aq) \rightarrow 2SO_4^{2-}(aq) + 2Fe^{3+}(aq)$$

Stage 2 – The Fe^{3+} then oxidises the I^- ions to I_2:

$$2Fe^{3+}(aq) + 2I^-(aq) \rightarrow 2Fe^{2+}(aq) + I_2(aq)$$

Autocatalysis

This occurs where one of the products in the reaction is also the catalyst for the reaction. In these reactions, the rate is slow to start with but speeds up as more of the catalyst is produced.

An example is the oxidation of ethanedioate ions by manganate (VII) ions.

The overall reaction is:

$$2MnO_4^-(aq) + 16H^+(aq) + 5C_2O_4^{2-}(aq) \rightarrow 2Mn^{2+}(aq) + 8H_2O(l) + 10CO_2(g)$$

The catalyst for the reaction is the Mn^{2+} ions, which are not present at the start of the reaction.

2.6 – Reactions of the ions in aqueous solution

The reactions of transition metal ions in aqueous solution provide a practical opportunity for students to show and to understand how transition metal ions can be identified by test-tube reactions in the laboratory.

<u>Lewis Acids and Bases</u>

We have already encountered the Brønsted-Lowry theory of acids and bases in terms of acids being proton donors and bases being proton acceptors. There is another theory of acids and bases, however, and this is called the Lewis theory. This theory defines acids as electron pair acceptors and bases as electron pair donors in the formation of coordinate (dative) covalent bonds.

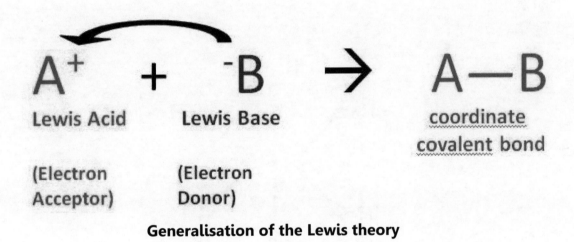

Generalisation of the Lewis theory

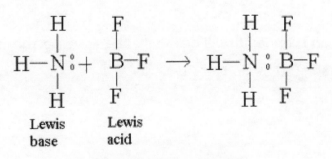

A more specific example

In the above example, the ammonia is acting as the Lewis base, as it is donating a pair of electrons, and the boron trifluoride is acting as the Lewis acid, as it is accepting the pair of electrons. The bond that is formed is a coordinate covalent bond.

NB. All Brønsted-Lowry acids are also Lewis acids.

Ligands that bond with transition metals using lone pairs of electrons are acting as Lewis bases and the transition metal is acting as a Lewis acid.

Metal-Aqua Ions

If we dissolve the salt of a transition metal in water, water molecules will actually cluster around the ion so that it essentially forms a complex ion (aqua ion). Consider Fe^{2+}. If iron (II) sulphate is dissolved in water, the following complex will form: $[Fe(H_2O)_6]^{2+}$

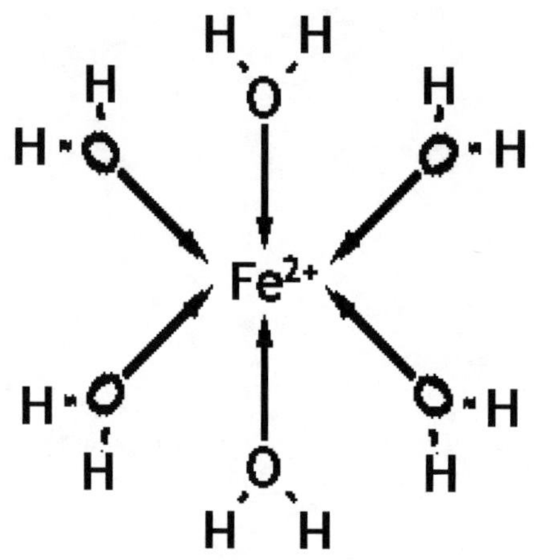

Salts of cobalt (II) and copper (II) will be exactly the same, i.e. the Fe^{2+} in the illustration above would be replaced by Co^{2+} or Cu^{2+}.

The same would occur with an iron (III) salt:

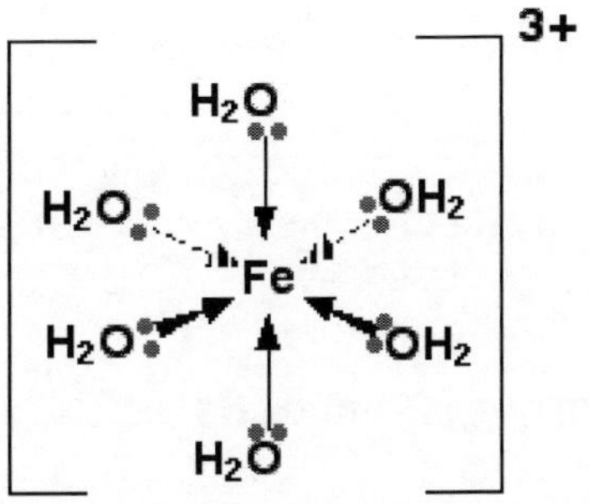

Salts of aluminium (III) and chromium (III) will be exactly the same, i.e. the Fe^{3+} in the illustration above would be replaced by Al^{3+} or Cr^{3+}.

(NB. Remember aluminium is not a transition metal, but the chemistry is the same.)

Acidity or Hydrolysis Reactions

The iron (II) and iron (III) complexes we looked at above look substantially the same, but there is a significant difference in their acidity. The solution of Fe^{2+}(aq) is not noticeably acidic, but the solution of Fe^{3+}(aq) has a pKa of 2.2.

The difference in acidity is caused by the Fe^{3+} ion being smaller and more highly charged than the Fe^{2+} ion. This higher charge density makes Fe^{3+} more strongly polarising.

In $[Fe(H_2O)_6]^{3+}$, the Fe^{3+} attracts the electrons of the oxygen atoms in the water ligands towards itself strongly, thus weakening the O–H bonds in those ligands. This complex then releases H^+ ions readily, making the solution acidic.

The Fe^{2+} ion is less polarising and therefore the O–H bonds are less weakened and fewer H^+ ions are released into the solution as a result.

The dissociation of H^+ from $[Fe(H_2O)_6]^{3+}$ can be written as the following equation:

$$[Fe(H_2O)_6]^{3+}(aq) \rightleftharpoons [Fe(H_2O)_5(OH)]^{2+}(aq) + H^+(aq)$$

As a general rule of transition metal chemistry, M^{3+} ions are more acidic than M^{2+} ions.

These reactions are called hydrolysis reactions, as they are reactions with water. They can also be written as:

$$[Fe(H_2O)_6]^{3+}(aq) + H_2O(l) \rightleftharpoons [Fe(H_2O)_5(OH)]^{2+}(aq) + H_3O^+(aq)$$

Note that the $[Fe(H_2O)_6]^{3+}(aq)$ donates an H^+ ion to the water. It is therefore acting as a Brønsted-Lowry acid.

Simple Reactions

If we add a base (i.e. OH^- ions) to either an M^{2+} or M^{3+} solution, it will remove protons from the aqueous complex.

There are three stages to this in the case of M^{3+}:

$$[M(H_2O)_6]^{3+}(aq) + OH^-(aq) \rightarrow [M(H_2O)_5(OH)]^{2+}(aq) + H_2O(l)$$

$$[M(H_2O)_5(OH)]^{2+}(aq) + OH^-(aq) \rightarrow [M(H_2O)_4(OH)_2]^+(aq) + H_2O(l)$$

$$[M(H_2O)_4(OH)_2]^+(aq) + OH^-(aq) \rightarrow M(H_2O)_3(OH)_3(s) + H_2O(l)$$

In the case of M^{2+}, it is a two stage process:

$$[M(H_2O)_6]^{2+}(aq) + OH^-(aq) \rightarrow [M(H_2O)_5(OH)]^+(aq) + H_2O(l)$$

$$[M(H_2O)_5(OH)]^+(aq) + OH^-(aq) \rightarrow M(H_2O)_4(OH)_2(s) + H_2O(l)$$

Ammonia, which is also a base, has the same effect of removing protons as does the hydroxide ion.

Reactions with the Base CO_3^{2-} (the Carbonate Ion)

The carbonate ion is able to remove protons from $[Fe(H_2O)_6]^{3+}(aq)$ to form carbon dioxide. $[Fe(H_2O)_6]^{2+}(aq)$ does not form carbon dioxide. This is because of the greater acidity of $[Fe(H_2O)_6]^{3+}(aq)$. $[Fe(H_2O)_6]^{2+}(aq)$ forms M(II) carbonates (precipitates).

$$2[Fe(H_2O)_6]^{3+}(aq) + 3CO_3^{2-}(aq) \rightarrow 2[Fe(H_2O)_3(OH)_3](aq) + 3CO_2(g) + 3H_2O(l)$$

Generally speaking, carbonates of transition metal ions in oxidation state +2 exist, whilst those of ions in oxidation state +3 do not.

Tests for Ions

We saw earlier that aqua ions of Fe^{2+} and Fe^{3+} exist. They are difficult to tell apart in solution, however, as the former is pale green and the latter pale brown. There is a simple test tube test to distinguish between them. If some dilute alkali is added, a precipitate is formed which has a more distinguishable colour. Fe^{2+} is green, while Fe^{3+} is brown.

The reactions are:

$$[Fe(H_2O)_6]^{2+}(aq) + 2OH^-(aq) \rightarrow Fe(H_2O)_4(OH)_2(aq) + 2H_2O(l)$$

$$[Fe(H_2O)_6]^{3+}(aq) + 3OH^-(aq) \rightarrow Fe(H_2O)_3(OH)_3(aq) + 3H_2O(l)$$

Amphoteric Hydroxides

Some substances show some of the characteristics of both acids and bases. These are called amphoteric.

For example, aluminium hydroxide will react with an acid and is therefore a base:

$$Al(H_2O)_3(OH)_3 + 3HCl \rightarrow Al(H_2O)_6{}^{3+} + 3Cl^-$$

But it will also react with sodium hydroxide (a base) and therefore acts as an acid in the following reaction:

$$Al(H_2O)_3(OH)_3 + OH^- \rightarrow [Al(OH)_4]^- + 3H_2O$$

Chromium has similar amphoteric properties:

$$Cr(H_2O)_3(OH)_3 + 3H_3O^+ \rightleftharpoons [Cr(H_2O)_6]^{3+} + 3H_2O$$

$$Cr(H_2O)_3(OH)_3 + 3OH^- \rightleftharpoons [Cr(OH)_6]^{3+} + 3H_2O$$

Anionic Transition Metal Compounds

In most of the examples we have looked at so far, the transition metal exists in a positively charged form (as a cation). When a transition metal has a high oxidation state, however, it can exist in a negatively charged form (as an anion).

Examples include:

- Manganese as MnO_4^-
- Chromium as CrO_4^-
- Chromium as $Cr_2O_7^{2-}$

An example of their reaction is:

$$2CrO_4^-(aq) + 2H^+(aq) \rightleftharpoons Cr_2O_7^{2-}(aq) + H_2O(l)$$

Required practical 11:

Carry out simple test-tube reactions to identify transition metal ions in aqueous solution.

Topic 3

Organic Chemistry

Topic 3

3.1 – Introduction to organic chemistry

Organic chemistryis the study of the millions of covalent compounds of the element carbon.

These structurally diverse compounds vary from naturally occuring petroleum fuels to DNA and the molecules in living systems. Organic compounds also demonstrate human ingenuity in the vast range of synthetic materials created by chemists. Many of these compounds are used as drugs, medicines and plastics.

Organic compounds are named using the International Union of Pure and Applied Chemistry (IUPAC) system, and the structure or formula of molecules can be represented in various different ways. Organic mechanisms are studied, which enable reactions to be explained.

In search for sustainable chemistry, for safer agochemicals and for new materials to match the desire for new technology, chemistry plays the dominant role.

3.1.1 - Nomenclature

Organic compounds can be represented by:

- Empirical formula
- Molecular formula
- General formula
- Structural formula
- Displayed formula
- Skeletal formula

Empirical formula

We encountered this concept earlier in the course, but to recap: the empirical formula is the simplest ratio of the atoms of each element present in a compound.

For example:

Pentene has the molecular formula:

- C_5H_{10}

Empirical formula:

- CH_2

Molecular formula

Again, we have encountered this concept too. The molecular formula is the actual formula of the given compound.

For example, a molecular formula could be:

- $C_{13}H_{26}$

The again the empirical formula would be:

- CH_2

General formula

A general formula is a type of empirical formula that represents the composition of any member of an entire class of compounds.

Every alkane, for example, would have the general formula:

C_nH_{2n+2}

given that n stands for any number.

For example the molecular formula for pentane is:

C_5H_{12}

Structural formula

The structural formula of a substance is the organisation of the atoms within the molecule.

Isomers are molecules with the same chemical (molecular) formula but a different structural formula. That is to say that the atoms are arranged differently, although there is the same total number of each one.

Consider hexane: C_6H_{14}. This can be arranged in a simple straight chain, or in a number of other possible structural arrangements, as illustrated below:

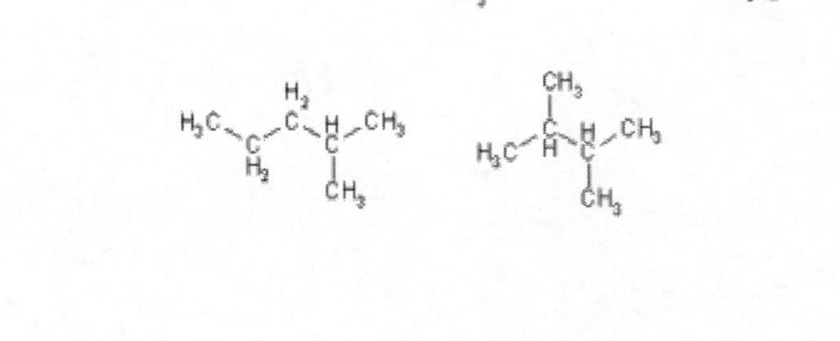

Count up the carbon and hydrogen atoms in each of the five molecules above and you will see that they all have the same molecular formula. They are all very different substances, however, with different physical and chemical properties because of their different structural arrangements.

Activity 35 – Draw the structural isomers of pentane (C_5H_{12}).

Displayed formula

The displayed formula is a pictorial representation of a molecule showing single bonds as a single line, double bonds as a double line and triple bonds as a triple line.

For example, ethane:

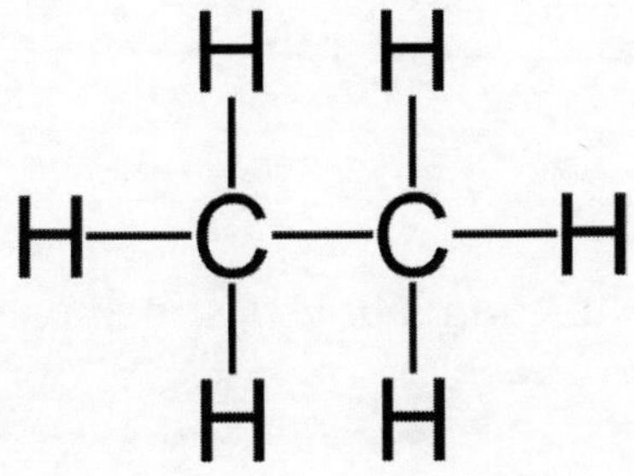

$$
\begin{array}{c}
\quad\; H \quad\;\; H \\
\quad\; | \qquad\; | \\
H - C - C - H \\
\quad\; | \qquad\; | \\
\quad\; H \quad\;\; H
\end{array}
$$

Ethene:

$$
\begin{array}{c}
H \qquad\qquad H \\
\;\;\diagdown \qquad\;\; \diagup \\
\quad\; C = C \\
\;\;\diagup \qquad\;\; \diagdown \\
H \qquad\qquad H
\end{array}
$$

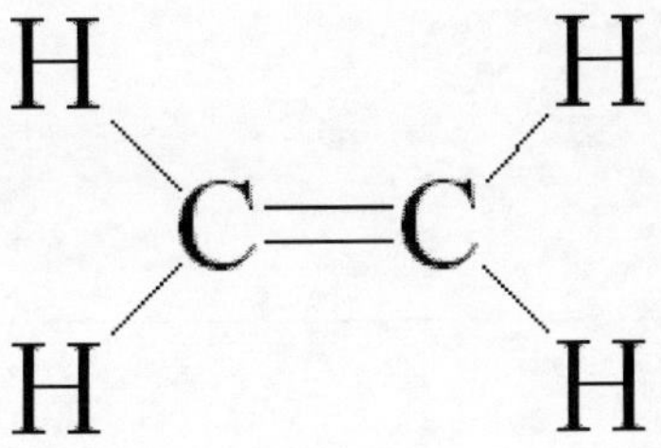

Ethyne:

$$
H - C \equiv C - H
$$

<u>Skeletal formula</u>

This is a simplified way of drawing the displayed formulae which omits the atoms.

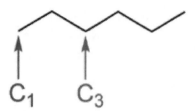

You should generally avoid this in exams unless specifically asked for it.

<u>Homologous Series</u>

To understand what this concept means, we should examine a series of organic compounds. We will examine the first 4 alkanes (we will look at what "alkanes" means soon):

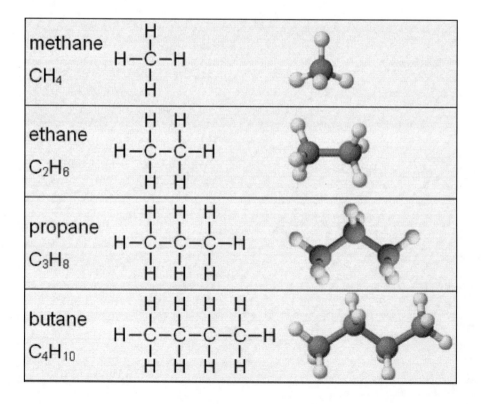

A homologous series is a series of compounds where each member differs from the previous member of the series by the same, specific amount.

- Ethane has 1 more carbon and 2 more hydrogen atoms than methane
- Propane has 1 more carbon and 2 more hydrogen atoms than ethane
- Butane has 1 more carbon and 2 more hydrogen atoms than propane

This continues to be the case as you move up the series, pentane being the next in this homologous series, then hexane, etc.

Functional Group

A functional group is a portion of a molecule that is a recognisable/classified group of bound atoms. In organic chemistry, it is very common to see molecules comprised mainly a carbon backbone with functional groups attached to the chain. The functional group gives the molecule its properties, regardless of what molecule contains it; they are the centres of chemical reactivity. The functional groups within a molecule need to be identified in their names.

This is best understood by looking at some illustrations:

$$
\begin{array}{ccc}
H & H & H \\
| & | & | \\
H-C-C-C-H \\
| & | & | \\
H & H & H \\
\end{array}
$$

```
   H  H  H                    H  H  Br                   H  H  H
   |  |  |                     |  |  |                    |  |  |
H–C–C–C–Br                  H–C–C–C–H                  H–C–C–C–H
   |  |  |                     |  |  |                    |  |  |
   H  H  H                     H  H  H                    H  H  Br


   H  H  H                    Br H  H                    H  H  H
   |  |  |                     |  |  |                    |  |  |
Br–C–C–C–H                  H–C–C–C–H                  H–C–C–C–H
   |  |  |                     |  |  |                    |  |  |
   H  H  H                     H  H  H                    Br H  H
```

In bromopropane, the bromine is the functional group and can appear on any of the carbon atoms.

Molecules can have more than one functional group. The molecule below is:

1,2-di-bromo 3-chloropropane

```
   H  H  H
   |  |  |
H–C–C–C–H
   |  |  |
   Br Br Cl
```

This has three functional groups: 1 chlorine atom and 2 bromine atoms.

The functional groups define the characteristics of the molecule. Examples include:

acyl halides (X = F, Cl, Br, I)   alcohols   aldehydes   alkyl halides (X = F, Cl, Br, I)   alkynes

alkenes   amines   amides   aromatic rings   aryl halides (X = F, Cl, Br, I)

carboxylic acids   disulfides   esters   ethers

imines   ketones   nitriles   nitro groups   phosphate esters

thioethers   thiols

You need to be aware of the standard naming system (the IUPAC system) for basic hydrocarbons of up to a 6 carbon atom chain in length.

Alkanes

The first part of the name of a hydrocarbon will tell you how many carbon atoms it has in its chain.

methane CH_4	H | H—C—H | H	
ethane C_2H_6	H H | | H—C—C—H | | H H	
propane C_3H_8	H H H | | | H—C—C—C—H | | | H H H	
butane C_4H_{10}	H H H H | | | | H—C—C—C—C—H | | | | H H H H	

The next two hydrocarbons in this series are called:

- Pentane (5 carbon atoms)
- Hexane (6 carbon atoms)

Activity 35 – Draw the structures of pentane and hexane.

Answer to Activity 35:

You know pentane has 5 carbon atoms and hexane has 6, and you know that they are in a straight line (as we are discussing alkanes), therefore:

Pentane:

$$\begin{array}{ccccccccc}
& H & & H & & H & & H & & H \\
& | & & | & & | & & | & & | \\
H- & C & - & C & - & C & - & C & - & C & -H \\
& | & & | & & | & & | & & | \\
& H & & H & & H & & H & & H
\end{array}$$

Hexane:

$$\begin{array}{ccccccccccc}
& H & & H & & H & & H & & H & & H \\
& | & & | & & | & & | & & | & & | \\
H- & C & - & C & - & C & - & C & - & C & - & C & -H \\
& | & & | & & | & & | & & | & & | \\
& H & & H & & H & & H & & H & & H
\end{array}$$

Alkenes

Alkenes are a little more difficult to name because of the presence of a double bond.

The first part of the name is the same as the corresponding alkane, but the first difference in the name is that the ending is different:

- -ane for alkanes
- -ene for alkenes

The other difficulty with naming alkenes is that the name needs to identify where the double bond is, that is to say between which two carbon atoms. The location of the double bond affects the properties of the material, so identifying its location in the name is important.

The first three alkenes are as follows:

Ethene
$$\begin{array}{cc} H & H \\ | & | \\ C &= C \\ | & | \\ H & H \end{array}$$

Propene
$$\begin{array}{ccc} H & H & H \\ | & | & | \\ C &= C - C - H \\ | & & | \\ H & & H \end{array}$$

Butene
$$\begin{array}{cccc} H & H & H & H \\ | & | & | & | \\ H - C - C &= C - C - H \\ | & & & | \\ H & & & H \end{array}$$

Activity 36 – Why is methene not the first in the series?

Answer to Activity 36:

Methene does not exist. An alkene needs to have a double bond between two carbon atoms, and methene would only have 1 carbon, therefore it cannot exist.

The names in the above table are not strictly accurate because they do not specifically identify the location of the double bond.

Look at the illustration of butane. The double bond could be on either the first carbon atom or the second (i.e. between the two central carbon atoms). In the illustration, it is on the first carbon atom (counting from the shortest end) and the name needs to reflect this. The actual name for that substance would be:

- But-1-ene

The 1 in the centre of the name indicates that the double bond is on the first carbon atom.

If the bond was on the second carbon atom, the substance would be called:

- But-2-ene

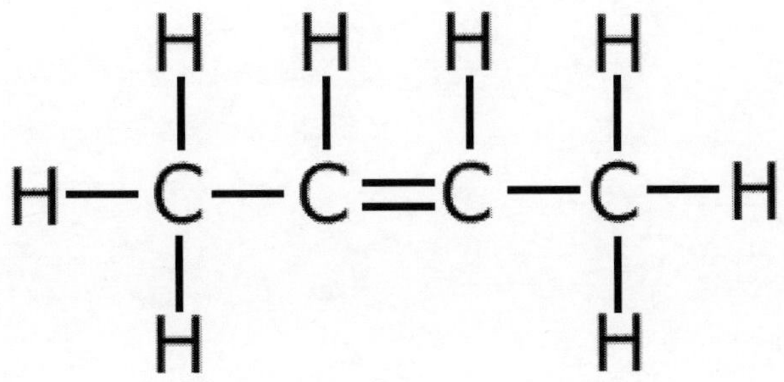

$$
\begin{array}{cccc}
H & H & H & H \\
| & | & | & | \\
H-C-C=C-C-H \\
| & & & | \\
H & & & H
\end{array}
$$

Let us now look at 5 and 6 carbon chain alkenes.

Activity 37 – Use what you have learned so far to draw the following:

Pent-1-ene

Pent-2-ene

Hex-2-ene

Hex-3-ene

Answer to Activity 37:

We know pent-1-ene has 5 carbon atoms (from "pent"), it has a double bond (from "ene") and the double bond is on the first carbon atom (from "-1-"). Therefore:

Pent-1-ene:

```
        H    H    H         H
        |    |    |         |
  H —— C —— C —— C —— C ==== C
        |    |    |    |     |
        H    H    H    H     H
```

We know pent-2-ene has 5 carbon atoms (from "pent"), it has a double bond (from "ene") and the double bond is on the second carbon atom (from "-2-"). Therefore:

Pent-2-ene:

We know hex-2-ene has 6 carbon atoms (from "hex"), it has a double bond (from "ene") and the double bond is on the second carbon atom (from "-2-"). Therefore:

Hex-2-ene:

```
        H              H    H    H
        |              |    |    |
  H —— C —— C ==== C —— C —— C —— C —— H
        |    |    |    |    |    |
        H    H    H    H    H    H
```

We know hex-3-ene has 6 carbon atoms (from "hex"), it has a double bond (from "ene") and the double bond is on the third carbon atom (from "-3-"). Therefore:

Hex-3-ene:

$$H-\underset{\underset{H}{|}}{\overset{\overset{H}{|}}{C}}-\underset{\underset{H}{|}}{\overset{\overset{H}{|}}{C}}-\underset{\underset{H}{|}}{\overset{}{C}}=\underset{}{\overset{\overset{H}{|}}{C}}-\underset{\underset{H}{|}}{\overset{\overset{H}{|}}{C}}-\underset{\underset{H}{|}}{\overset{\overset{H}{|}}{C}}-H$$

Haloalkanes

The final family you need to be able to name are the haloalkanes.

Haloalkanes are alkanes with a halogen somewhere in the structure (halogens are the group 7 elements – Fluorine to Antimony).

The rules for naming haloalkanes are very similar to those for naming alkenes, in that the location of the halogen needs to be identified in the name, and that is done with a number representing which carbon atom the halogen is bonded to. This time, however, the number is at the start of the name.

In the following example, the substance has 3 carbon atoms in its longest chain (starts with "Prop"), it has only single bonds (ends in "ane") and the halogen is on the second carbon atom. It is therefore called:

- 2 - bromopropane

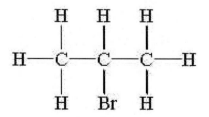

Haloalkanes can also have more than one halogen present, but the naming system follows the same rules.

In the next example, the substance has 4 carbon atoms in its longest chain (starts with "But"), it has only single bonds (ends in "ane") and the halogens are both on the first carbon atom (counting from the shortest end). The halogens are named alphabetically. It is therefore called:

- 1-bromo 1-chlorobutane

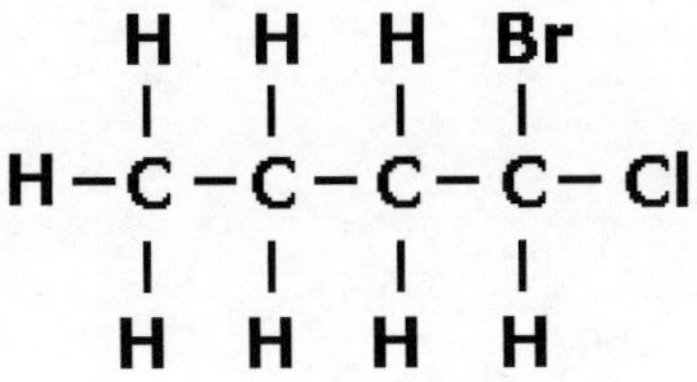

<pre>
      H   H   H   Br
      | | | |
  H − C − C − C − C − Cl
      | | | |
      H   H   H   H
</pre>

Names can often look complex and daunting, but when broken down they are quite simple.

If the halogens are on different carbon atoms, then the halogens still need to be identified as to which carbon they are each on, as follows:

In the following example, the haloalkane has a bromine atom on the 1st and 3rd carbon and a chlorine on the 2nd. It is therefore called:

- 1,3 - dibromo 2 - chlorobutane

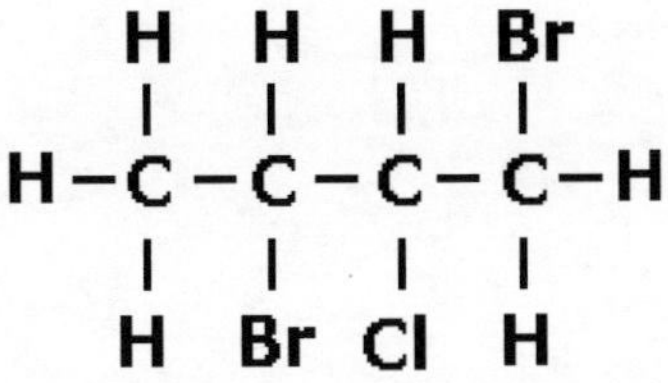

<pre>
      H   H   H   Br
      | | | |
  H − C − C − C − C − H
      | | | |
      H   Br Cl H
</pre>

Note: Use commas to separate numbers in the name and hyphens to separate numbers and letters.

3.1.2 – Reaction mechanisms

Reactions of organic compounds can be explained using mechanisms.

<u>Free-radical mechanisms</u>

Haloalkanes are produced by mixing a halogen with an alkane. If they are mixed in the dark, however, no reaction will occur.

If the mixture is exposed to bright sunlight, they react together to form the appropriate haloalkane. For example:

$$CH_4(g) \ + \ Cl_2(g) \ \rightarrow \ CH_3Cl(g) \ + \ HCl(g)$$

The above reaction is called a **free radical substitution** reaction and it occurs in three stages:

- Initiation
- Propagation
- Termination

<u>Initiation</u>

First the Cl–Cl bond breaks to form two Cl· free radicals (these are very reactive). The · is used to indicate an unpaired electron. This is achieved by the bond absorbing a single quantum of UV light, whose energy is greater than the strength of the bond, and so the bond breaks. The reaction is as follows:

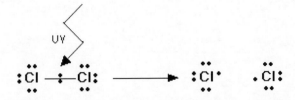

Activity 63 – Why do both Cl free radicals have 1 outer electron?

Answer to Activity 63:

They each take one of the electrons in the covalent bond, rather than one of the Cl atoms taking both. If it was a bond between two different substances, then the electrons might be distributed unevenly. The Cl–Cl bond breaks homolytically, essentially right down the middle.

Free radicals are always highly reactive and don't exist for long before they attack another substance.

Propagation

This is not a single stage, but occurs in two sub-stages.

1st sub-stage:

A chlorine free radical reacts with methane to produce a methyl free radical:

$$Cl\cdot + CH_4 \rightarrow HCl + CH_3\cdot$$

2nd sub-stage:

The methyl free radical, which is also highly reactive, reacts with a chlorine molecule:

$$CH_3\cdot + Cl_2 \rightarrow CH_3Cl + Cl\cdot$$

Termination

This is the final step, where free radicals combine to end their reactions. There are three possible termination reactions:

1st:

$$Cl\cdot + Cl\cdot \rightarrow Cl_2$$

2nd:

$$CH_3\cdot + CH_3\cdot \rightarrow C_2H_6$$

3rd:

$$Cl\cdot + CH_3\cdot \rightarrow CH_3Cl$$

Ozone

Ozone is a naturally occurring substance with the formula O_3. It decomposes in the upper atmosphere to form oxygen (O_2). In the upper atmosphere, ozone has a vital role in protecting the earth from harmful UV radiation from the sun. If too much UV was reaching the earth, life would be almost impossible for most creatures.

A C–Cl bond in a chlorofluorocarbon (CFC) will break homolytically in the upper atmosphere to form a Cl• free radical (as well as a free radical of the carbon compound). These Cl• free radicals will react with O_3 in the upper atmosphere in the following reactions:

$$Cl\cdot + O_3 \rightarrow ClO\cdot + O_2$$

and:

$$ClO\cdot + O_3 \rightarrow 2O_2 + Cl\cdot$$

From these two equations, you can see that the Cl• free radical is not used up in the reaction and is therefore a catalyst in the breakdown of ozone to oxygen.

We have seen that CFCs facilitated the breakdown of O_3 in the upper atmosphere to O_2. We have also seen how important O_3 is in terms of protecting the Earth's surface from the harmful effects of UV radiation.

Legislation was implemented to ban the use of CFCs as the ozone layer was becoming gradually depleted. This act was supported by chemists, and different substances were developed to replace CFCs in a variety of products such as aerosols and refrigerators.

Addition Reactions of Alkenes

Alkene reactions are typically electrophilic addition reactions. The C=C bond contains four electrons and is therefore a region of high electron density. Electrophiles will be attracted to this electron concentration and will form a bond using two of these electrons, thus breaking the double bond.

Addition Mechanism

The electrophile is attracted to the high electron density of the double bond. These electrophiles are positively charged (being either an ion or having a slightly positively charged bond) and will accept a pair of electrons from the C=C double bond. Once this occurs, a temporary C^+ ion is formed (called a carbocation). This C^+ ion will be extremely reactive and will bond with a negatively charged ion.

Activity 68 – Draw the reaction you would expect between the following:

Ethene + Hydrogen chloride

Answer to Activity 68:

$$C_2H_4 + HCl \rightarrow C_2H_5Cl$$

The mechanism for this is illustrated below, but split into two phases.

Firstly, as described above, the hydrogen in the HBr acts as an electrophile because the bromine attracts the electrons in the bond towards itself, creating a slight positive charge on the hydrogen. This hydrogen then breaks the double bond and forms a single bond with one of the carbon atoms. The other carbon atom is now deficient by 1 electron (and has gained a positive charge, C^+) and the bromine is now a Br^- ion.

In the second stage, the bromide ion bonds with the carbocation to form the final product, bromoethane.

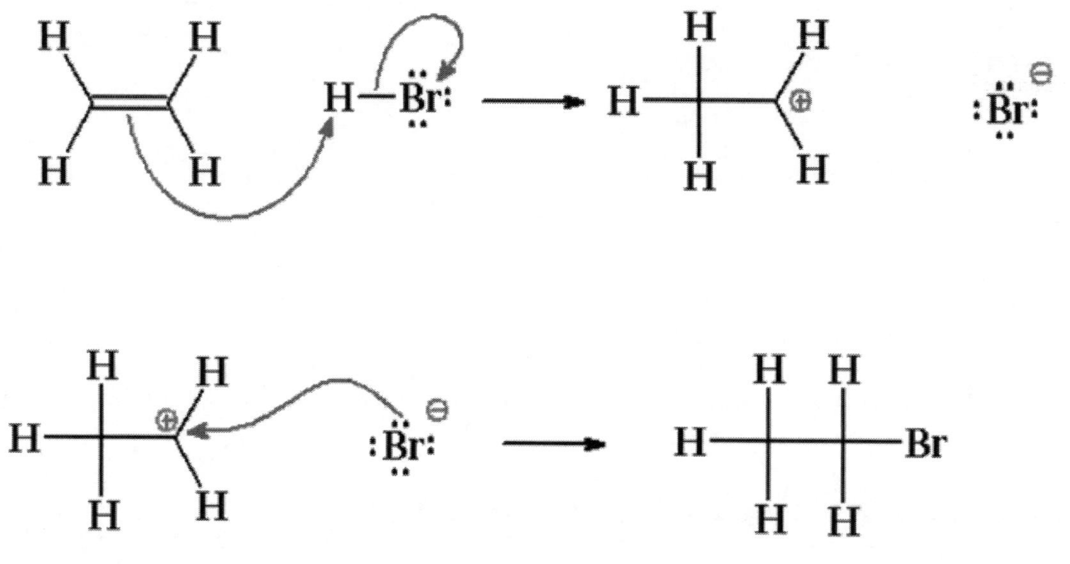

You must understand:

- The formation of a covalent bond is shown by a curly arrow that starts from a lone electron pair or from another covalent bond
- The breaking of a covalent bond is shown by a curly arrow starting from the bond

3.1.3 - Isomerism

You should remember from earlier what an isomer is; if you cannot remember, then please look back over the relevant material to remind yourself.

Isomers are essentially compounds with the same molecular formula but a different structural formula.

Activity 81 – Name the following isomers:

Answer to Activity 81:

Pentane

2-methylbutane

2,2-dimethylpropane

Stereoisomers

Stereoisomerism occurs when two or more compounds have the same structural formula but differ in the arrangement of the atoms in space. There are two types of stereoisomer:

- E – Z isomers
- Optical isomers

The E-Z isomers of 1,2-dichloroethene would be:

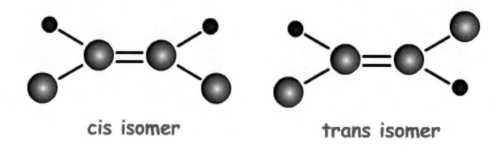

cis isomer   trans isomer

- The Z isomer occurs when the functional groups are on the same side of the compound. It is often called a cis-isomer.
- The E isomer occurs when the functional groups are on different sides. It is often called a trans-isomer.

Remember that there is no rotation of the double bond.

Optical Isomers

Optical isomers can occur when a substance has 4 different groups attached to one of its carbon atoms. This can result in two substances that are mirror images of each other.

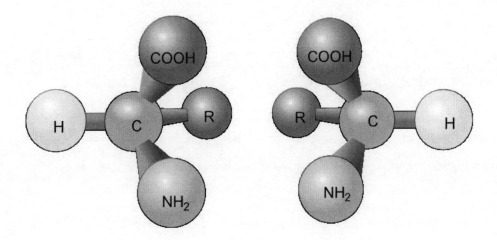

Chirality

Optical isomers are chiral, which is to say they are either left or right handed. The carbon atom that is bonded to the four different groups is called the chiral centre. Chiral atoms cannot be superimposed on each other, in the same way that left and right hands cannot be superimposed. Optical isomers that are mirror images like this are sometimes called **enantiomers**.

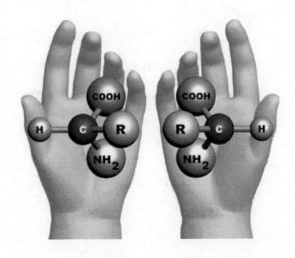

Chiral molecules differ in their effect on polarised light.

Light can be considered as a wave with vibrations occurring in every direction at right angles to the direction of movement of the light. If this light is passed through a polarising substance, then all of the planes of light are eliminated with the exception of the vertical plane.

This light is now considered to be vertically polarised and it will have a different impact on different optical isomers.

If we pass this light through a solution of one type of the optical isomer, the light will be rotated clockwise. This is called the positive isomer.

The other isomer will cause the light to be rotated in an anti-clockwise direction. This is called the negative isomer.

A **racemate** is a solution that is an equal mixture of left and right handed **enantiomers** (optical isomers).

In any normal reaction that produced enantiomers, unless the conditions of the reaction are designed to favour either the left or right hand optical isomer, both will form in approximately equal numbers.

Optical Isomers in the Drug Industry

In the drug industry, optical isomers are often produced because of the complexity of the chemicals involved. Sometimes a racemate mixture is acceptable, but at other times only one of the enantiomers is required, and conditions in the reaction must be adjusted to ensure this occurs.

In the case of a painkiller like ibuprofen, a racemate mixture is acceptable. With some other drugs, one of the enantiomers will be an effective medicine, the other may be toxic.

Cahn-Ingold-Prelog (CIP) priority rules

The method of unambiguously assigning the handedness of molecules was originated by three chemists: R.S. Cahn, C. Ingold, and V. Prelog and, as such, is also often called the Cahn-Ingold-Prelog priority rules.

The sign of optical rotation, although different for the two enantiomers of a chiral molecule, at the same temperature, cannot be used to establish the absolute configuration of an enantiomer; this is because the sign of optical rotation for a particular enantiomer may change when the temperature changes.

Stereocenters are labelled R or S

The "right hand" and "left hand" nomenclature is used to name the enantiomers of a chiral compound. The stereocenters are labelled as R or S.

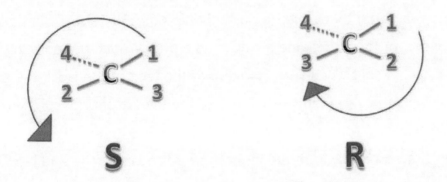

Consider the first illustration above: a curved arrow is drawn from the highest priority (1) substituent to the lowest priority (4) substituent. If the arrow points in a anticlockwise direction, the configuration at stereocenter is considered S (meaning "Sinister", Latin for left). If, however, the arrow points clockwise, then the stereocenter is labeled R ("Rectus", Latin for right).

The R or S is then added as a prefix, in parenthesis, to the name of the enantiomer of interest.

Sequence rules to assign priorities to substituents

Before applying the R and S nomenclature to a stereocenter, the substituents must be prioritised according to the following rules:

Rule 1

First, examine at the atoms directly attached to the stereocenter of the compound. A substituent with a higher atomic number takes precedence over a substituent with a lower atomic number. Hydrogen is the lowest possible priority substituent, because it has the lowest atomic number.

1. When dealing with isotopes, the atom with the higher atomic mass receives higher priority.
2. When visualising the molecule, the lowest priority substituent should always point away from the viewer (a dashed line indicates this). To understand how this works or looks, imagine a clock and a pole. Attach the pole to the back of the clock, so that when when looking at the face of the clock the pole points away from the viewer in the same way the lowest priority substituent should point away.
3. Then, draw an arrow from the highest priority atom to the 2nd highest priority atom to the 3rd highest priority atom. Because the 4th highest priority atom is placed in the back, the arrow should appear like it is going across the face of a clock. If it is going clockwise, then it is an R-enantiomer; If it is going counterclockwise, it is an S-enantiomer.

When looking at a problem with wedges and dashes, if the lowest priority atom is not on the dashed line pointing away, the molecule must be rotated. Remember that:

- Wedges indicate coming towards the viewer.
- Dashes indicate pointing away from the viewer.

Rule 2

If there are two substituents with equal rank, proceed along the two substituent chains until there is a point of difference. First, determine which of the chains has the first connection to an atom with the highest priority (the highest atomic number). That chain has the higher priority.

If the chains are similar, proceed down the chain, until a point of difference.

For example: an ethyl substituent takes priority over a methyl substituent. At the connectivity of the stereocenter, both have a carbon atom, which are equal in rank. Going down the chains, a methyl has only has hydrogen atoms attached to it, whereas the ethyl has another carbon atom. The carbon atom on the ethyl is the first point of difference and has a higher atomic number than hydrogen; therefore the ethyl takes priority over the methyl.

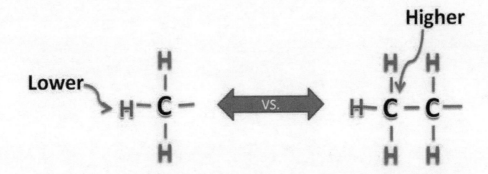

The "H-" (left) ranks lower than the "C-" (right) based on the <u>first point of difference</u> and their relative molecular weights

Rule 3

If a chain is connected to the same kind of atom twice or three times, check to see if the atom it is connected to has a greater atomic number than any of the atoms that the competing chain is connected to:

- If none of the atoms connected to the competing chain(s) at the same point has a greater atomic number, the chain bonded to the same atom multiple times has the greater priority.
- If however, one of the atoms connected to the competing chain has a higher atomic number, that chain has the higher priority[6].

6

http://chemwiki.ucdavis.edu/Wikitexts/Purdue/Purdue%3A_Chem_26505/Chapter_3._Stereochemistry/3.6_Cahn-Ingold_Prelog_Rules

3.2 - Alkanes

Alkanes are the main constituent of crude oil, which is an important raw material for the chemical industry. Alkanes are also used as fuels and the environmental consequences of this use are considered in this section.

3.2.1 – Fractional distillation of crude oil

Crude oil is one of the most important substances in the world today. It consists of a large number of different chemicals, mainly the type of hydrocarbon called "alkanes".

In order for crude oil to be commercially useful, these different alkanes need to be separated out. Alkanes are often called "saturated", as they only have single bonds between carbon-carbon and carbon-hydrogen, i.e. if the carbon atoms cannot be bonded with any more atoms, they are saturated.

Propane is an example of a saturated hydrocarbon. Note that there are no double bonds and no space for any more hydrogen atoms on the structure:

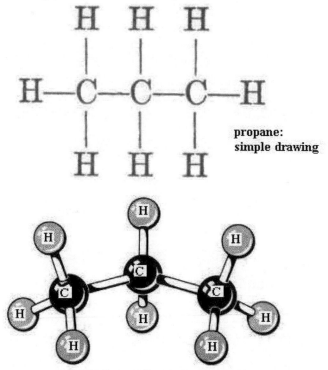

propane:
simple drawing

propane: ball-and-stick model

In order to separate out the various fractions (different component parts) of crude oil, a fractional distillation column is used.

This is done on an industrial scale at an oil refinery. Refineries are huge, complex and very dangerous chemical plants.

The crude oil is separated by pumping the heated oil into the bottom of a fractional distillation column. The oil is then further heated to around 350°C; most of the components of the oil vaporise at that temperature and rise up the column. The various constituent parts of the crude oil all have different temperatures at which they condense, and the temperature in the column is very carefully controlled at different levels in the column.

The temperature at the bottom of the column will be around 350°C and the temperature at the very top is around 40°C or less. All of the fractions have condensation temperatures between those two levels.

For example, diesel fuel condenses at around 270°C. Given that the temperature at various levels is very carefully controlled, it is possible to know exactly how far up the column the diesel vapour will travel before it condenses. The diesel fraction of the crude oil can then be collected at this level.

Petrol, however, does not condense until the temperature is 120°C. It will therefore remain in its vapour form as it passes the diesel condensation level and will itself condense higher up the tower. At the 120°C point, the petrol can be collected.

Fractional distillation works because all of the fractions of crude oil have a different condensation temperature, and as long as the temperature in the tower is carefully controlled, the different fractions can be separated out by using their condensation temperatures in this way.

Note that condensation temperature and boiling point are the same.

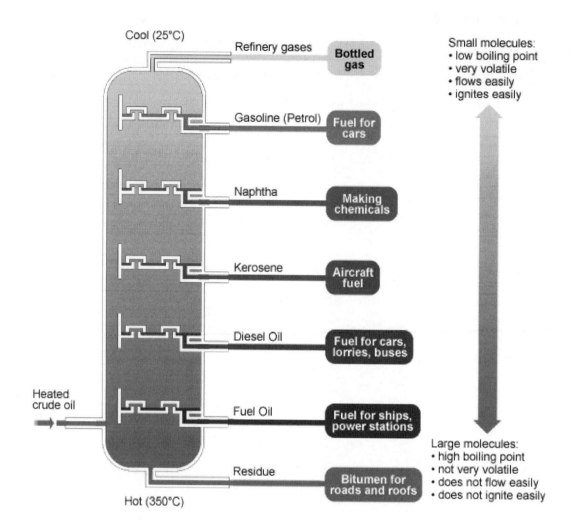

There are trends in properties; smaller molecules have the lowest boiling point. Also:

- they are very volatile
- they flow easily
- they ignite easily

Larger molecules have a much higher boiling point. They also:

- have a low volatility
- do not flow easily
- do not ignite easily

3.2.2 - Modification of Alkanes by Cracking

Crude oil is different depending on where in the world it was sourced. Some sources will have more of particular fractions and less of others, depending on their location. Most samples of crude oil will, in fact, produce more of the larger and longer chain fractions than the smaller, short chain ones. The larger molecular fractions can be further processed (known as cracking) into smaller molecules. For example, heptanes can be broken down into ethene and an alkane:

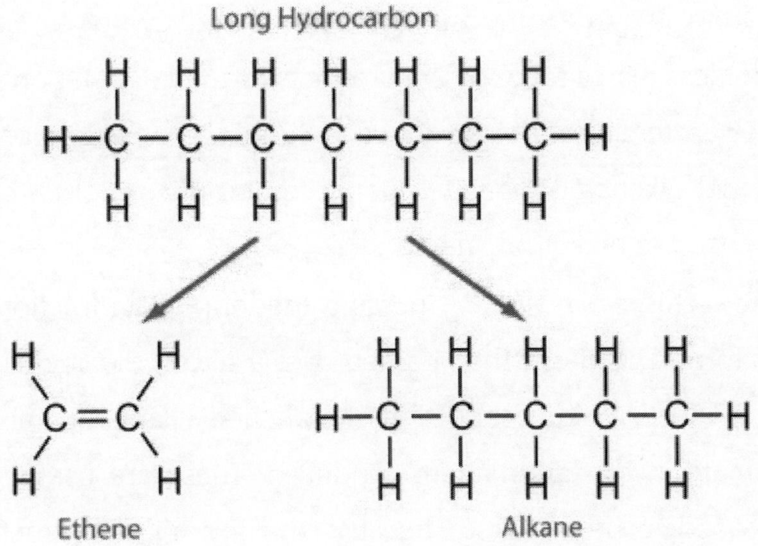

Long Hydrocarbon

Ethene   Alkane

Activity 41 – What would the alkane in the above illustration be called?

Answer to Activity 41:

The alkane has 5 carbon atoms in a line with no double or triple bonds; it would therefore be pentane.

There are two types of cracking:

- **Thermal** – This happens at high temperatures (450 – 900 $^\circ$C) and pressures (up to 7000 kPa). Air is kept out to prevent combustion. If the alkanes are heated for too long, they decompose into carbon and hydrogen, so they are only heated for less than a second. The products formed depend on the temperature used. Lower temperatures produce a higher proportion of medium sized alkanes and alkenes. Higher temperatures produce more small alkenes, e.g. ethene – used to make polymers.
- **Catalytic** – This is achieved by heating the long chain fraction until it is in its gaseous form. This gas is then passed over a silicon dioxide (silica) and zeolite catalyst at 450°C. A high proportion of branched alkanes and alkenes, and cyclic and aromatic hydrocarbons, are produced. These are useful as motor fuels. Alkanes need to be "cracked" because the shorter chain materials are more commercially valuable (as motor fuel, for example). Also, the alkenes produced, ethene for example, can undergo a polymerisation reaction to produce polymers. Ethene produces poly(ethene), for example:

	Thermal	**Catalytic**
Temperature	450-900°C	450°C
Pressure	High	Moderate
Catalyst	None	Zeolite
Products	High proportion of straight-chain alkanes and alkenes. Useful as raw materials for the chemical industry.	High proportion of branched alkanes, alkenes, cyclic and aromatic hydrocarbons. Useful for motor fuels.

3.2.3 - Combustion of alkanes

What makes fossil fuels, including fractions of crude oil, commercially useful is the fact that they can be burned in air (although with some of the fractions, like bitumen, this is very difficult to achieve).

Consider gasoline, for example. One of the main constituents is octane. This will burn in air as follows:

$$C_8H_{18}(l) + O_2(g) \rightarrow CO_2(g) + H_2O(l)$$

Activity 42 – The above reaction is obviously not balanced. Try balancing it.

Answer to Activity 42:

The reaction for the complete combustion of octane in air is:

$$2C_8H_{18}(l) + 25O_2(g) \rightarrow 16CO_2(g) + 18H_2O(l)$$

Not all combustion reactions are the same. For example, the complete combustion of propane is:

C_3H_8 +	$5\,O_2$	$3\,CO_2$ +	$4\,H_2O$	+ Heat
				and
Propane	Oxygen gas	Carbon dioxide	Water	light

Not all combustion reactions are this efficient either, as you know. Some combustion reactions are incomplete.

Consider octane again, but this time we will draw the equation for its **incomplete** combustion:

$$2C_8H_{18}(l) + 17O_2(g) \rightarrow 16CO(g) + 18H_2O(l)$$

With an incomplete combustion reaction, carbon monoxide is produced rather than carbon dioxide. Carbon monoxide is a particularly dangerous molecule. It is toxic and if you breathe it in, it will fill your lungs and reduce the blood's ability to carry oxygen to your cells.

Combustion Engines

In the internal combustion engine (in cars in particular), the reaction chamber can get so hot that nitrogen and oxygen from the air intake can react together to produce oxides of nitrogen. Nitrous oxides (NOx for short, the x referring to the fact that there are several different types) contribute to acid rain.

When the combustion reaction involves a hydrocarbon mixed with sulphur, sulphur dioxide will be a by-product of the reaction. This is a dangerous pollutant and is another major cause of acid rain.

Some of the hydrocarbon fuel can pass through the engine without being burnt. These unburned hydrocarbons are volatile and can react with NOx to produce a photochemical smog. This can cause health problems.

These pollutants should be removed from the waste gases if at all possible, rather than simply being released into the atmosphere. These pollutants can be removed from the exhaust gases by means of a catalytic converter, now standard in most cars.

You need to know the chemical equations for the removal of pollutants that takes place in a catalytic converter.

$$2NO_{(g)} \rightarrow N_{2(g)} + O_{2(g)}$$
$$C_9H_{20(g)} + 14O_{2(g)} \rightarrow 9CO_{2(g)} + 10H_2O_{(g)}$$

Most power stations in Europe will remove the majority of the sulphur in their emissions in the chimney (flue) before it reaches the atmosphere. This is done using either calcium oxide (CaO) or limestone ($CaCO_3$). Either of these will react with the sulphur in the flue gas, thereby removing it. The reaction produces gypsum ($CaSO_4$), which is used as plaster. This is a process known as flue gas desulphurisation (FGD). You will need to know the chemical equations for these reactions.

$$CaCO_{3(s)} + SO_{2(g)} \rightarrow CaSO_{3(s)} + CO_{2(g)}$$

$$CaCO_{3(s)} \rightarrow CaO_{(s)} + CO_{2(g)}$$

$$CaO_{(s)} + SO_{2(g)} \rightarrow CaSO_{3(s)}$$

$$CaSO_{3(s)} + \tfrac{1}{2}O_{2(g)} + 2H_2O_{(l)} \rightarrow CaSO_4.2H_2O_{(s)}$$

Note the use of the term "$\tfrac{1}{2}O_{2(g)}$" in the final equation. Using halves is acceptable, or multiples, to balance an equation.

Combustion results in the release of recognisable pollutants, like sulphur dioxide, carbon dioxide and nitrous oxides, but also less obvious ones.

The combustion process also produces water vapour, which is released into the atmosphere. This water vapour, along with carbon dioxide and methane, are referred to as greenhouse gases and these in all likelihood contribute to global warming.

3.2.4 – Chlorination of alkanes

We looked at this particular process when we examined reaction mechanisms in 3.1.2, but the specification notes that you need to understand this specific process.

Haloalkanes are produced by mixing a halogen with an alkane. If they are mixed in the dark, however, no reaction will occur. If the mixture is exposed to bright sunlight, they react together to form the appropriate haloalkane. For example:

$$CH_4(g) \ + \ Cl_2(g) \ \rightarrow \ CH_3Cl(g) \ + \ HCl(g)$$

The above reaction is called a free radical substitution reaction and it occurs in three stages:

- Initiation
- Propagation
- Termination

Initiation

First the Cl–Cl bond breaks to form two Cl· free radicals (these are very reactive). The · is used to indicate an unpaired electron. This is achieved by the bond absorbing a single quantum of UV light, whose energy is greater than the strength of the bond, and so the bond breaks. The reaction is as follows:

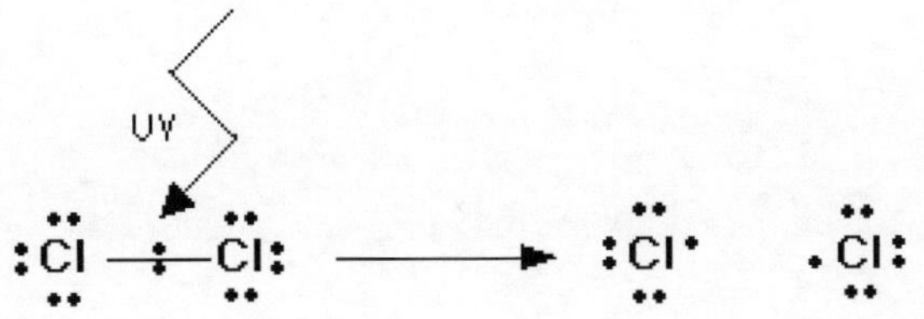

Free radicals are always highly reactive and don't exist for long before they attack another substance.

Propagation

This is not a single stage, but occurs in two sub-stages.

1st sub-stage:

A chlorine free radical reacts with methane to produce a methyl free radical:

$$Cl\cdot \; + \; CH_4 \; \rightarrow \; HCl \; + \; CH_3\cdot$$

2nd sub-stage:

The methyl free radical, which is also highly reactive, reacts with a chlorine molecule:

$$CH_3\cdot \; + \; Cl_2 \; \rightarrow \; CH_3Cl \; + \; Cl\cdot$$

Termination

This is the final step, where free radicals combine to end their reactions. There are three possible termination reactions:

1st:

$$Cl\cdot \; + \; Cl\cdot \; \rightarrow \; Cl_2$$

2nd:

$$CH_3\cdot \; + \; CH_3\cdot \; \rightarrow \; C_2H_6$$

3rd:

$$Cl\cdot \; + \; CH_3\cdot \; \rightarrow \; CH_3Cl$$

The chlorination of methane does not necessarily stop after one chlorination. It may actually be very hard to get a monosubstituted chloromethane. Instead di-, tri- and even tetra-chloromethanes are formed.

One way to avoid this problem is to use a much higher concentration of methane in comparison to chloride. This reduces the chance of a chlorine radical running into a chloromethane and starting the mechanism over again to form a dichloromethane.

Through this method of controlling product ratios one is able to have a relative amount of control over the product.

3.3 - Halogenoalkanes

Halogenoalkanes are much more reactive than alkanes. They have many uses, including as refrigerants, as solvents and in pharmaceuticals. The use of some halogenoalkanes has been restricted due to the effect of chlorofluorocarbons (CFCs) on the atmosphere.

3.3.1 – Nucleophilic substitution

We encountered nucleophiles in the previous section. You will remember that they are reagents that attack and form bonds with positively charged carbon atoms. They are:

- Negatively charged ions (for example, OH^- and CN^-)
- A substance with a lone and unshared pair of electrons (for example H_2O and NH_3)

Examples of nucleophiles include:

- OH^-
- NH_3
- CN^-

Each of these three substances will act to replace the halogen in a haloalkane by nucleophilic substitution reactions. They can do this because of the polar nature of the C – X bond.

Reactions

In the following equations:

- Nu⁻ represents any nucleophile
- X represents any halogen
- R represents an alkane group consisting of any number of carbon atoms in length

The general reaction for a nucleophilic substitution is:

$$
\begin{array}{ccc}
\quad\quad H & & \quad\quad H \\
\quad\quad | & & \quad\quad | \\
R-C-X + Nu^- & \rightarrow & R-C-Nu + X^- \\
\quad\quad | & & \quad\quad | \\
\quad\quad H & & \quad\quad H
\end{array}
$$

This basic reaction is the same for any of the halogens, although the rate varies depending on the reactivity of the halogen involved. The C – F bond is strong and fairly unreactive. As we move down the group, the bond weakens and as a result the reactivity increases.

Reaction with OH⁻

The general reaction of a haloalkane with hydroxide ions is:

$$R-X + OH^- \rightarrow ROH + X^-$$

The haloalkane will react with the hydroxide ion to form an alcohol and a halide ion.

Reaction with CN⁻

The general reaction of a haloalkane with cyanide is:

$$R - X \ + \ CN^- \ \rightarrow \ RCN \ + \ X^-$$

The haloalkane will react with the cyanide to form a nitrile and a halide ion. This reaction increases the carbon chain length.

Reaction with NH_3

The general reaction of a haloalkane with ammonia is:

$$R - X \ + \ 2NH_3 \ \rightarrow \ RNH_2 \ + \ NH_4X^-$$

The haloalkane will react with the ammonia to form a product called an amine and an ammonium halide. Excess ammonia is used to prevent the product from reacting with more of the haloalkane.

Activity 64 - Write the specific equations for the following reactions:

Chloroethane + hydroxide ions
Chloroethane + cyanide ions
Chloroethane + ammonia

Answer to Activity 64:

Chloroethane + hydroxide ions:

$$C_2H_5Cl + OH^- \rightarrow C_2H_5OH + Cl^-$$

Chloroethane + cyanide ions:

$$C_2H_5Cl + CN^- \rightarrow C_2H_5CN + Cl^-$$

Chloroethane + ammonia:

$$C_2H_5Cl + 2NH_3 \rightarrow C_2H_5NH_2 + NH_4Cl$$

Nucleophilic substitution reactions are useful because they are a mechanism for the introduction of new functional groups into an organic compound. In these three reactions, you can see that the haloalkane can be converted into:

- An alcohol
- An amine
- A nitrile

3.3.2 - Elimination

We have just seen that haloalkanes typically react by nucleophilic substitution, but under different conditions they can undergo elimination reactions.

In an elimination reaction, a hydrogen halide forms, leaving a double bond on the main carbon chain and thus forming an alkene.

OH⁻ as a Base

Hydroxide ions (OH⁻) can act as a base and remove an H^+ ion from a haloalkane.

For example, chloroethane can react with potassium hydroxide as follows:

$$C_2H_5Cl + KOH \rightarrow C_2H_4 + KCl + H_2O$$

A double bond is formed on the alkane skeleton creating an alkene, in this case ethene.

Mechanism

Hydrogen chloride is eliminated first. The electrons in one of the C – H bonds move to the carbon atom and an H^+ ion is eliminated. The electrons in the C – Cl bond move to the chlorine atom, which is also eliminated. The C – C bond then becomes a C = C bond with H^+ and Cl^- eliminated.

This reaction is a useful way of creating organic compounds with double bonds.

Substitution or Elimination

A hydroxide ion can act as a nucleophile or as a base and therefore can undergo a substitution or an elimination reaction. In most situations, a certain amount of both will occur.

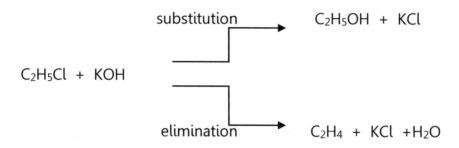

$$C_2H_5Cl + KOH$$

substitution $\longrightarrow$ $C_2H_5OH + KCl$

elimination $\longrightarrow$ $C_2H_4 + KCl + H_2O$

The reaction that predominates in the reaction chamber depends upon the following:

- The reaction conditions:
  - Elimination - high temp/conc. OH⁻ (base) in ethanol
  - Nucleophilic Substitution - low temp/dilute OH⁻(aq)
- The type of haloalkane (primary, secondary or tertiary)

3.3.3 – Ozone depletion

Ozone is a naturally occurring substance with the formula O_3. It decomposes in the upper atmosphere to form oxygen (O_2). In the upper atmosphere, ozone has a vital role in protecting the earth from harmful UV radiation from the sun. If too much UV was reaching the earth, life would be almost impossible for most creatures.

A C–Cl bond in a chlorofluorocarbon (CFC) will break homolytically in the upper atmosphere to form a Cl• free radical (as well as a free radical of the carbon compound). These Cl• free radicals will react with O_3 in the upper atmosphere in the following reactions:

$$Cl• + O_3 \rightarrow ClO• + O_2$$

And:

$$ClO• + O_3 \rightarrow 2O_2 + Cl•$$

From these two equations, you can see that the Cl• free radical is not used up in the reaction and is therefore a catalyst in the breakdown of ozone to oxygen.

We have seen that CFCs facilitated the breakdown of O_3 in the upper atmosphere to O_2. We have also seen how important O_3 is in terms of protecting the Earth's surface from the harmful effects of UV radiation.

Legislation was implemented to ban the use of CFCs as the ozone layer was becoming gradually depleted. This act was supported by chemists, and different substances were developed to replace CFCs in a variety of products such as aerosols and refrigerators.

3.4 - Alkenes

In alkenes, the high electron density of the carbon-carbon double bond leads to attack on these molecules by electrophiles. This section also covers the mechanism of addition to the double bond and introduces addition polymers, which are commercially important and have many uses in modern society.

3.4.1 – Structure, bonding and reactivity

Alkenes are unsaturated hydrocarbons. They have a double bond in their structure between two carbon atoms.

The general formula of an alkene is:

- C_nH_{2n}

So if there are 3 carbon atoms, n=3, therefore there will be 6 hydrogen atoms.

The double bond in all alkenes is a double covalent bond and involves the sharing of two pairs of electrons. The double bond in an alkene acts as a concentration of electrons, as it is formed by two pairs of shared electrons (rather than a single shared pair, as in a single bond).

Shape of Alkenes

The bond angles in ethene are as follows:

Always remember that the C=C bond is planar and it cannot rotate.

Isomers and Isomerism

Isomers are molecules with the same chemical (molecular) formula but a different structural formula.

Alkenes with more than three carbon atoms in their structure can form isomers, and these are named according to the rules of the IUPAC system, and always using the suffix "–ene" to denote the double bond.

As well as chain isomers that are found in alkanes, alkenes can form isomers that involve the double bond. These are:

- Position isomers
- Geometric isomers

Some of the following detail on naming will be revision as you have dealt with it before.

Position Isomers

A position isomer occurs when the double bond is in a different position on the carbon skeleton.

If we consider butene (C_4H_8), for example, it has 2 position isomers:

But-1-ene:

The "1" indicates the double bond is on the first carbon atom.

But-2-ene:

The "2" indicates the double bond is on the second carbon atom.

Activity 65 – Why is there not a but-3-ene?

Answer to Activity 65:

There is not a but-3-ene because the IUPAC system counts from the carbon that will give the lowest number. But-3-ene would have the double bond on the third carbon, but counting from the other end of the chain this would be on the first carbon, so the actual name for that substance would be but-1-ene.

Geometric Isomers

In a geometric isomer, the two isomers have the same formula but the bond is arranged differently in space.

There are two geometric isomers of butene:

- Z But-2-ene (sometimes called *cis* But-2-ene)
- E But-2-ene (sometimes called *trans* But-2-ene)

With a Z (or *cis*) isomer, the CH_3 (or any other groups in question) are on the same side of the substance.

With a E (or *trans*) isomer, the CH_3 (or any other groups in question) are on the opposite side of the substance.

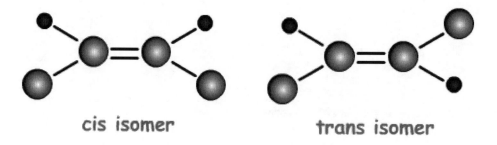

cis isomer   trans isomer

For example:

cis   trans

Activity 66 – What do you think these two substances would be called?

Answer to Activity 66:

The first would be:

Cis – 1,2-dichloroethene

The second would be:

Trans – 1,2-dichloroethene

Activity 67 – Draw the Z and E isomers of but-2-ene.

Answer to Activity 67:

cis-2-Butene   trans-2-Butene

Remember that the C=C bond cannot rotate. These isomers have different properties.

3.4.2 - Addition Reactions of Alkenes

Alkene reactions are typically electrophilic addition reactions. The C=C bond contains four electrons and is therefore a region of high electron density. Electrophiles will be attracted to this electron concentration and will form a bond using two of these electrons, thus breaking the double bond.

Addition Mechanism

The electrophile is attracted to the high electron density of the double bond. These electrophiles are positively charged (being either an ion or having a slightly positively charged bond) and will accept a pair of electrons from the C=C double bond. Once this occurs, a temporary C^+ ion is formed (called a carbocation). This C^+ ion will be extremely reactive and will bond with a negatively charged ion.

Activity 68 – Draw the reaction you would expect between the following:

Ethene + Hydrogen chloride

Answer to Activity 68:

$$C_2H_4 + HCl \rightarrow C_2H_5Cl$$

The mechanism for this is illustrated below, but split into two phases.

Firstly, as described above, the hydrogen in the HBr acts as an electrophile because the bromine attracts the electrons in the bond towards itself, creating a slight positive charge on the hydrogen. This hydrogen then breaks the double bond and forms a single bond with one of the carbon atoms. The other carbon atom is now deficient by 1 electron (and has gained a positive charge, C^+) and the bromine is now a Br^- ion.

In the second stage, the bromide ion bonds with the carbocation to form the final product, bromoethane.

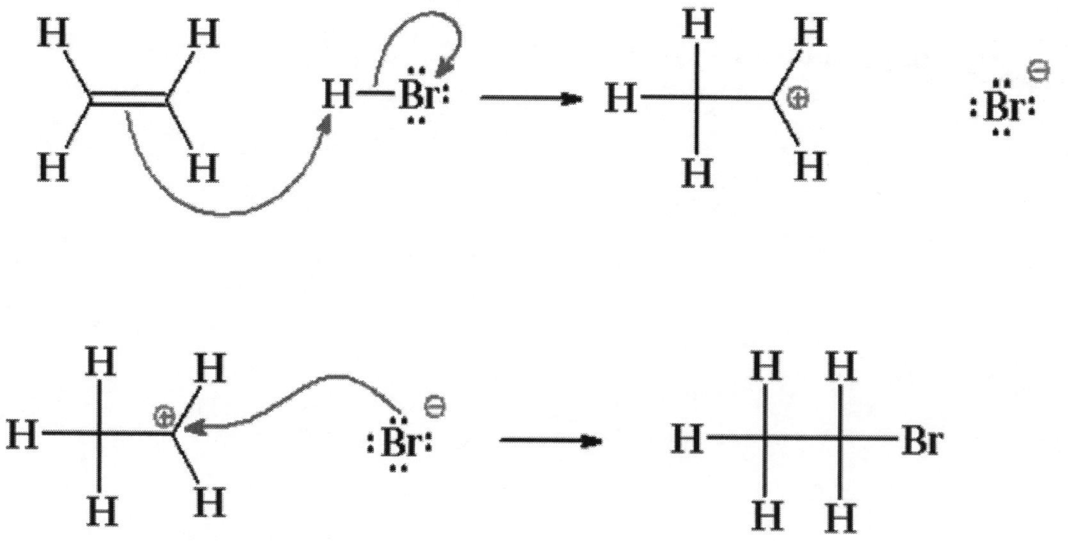

Asymmetrical Alkenes

In the reaction we have just considered, choroethene is the only possible product because ethene has only 2 carbon atoms, therefore there are no isomers.

When the double bond is not in the exact middle of the chain, however, there are two possible products. In the reaction below, the bromine could bond with either one of the two carbon atoms at either side of the C=C bond.

Two reactions could occur between propene and hydrogen bromide, although the generic formula is the same:

$$C_3H_6 + HBr \rightarrow C_3H_7Br$$

The two separate products can be illustrated as 2-bromopropane:

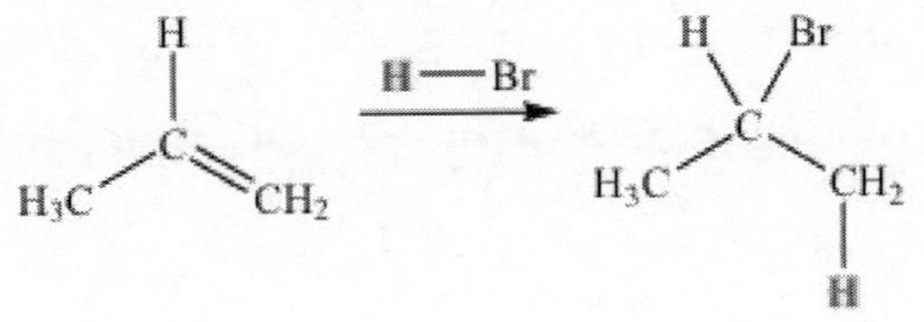

And 1-bromopropane:

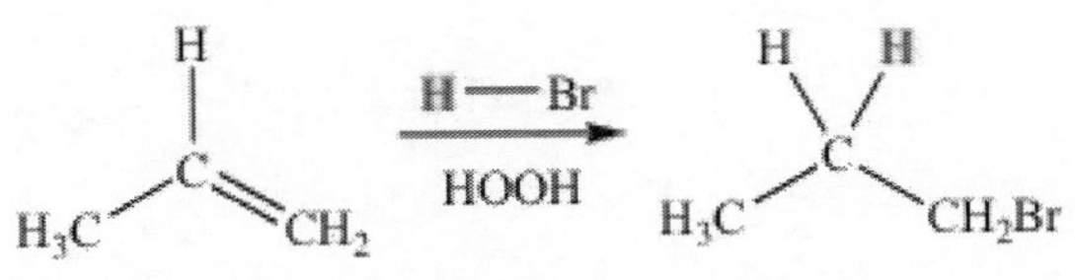

2-bromopropane is much more common as the product in this reaction, unless the reaction occurs in the presence of a peroxide catalyst (HOOH in the second reaction).

To explain the predominance of the 2-bromopropane product (under normal, uncatalysed reaction conditions) we need to understand that an alkyl group (i.e. the CH_3 group in C_2H_5) that is part of a larger structure will have a tendency to release electrons. This effect is called a positive induction effect.

This electron releasing effect will stabilise the positive charge on a neighbouring carbocation. The more alkyl groups that are attached to a carbocation, the more stable it becomes because they will all be pushing electrons towards the C^+ and thus having a stabilising effect by reducing the positive charge.

- If a carbocation has three alkyl groups bonded to it, it is the most stable and is called a **tertiary carbocation**
- If a carbocation has two alkyl groups bonded to it, it is the next most stable and is called a **secondary carbocation**
- If a carbocation has one alkyl group bonded to it, it is the least stable and is called a **primary carbocation**

Activity 69 – Draw an example of a primary, secondary and tertiary carbocation.

Answer to Activity 69:

In the following illustrations, remember that "R" refers to an alkyl group.

Tertiary carbocation (3 alkyl groups):

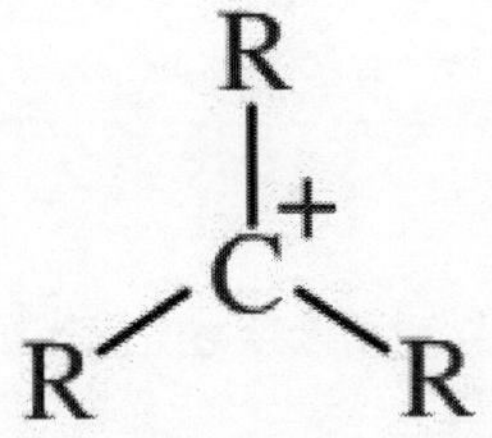

$$R-\overset{\overset{\displaystyle R}{|}}{\underset{}{C}}{}^{+}$$

$$R \qquad R$$

Secondary carbocation (2 alkyl groups):

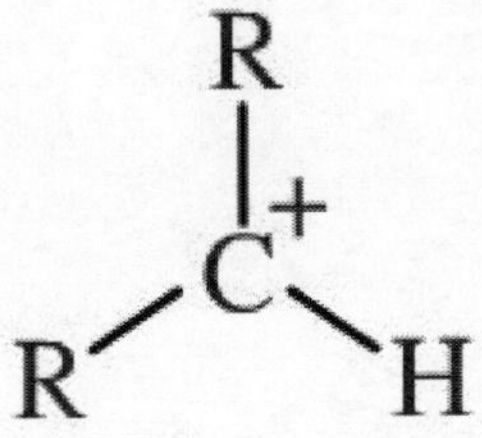

$$R-\overset{\overset{\displaystyle R}{|}}{\underset{}{C}}{}^{+}$$

$$R \qquad H$$

Primary carbocation (1 alkyl group):

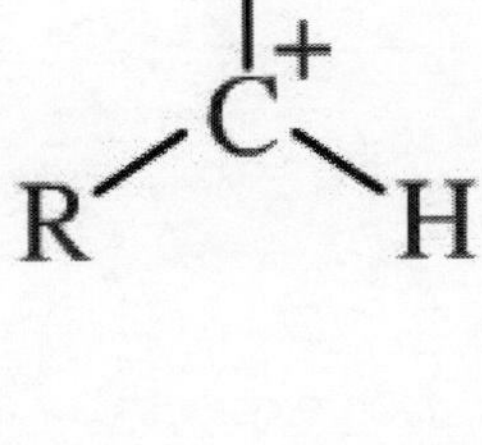

$$R-\overset{\overset{\displaystyle H}{|}}{\underset{}{C}}{}^{+}$$

$$R \qquad H$$

The tertiary carbocation is the most stable and the primary carbocation is the least stable. The product of the reaction will tend to come from the more stable carbocation.

Propene will produce two carbocations when it reacts with hydrogen bromide:

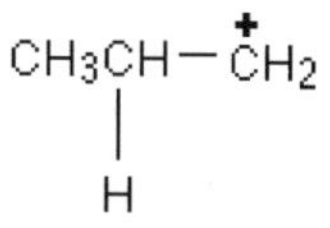

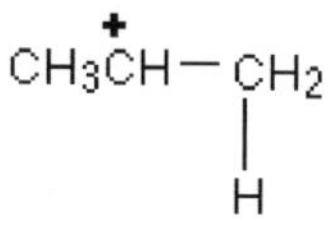

$$CH_3CH - \overset{+}{C}H_2 \qquad\qquad CH_3\overset{+}{C}H - CH_2$$
$$| \qquad\qquad\qquad\qquad\qquad |$$
$$H \qquad\qquad\qquad\qquad\qquad H$$

The secondary carbocation is more stable and therefore tends to be the one that reacts with HBr to produce 2-bromopropane:

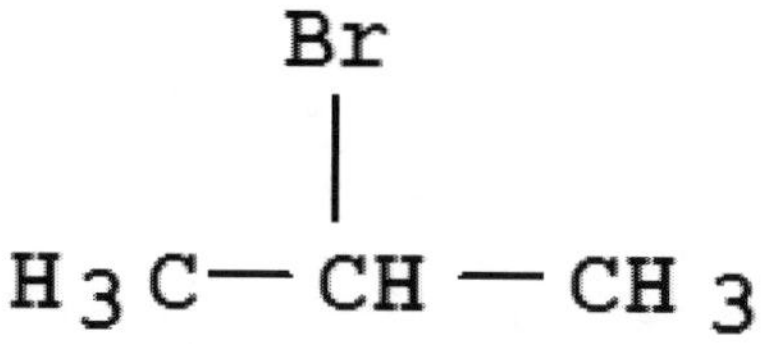

$$\overset{\displaystyle Br}{\underset{\displaystyle H_3C-CH-CH_3}{|}}$$

Alkenes and Halogens

Alkenes will react with halogens to produce a di-haloalkane as follows:

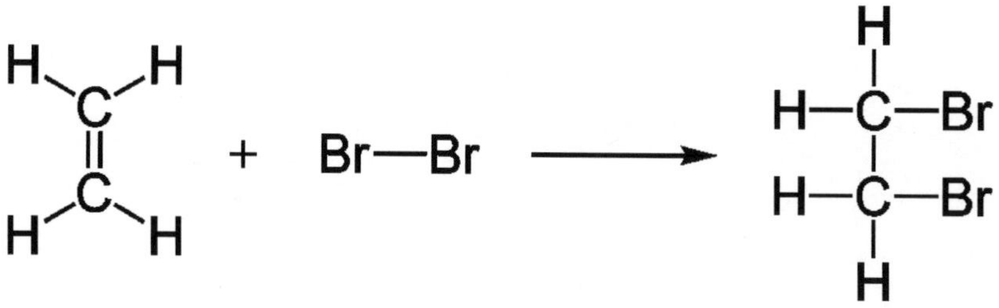

The Br–Br bond is one you would not expect to carry a charge as each bromine atom will attract the electrons in the same way.

What actually occurs, however, are a series of instantaneous charges, positive and negative, across the bond, because the electrons are mobile. Sometimes they will be closer to one atom of bromine for an instant, the next instant they may be in the middle or closer to the other bromine.

The electrons in the double bond will be attracted to the instantaneous positive charge formed on one of the bromine atoms, the bond will break and one bromine atom will bond to one of the carbon atoms. The other carbon then becomes positively charged and the remaining negative Br⁻ ion is attracted to that carbon, bonding with it. Therefore, the two bromine atoms become bonded with the two separate carbon atoms.

This addition reaction is used as a test for a C=C double bond. The unsaturated ethene reacts with the bromine to form the saturated 1,2-dibromoethane.

Bromine water can also be used as a test for alkenes. Bromine water is an orangey colour in its normal state. Add an unknown hydrocarbon to it and shake the test tube. If the liquid turns clear (as in the illustration below) then you know that the sample contained a double bond. It was therefore an alkene (although you do not yet know which one).

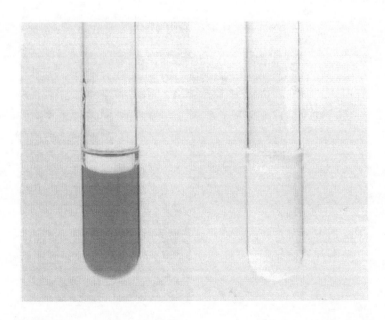

Reactions with Concentrated Sulphuric Acid and Water

H_2SO_4 and H_2O also react, in an addition reaction, to the double bond in an alkene.

The reaction of ethene with sulphuric acid will produce ethyl hydrogen sulphate:

$$C_2H_4 \ + \ H_2SO_4 \ \rightarrow \ C_2H_5SO_4H$$

The reaction of ethene with water will produce ethanol:

$$C_2H_4 \ + \ H_2O \ \rightarrow \ C_2H_5OH$$

Mechanism

3.4.3 - Polymerisation of Alkenes

The simplest polymer is poly(ethene), often called polythene. It is produced from polymerisation of the smallest hydrocarbon that contains a C=C double bond (ethene).

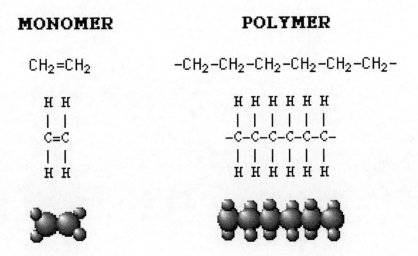

MONOMER

$CH_2=CH_2$

POLYMER

$-CH_2-CH_2-CH_2-CH_2-CH_2-CH_2-$

A monomer is the molecule which reacts to form the polymer. Many monomers go into a polymer chain.

In order for polymerisation to occur, the C=C double bonds must be broken. This creates a requirement for both carbon atoms in the monomer to gain another electron to fill their outer shells.

In a polymerisation reaction, this is achieved when the monomer bonds with other monomers in a continuous chain.

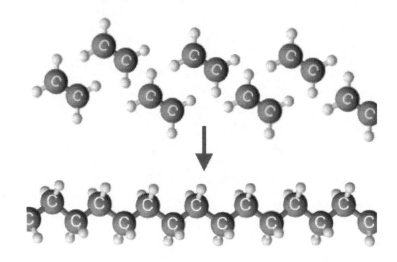

The polymerisation reaction requires heat to break the double bonds in the ethane. It also requires high pressure and the presence of an initiator; this is not a catalyst because it is used up in the reaction.

This reaction is called an addition polymerisation reaction. Many monomers are added together to form the resultant polymer.

Poly(propene) is also produced by an addition polymerisation reaction. This time the monomer is propene:

$$\begin{array}{c} H \\ \end{array} \overset{H}{\underset{H}{C}} = \overset{H}{\underset{CH_3}{C}} \longrightarrow \left(\overset{H\ \ H}{\underset{H\ \ CH_3}{C-C}} \right)_n$$

Note the use of the "n" to represent the repeat unit in poly(propene). This is a standard notation where the "n" is taken to be any very large number. That is to say that there could be hundreds or tens of thousands of the repeat unit in the polymer.

Poly(choroethene) is also produced via an addition polymerisation reaction. Chloroethene is also known as vinyl chloride, and therefore poly(chloroethene) is sometimes called poly(vinylchloride), or PVC for short.

$$n \ \ \overset{H}{\underset{H}{C}} = \overset{H}{\underset{Cl}{C}} \longrightarrow \left(\overset{H\ \ \ \ H}{\underset{H\ \ \ \ Cl}{C-C}} \right)_n$$

Note again the use of the notation "n", this time both before the chloroethene and after the repeat unit. It means the same in both cases: it should be taken to be a very large number.

It is saying that a very large number of chloroethene molecules bond together to form a very long polymer of the repeat units.

The repeat units of some common polymers:

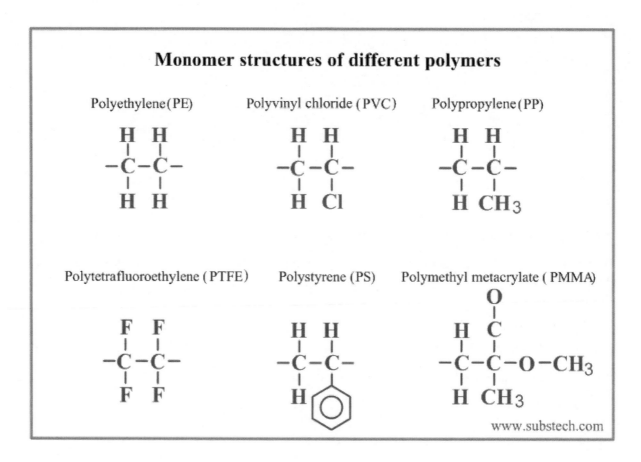

Uses of Polythene

Low density polythene (polyethene) is produced by polymerising ethene at high temperature and pressure, using a free radical reaction. This results in a product that has a degree of chain branching, rather than just straight chains.

Branched chains do not pack together as tightly as non-branched chains and they produce a product that is flexible, stretchy and has a low density. These properties make it suitable for plastic bags, insulation for electrical cables and sheeting.

Polythene can also be recycled.

3.5 - Alcohols

Alcohols have many scientific, medicinal and industrial uses. Ethanol is one such alcohol and it is produced using different methods, which are considered in this section. Ethanol can be used as a biofuel.

3.5.1 – Alcohol production

<u>Background</u>

With an alcohol, the ending to the name is typically "-ol". The simplest alcohol (the one with the fewest carbon atoms) is methanol:

$$
\begin{array}{c}
\text{H} \\
| \\
\text{H}-\text{C}-\text{O}-\text{H} \\
| \\
\text{H}
\end{array}
$$

When the chain is longer than ethanol (2 carbon atoms) we need to assign a number to show which carbon atom the OH group is bonded to (as you have done before with halogens and double bonds).

For example, in the following, the OH group is on the first carbon atom in the chain. It will therefore be called propan-1-ol:

$$
\begin{array}{c}
\text{H} \quad \text{H} \quad \text{H} \\
| \quad\quad | \quad\quad | \\
\text{H}-\text{C}-\text{C}-\text{C}-\text{O}-\text{H} \\
| \quad\quad | \quad\quad | \\
\text{H} \quad \text{H} \quad \text{H}
\end{array}
$$

When the OH group is on the second carbon atom in the chain, the substance will be called propan-2-ol:

$$
\begin{array}{c}
 \quad\quad\quad H \\
 \quad\quad\quad | \\
 \quad\quad O \\
H \quad\quad | \quad\quad H \\
| \quad\quad | \quad\quad | \\
H-C-C-C-H \\
| \quad\quad | \quad\quad | \\
H \quad\quad H \quad\quad H
\end{array}
$$

When there is more than one OH group, we need to add di-, tri-, tetra- (etc.).

In the following example, there are 2 x OH groups, one on each end of the carbon skeleton. One will be considered to be on the 1st carbon, and the other on the 3rd carbon. This substance is called propan 1,3-diol:

$$
\begin{array}{c}
H \quad H \quad\quad H \\
| \quad\quad | \quad\quad O \\
H-C-C-C-H \\
_1| \quad _2| \quad _3| \\
O \quad H \quad H \\
H
\end{array}
$$

Ethanol Production

Ethanol is a remarkably important molecule in the modern world, and in the future its importance is only likely to increase. Its most obvious use is in alcoholic drinks, but it is also increasingly produced as a fuel source. Large scale manufacture is becoming big business.

Ethanol can be manufactured by hydrating ethene. In this process, the ethanol is produced by reacting ethene with steam in the presence of a catalyst:

$$\underset{H}{\overset{H}{\diagdown}}C=C\underset{H}{\overset{H}{\diagup}} + H_2O \underset{\text{catalyst}}{\overset{\text{phosphoric acid}}{\rightleftharpoons}} H-\underset{\underset{H}{|}}{\overset{\overset{H}{|}}{C}}-\underset{\underset{H}{|}}{\overset{\overset{H}{|}}{C}}-OH$$

The reaction requires the use of a phosphoric acid catalyst; it also requires temperatures of 300°C and 7MPa pressure.

This illustration shows exactly what happens to the water molecules:

$$\underset{H}{\overset{H}{\diagdown}}C=C\underset{H}{\overset{H}{\diagup}} + H_2O \rightarrow H-\underset{\underset{H}{|}}{\overset{\overset{H}{|}}{C}}-\underset{\underset{OH}{|}}{\overset{\overset{H}{|}}{C}}-H$$

This is a very inefficient reaction, as only some of the ethene will react to produce ethanol. The ethanol that is produced can be collected as a condensate. Even though this reaction is quite inefficient, the unreacted ethane can remain in the reaction chamber until it is hydrated.

This is the process of manufacture used in large-scale chemical plants. It uses non-renewable ethene, has high energy costs and is a continuous process.

Fermentation is the other process for manufacturing ethanol. Ethanol can be produced through the fermentation of sugars by the addition of yeast to a starch solution at around 30°C. This mixture must be left in an anaerobic (no air) environment for several days. The yeast catalyses the reaction from sugar to ethanol, with carbon dioxide as a by-product:

$$C_6H_{12}O_6(aq) + H_2O(l) \rightarrow C_2H_5OH(aq) + CO_2(g)$$

This reaction will not occur if the temperature is not around 30°C, if there is no yeast or if the atmosphere is aerobic. Fermentation uses renewable materials, has low energy costs, but uses a batch process.

This simple and well-established reaction is generating a whole new industry: biofuels.

In some parts of the world, crops are now being grown with the specific intention to produce ethanol for use as biofuel.

This is a controversial fuel source, although some speculate it could eventually relieve us of our dependence on oil.

There are a number of factors that can affect the choice of the manufacturing process to be used, and these include:

	Fermentation	Hydration of Ethene
Type of process	A batch process. Everything is put into a container and then left until fermentation is complete. That batch is then cleared out and a new reaction set up. This is inefficient.	A continuous flow process. A stream of reactants is passed continuously over a catalyst. This is a more efficient way of doing things (despite the reaction actually being very inefficient).
Rate of reaction	Very slow.	Very rapid.
Quality of product	Produces very impure ethanol which needs further processing (at some expense).	Produces much purer ethanol.
Reaction conditions	Uses gentle temperatures and atmospheric pressure.	Uses high temperatures and pressures, needing lots of energy input and very expensive/specialised industrial equipment.
Use of resources	Uses renewable resources based on plant material. It does, however, take food that could be used to feed people thus (potentially) driving up food prices and creating shortages.	Uses finite resources based on crude oil.

At the current time, crude oil and the hydration process produces far more ethanol than does the fermentation process, but as world supplies of crude oil begin to run out (which is inevitable, as it is a finite resource) then that balance will almost certainly change.

One drawback of biofuel is that it takes land to grow the crops, and in a world with an ever-increasing population, is it really viable to use more and more land for growing fuel instead of food?

Dehydration of Ethanol

The reaction to produce ethanol can be reversed, given the right conditions. Ethanol can be dehydrated to form ethene.

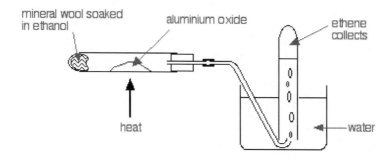

The term 'dehydration' refers to the removal of water, and is therefore the opposite of hydration. The below apparatus can be used on a laboratory scale to dehydrate ethanol:

In this experiment, ethanol vapour passes over the aluminium oxide (which catalyses the dehydration reaction) and converts it to ethene. The ethene is bubbled through water and collected in an inverted test tube.

The double bond is re-formed and the hydroxyl group (OH) is removed and reacts with the other hydrogen (which is also removed from the ethanol) to produce water as a by-product.

Carbon Neutral

Ethanol that is manufactured from ethene is not a renewable fuel, as the ethene will likely come from crude oil. Ethanol that is produced from fermentation is renewable, however, as it comes from the sugars in plants.

Ethanol that is manufactured by fermentation is sometimes called carbon neutral. This means that the carbon dioxide released when the fuel is burned is balanced by the carbon dioxide absorbed by the plant as it is growing. The net carbon output of the fuel is therefore zero.

3.5.2 – Oxidation of alcohols

Alcohols can be oxidised; this is typically a slow and gentle process.

Primary alcohols are oxidised to the equivalent aldehyde. These can then be further oxidised to carboxylic acids.

Secondary alcohols are oxidised to ketones (with the use of a suitable oxidising agent, like potassium dichromate (VI), for example. "O" is acceptable in the equation to demonstrate this oxidising agent). Ketones are not oxidised further.

The reactions are:

$$R-CH_2-O-H \longrightarrow R-\overset{\overset{\textstyle O}{\|}}{C}-OH$$

Primary alcohol → Carboxylic acid

$$R-CH_2-O-H \longrightarrow R-\overset{\overset{\textstyle O}{\|}}{C}-H$$

Primary alcohol → Aldehyde

$$R\overset{\overset{\textstyle O-H}{|}}{\underset{\underset{\textstyle H}{|}}{C}}-R' \longrightarrow R-\overset{\overset{\textstyle O}{\|}}{C}-R'$$

Secondary alcohol → Ketone

Tertiary alcohols are not easily oxidised.

Test for Aldehydes and Ketones

As you can see from their structure, aldehydes and ketones are similar substances with similar properties, but there are two chemical tests that can be used to detect the difference.

These tests use the fact that aldehydes can be oxidised to carboxylic acids, and that ketones are not easily oxidised.

Tollens' reagent is a solution of silver nitrate and aqueous ammonia. It can be used as a gentle oxidising agent. It will oxidise an aldehyde but have no effect upon a ketone.

If a solution of an aldehyde has some Tollens' reagent added to it and is then gently heated, metallic silver will be deposited on the inside of the test tube. This test is sometimes, therefore, called the "silver mirror test".

Fehling's reagent can also be used in the same way. They both contain copper II ions that will oxidise an aldehyde (when warmed) but have no effect upon a ketone.

A positive test result is the formation of a bright red precipitate that gradually forms in the solution.

Activity 72 – Without looking back over the course, draw the functional groups for the following:

- **Aldehydes**
- **Ketones**
- **Carboxylic acids**
- **Alcohols**
- **Alkenes**

3.5.3 - Elimination

Elimination reactions are essentially the opposite of addition reactions. In an elimination reaction, a small molecule is eliminated from the starting molecule. In the case of alcohols, the eliminated molecule is always water.

The water is formed from the hydroxide group that defines the alcohol (OH) and a hydrogen atom on the adjacent carbon atom. A double bond is then formed between these two adjacent carbon atoms in the chain.

This reaction occurs in the presence of an acid catalyst.

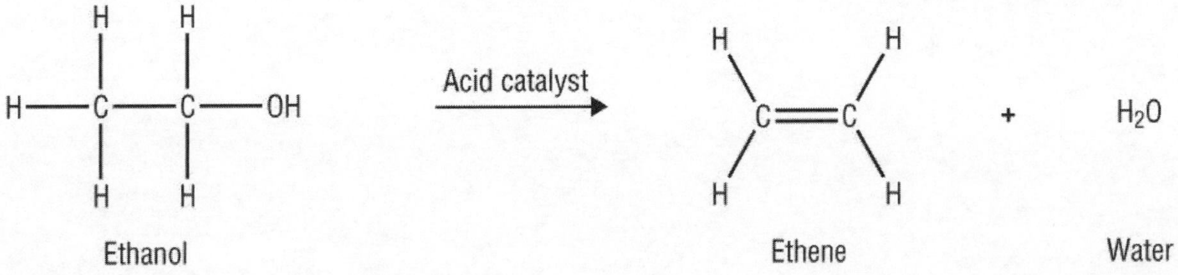

Ethanol   Ethene   Water

This type of reaction could become commercially very valuable in the future as it produces an alkene, in the above case ethene, which can then be polymerised. This is a potential route to the manufacture of polymers without relying on crude oil.

Required practical 5:

Distillation of a product from a reaction.

3.6 – Organic analysis

Our understanding of organic molecules, their structure and the way they react, has been enhanced by organic analysis. This section considers some of the analytical techniques used by chemists, including test-tube and spectroscopic techniques.

3.6.1 – Identification of functional groups by test-tube reactions

One of the most important things in identifying an organic compound is to identify the functional group. There are some simple tests that you can apply to help you identify a compound:

- If the substance is acidic, it may be a carboxylic acid
- If the substance is basic, it may be an amine
- If the compound is a solid, it may have a long carbon chain or ionic bonding
- If the compound is a liquid, it may have a medium carbon chain or have polar or hydrogen bonds
- If the compound is a gas, it may have short carbon chains with little or no polarity
- If the compound dissolves in water, it may have polar groups
- If the compound burns with a smoky flame, it likely has a high C:H ratio and may be aromatic
- If the compound burns with a non-smoky flame, it likely has a low C:H ratio and is possibly non-aromatic

Summary of functional group tests

test	functional group	positive result
Baeyer test	alkenes and alkynes	clear purple solution turns to brown precipitate
Bromine test	alkenes and alkynes	brown color disappears
Dinitrophenylhydrazine test	aldehydes and ketones	yellow to orange red precipitate
Ferrox test	any functional group containing oxygen	reddish-purple color
Hydroxamate test	amides and esters	red-purple color appears
Iodoform test	methyl ketones	yellow precipitate
Iron hydroxide test	nitro groups	red-brown precipitate
Jones test	1° and 2° alcohols	orange reagent turns blue-green
Lucas test	2°, 3°, and benzylic alcohols	cloudy solution or separate layer
Tollen's test	aldehydes	silver mirror forms

Test for alcohol

Jones Oxidation for Primary and Secondary Alcohols

$$3\ R_2CHOH \quad + \quad 2\ CrO_3 \quad + \quad 3\ H_2SO_4 \quad \longrightarrow$$

$$\underset{R\quad\quad R}{\overset{O}{\|}}\ C \quad + \quad 6\ H_2O \quad + \quad \underset{green}{Cr_2(SO_4)_3}$$

Procedure

Dissolve 10 mg or 2 drops of the unknown in 1 ml of propanone in a test tube and add to the solution 1 small drop of Jones reagent. A positive test is marked by the formation of a green colour within 15 seconds upon addition of the orange-yellow reagent to a primary or secondary alcohol. Aldehydes also give a positive test, but tertiary alcohols do not.

Positive Test

A positive test for aldehydes and primary or secondary alcohols consists in the production of an opaque suspension with a green to blue colour. Tertiary alcohols give no visible reaction within 2 seconds, the solution remaining orange in colour. Disregard any changes after 15 seconds.

Lucas Test for Secondary and Tertiary Alcohols

$$R' \overset{R}{\underset{R''}{\overset{|}{\underset{|}{C}}}} OH \;+\; HCl \;\xrightarrow{\;ZnCl_2\;}\; R' \overset{R}{\underset{R''}{\overset{|}{\underset{|}{C}}}} Cl \;+\; H_2O$$

Procedures

To 0.2 ml or 0.2 g of the unknown in a test tube add 2 ml of the Lucas reagent at room temperature. Stopper the tube and shake vigorously, then allow the mixture to stand. Note the time required for the formation of the alkyl chloride, which appears as an insoluble layer or emulsion.

Positive test

Appearance of a cloudy second layer or emulsion
- 3° alcohols: immediate to 2-3 minutes
- 2° alcohols: 5 -10 minutes
- 1° alcohols: no reaction[7]

---

[7] http://academics.wellesley.edu/Chemistry/chem211lab/Orgo_Lab_Manual/Appendix/ClassificationTests/alcohol.html

Test for Aldehydes and Ketones

You looked at these only a few pages ago, but they are raised again in the specification here. As you can see from their structure, aldehydes and ketones are similar substances with similar properties, but there are two chemical tests that can be used to detect the difference. These tests use the fact that aldehydes can be oxidised to carboxylic acids, and that ketones are not easily oxidised.

Tollens' reagent is a solution of silver nitrate and aqueous ammonia. It can be used as a gentle oxidising agent. It will oxidise an aldehyde but have no effect upon a ketone. If a solution of an aldehyde has some Tollens' reagent added to it and is then gently heated, metallic silver will be deposited on the inside of the test tube. This test is sometimes, therefore, called the "silver mirror test".

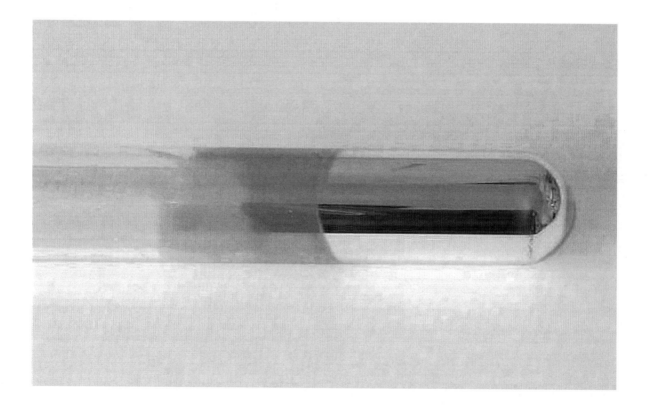

Fehling's reagent can also be used in the same way. They both contain copper II ions that will oxidise an aldehyde (when warmed) but have no effect upon a ketone. A positive test result is the formation of a bright red precipitate that gradually forms in the solution.

Test for alkenes

Bromine water can be used as a test for alkenes. Bromine water is an orangey colour in its normal state. Add an unknown hydrocarbon to it and shake the test tube. If the liquid turns clear (as in the illustration below) then you know that the sample contained a double bond. It was therefore an alkene (although you do not yet know which one).

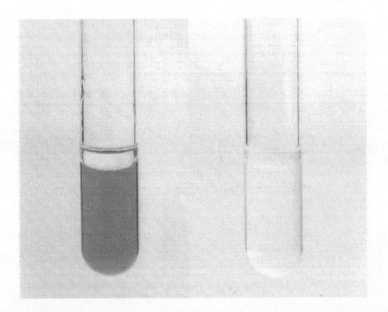

For the exam you should be able to identify the functional groups using reactions discussed in the specification

Required practical 6:

Tests for alcohol, aldehyde, alkene and carboxylic acid.

3.6.2 – Mass spectrometry

We looked at mass spectrometry earlier in the course (1.1.2), but the specification includes another section on the subject, so this should be revision.

A mass spectrometer is complex piece of equipment that can measure the relative atomic mass of an atom or the relative molecular mass of a substance.

We use the term "relative" because the mass is relative to the mass of carbon-12; you will learn more about this later in the course.

Carbon-12 is considered to have a mass of EXACTLY 12 (there are no units). No other isotope has an exact whole number as its mass. This is because the mass of protons and neutrons is not exactly 1.

A mass spectrometer can be used by scientists to determine the masses of a given substance, but it also determines the relative amount of that material in the sample, for example, it will tell you if something is 95% carbon, 5% hydrogen. So a sample of an unknown material can be analysed, and the machine will determine the constituent parts to that substance, and therefore what it is.

Activity 5 – Can you think of an example where this could be useful?

Answer to Activity 5:

In truth, there are thousands of potential applications for such a piece of technology. One would be in law enforcement to test an unknown substance to see if it is an illegal drug or something harmless. Another would be in a planetary space probe to identify elements in space.

The basic operation of a mass spectrometer is very simple. A sample is vaporised, ionised, accelerated through magnetic deflectors and the amount of deflection is measured. Heavier atoms are deflected less than lighter ones.

There are a number of stages that occur in the mass spectrometer that allow the unknown substance to be analysed:[8]

1) Ionisation - The atom is ionised by knocking one or more electrons off to give a positive ion. This is true even for things which you would normally expect to form negative ions (chlorine, for example) or never form ions at all (argon, for example). Mass spectrometers always work with positive ions.

2) Acceleration - The ions are accelerated so that they all have the same kinetic energy.

3) Deflection - The ions are then deflected by a magnetic field according to their masses. The lighter they are, the more they are deflected. The amount of deflection also depends on the number of positive charges on the ion - in other words, on how many electrons were knocked off in the first stage. The more the ion is charged, the more it gets deflected.

4) Detection - The beam of ions passing through the machine is detected electrically.

---

[8] http://www.chemguide.co.uk/analysis/masspec/howitworks.html

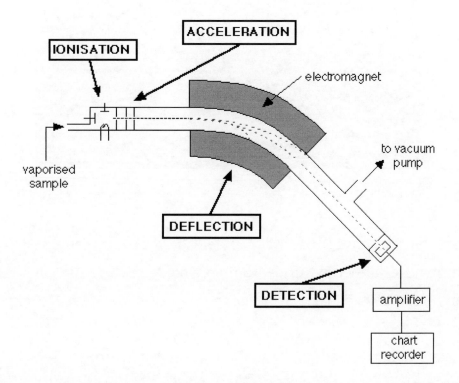

Why does it need a vacuum?

It's important that the ions produced in the ionisation chamber do not impact any air molecules as they pass through the machine, as this would change the results dramatically.

Ionisation Process

The vaporised sample passes into the ionisation chamber where the electrically heated metal coil gives off electrons. These electrons are attracted to the electron trap, which has a positively charged plate.

The particles in the sample, either atoms or molecules, are therefore bombarded with a stream of electrons, and some of the collisions are energetic enough to remove one or more electrons from the sample to produce positively charged ions.

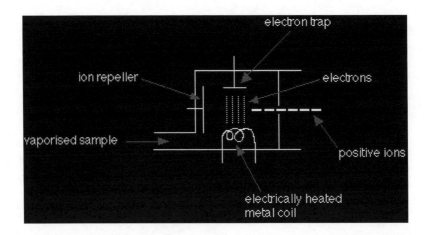

Most of the positive ions formed will carry a charge of 1^+ because it is much more difficult to remove further electrons from an already positive ion, although a small percentage, around 5%, do carry a 2^+ charge.

These ions are then directed out of the ionisation chamber by a "repeller", which is another metal plate carrying a slight positive charge.

Acceleration of the Ion Stream

As the positive ions leave the ionisation chamber, they pass through three slits. These slits have the effect of creating a beam of ions, as those not part of the beam are stopped by the plate that the slits are cut into.

Deflection

The ions are then deflected by a magnetic field; this deflection will be by different amounts. The amount of deflection depends on:

- The mass of the ion. Heavier ions are deflected less than lighter ones.
- The charge on the ion. Ions with 2^+ or greater charge are deflected more than 1^+ ions.

These two factors are combined into the mass/charge ratio. Mass/charge ratio is given the symbol m/z (or sometimes m/e).

For example, if an ion had a mass of 28 and a charge of 1^+, its mass/charge ratio would be 28. An ion with a mass of 56 and a charge of 2^+ would also have a mass/charge ratio of 28.

Look at the deflection of ions in the following diagram:

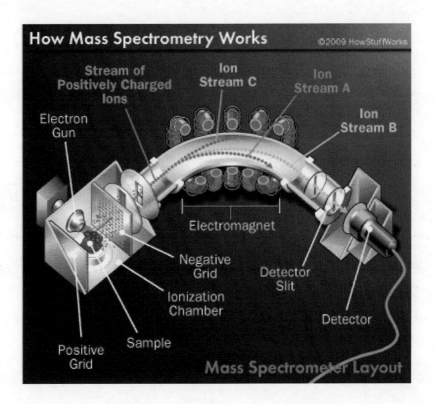

- Ion stream A is most deflected, therefore it will contain ions with the smallest mass/charge ratio.
- Ion stream C is the least deflected, therefore it contains ions with the greatest mass/charge ratio.

It makes it simpler to talk about this if we assume that the charge on all the ions is 1^+. Most of the ions passing through the mass spectrometer will have a charge of 1^+, so that the mass/charge ratio will be the same as the mass of the ion.

For the exam, you must be aware of the possibility of 2^+ (and those of a greater charge than this) ions, but the vast majority of A-Level questions will give you mass spectra which only involve 1^+ ions. Unless there is some hint in the question, you can reasonably assume that the ions you are talking about will have a charge of 1^+.

Assuming the ions are all 1^+ ions:

- Stream A has the lightest ions
- Stream B the next lightest
- Stream C the heaviest

This is because the lighter ions are going to be deflected more than the heavier ones.

Detection

Only the ions in stream B will reach the detector. When the ions reach the detector, they hit a wall where they collect electrons and are therefore essentially neutralised. Eventually, they are removed from the mass spectrometer by a vacuum pump.

When an ion hits the metal plate at the detector, its charge is neutralised by an electron migrating from the metal onto the ion. That leaves a space amongst the electrons in the metal, and the electrons in the wire that connects to the metal plate move along to fill it.

A flow of electrons in the wire is detected as an electric current, which can be amplified and recorded; the more ions that impact on the detector plate, the greater the current.

Detecting the other Ions

How might the other ions be detected - those in streams A and C which have been lost in the machine?

Remember that stream A was most deflected - it has the smallest value of m/z (the lightest ions if the charge is 1^+). To bring them onto the detector, you would need to deflect them less - by using a smaller magnetic field (a smaller sideways force).

To bring those with a larger m/z value (the heavier ions if the charge is 1^+) onto the detector, you would have to deflect them more by using a larger magnetic field.

If you vary the magnetic field, you can bring each ion stream in turn onto the detector to produce a current which is proportional to the number of ions arriving. The mass of each ion being detected is related to the size of the magnetic field used to bring it onto the detector. The machine can be calibrated to record current (which is a measure of the number of ions) against m/z directly. The mass is measured on the 12C scale.[9]

Activity 6 – How do you think you know the amount of a substance?

---

[9] http://www.chemguide.co.uk/analysis/masspec/howitworks.html

A read out might look like the following:

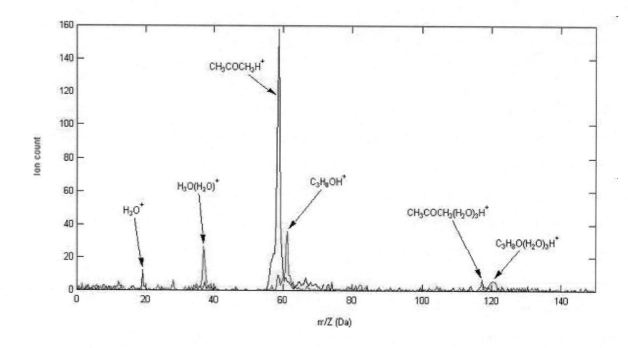

A mass spectrum can be used to identify the isotopes than make up an element. Different isotopes are detected separately in the detector because they have a different mass.

The following is the mass spectrum of a sample of chlorine illustrating two isotopes, Cl^{35} and Cl^{37} and their relative abundance in the sample:

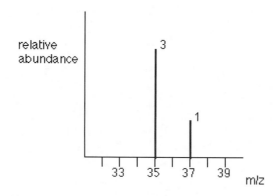

There are two basic types of mass spectrometry:

- High Resolution – Detects relative atomic mass up to 5 decimal places
- Low Resolution – Detects relative atomic mass to the nearest whole number. This is the more common of the two

From a mass spectrograph of the isotopes of an element in a sample, we can calculate the relative atomic mass of the sample easily.

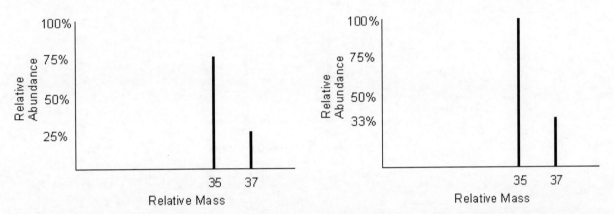

Consider these two graphs for a moment. Sometimes the mass spectrograph will be of the form on the right. In this graph the largest isotope will be adjusted to 100% and the others have their relative abundance adjusted to suit. So we see that Cl^{37} is 33% of the sample. The more typical, and in many ways more useful form, is that on the left. Here we see the following:

- Cl^{35} – 75% of sample
- Cl^{37} – 25% of sample

The relative atomic mass of chlorine in this sample can be calculated as follows:

$$\frac{(75 \times 35) + (25 \times 37)}{100} = \textbf{35.5}$$

The relative atomic mass for this sample of chlorine is, therefore, 35.5.

Activity 7 – Calculate the relative atomic mass of uranium from the graph:

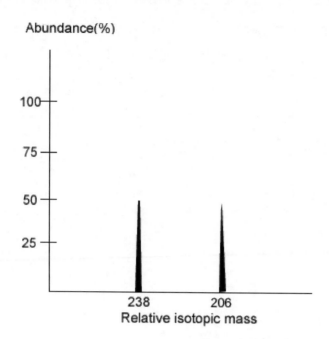

Answer to Activity 7:

$$\frac{(50 \times 238) + (50 \times 206)}{100} = \mathbf{222}$$

The relative atomic mass for the above illustrated sample of uranium would be 222.

3.6.3 – Infrared spectroscopy

Infrared spectroscopy is a very common tool used by chemists to help identify unknown compounds.

It works because every chemical bond vibrates. Generally speaking, stronger bonds vibrate faster and therefore at a higher frequency. Heavier atoms cause the bond to vibrate less, and therefore at a lower frequency. These vibrating bonds do so at a very specific frequency that is in the IR region of the electromagnetic spectrum.

When a beam of infrared radiation is shone through a sample, the bond absorbs the radiation of the same frequency as the natural vibration frequency of the bonds in the sample. The radiation that emerges from the sample will consist of every frequency EXCEPT the frequency of the bonds in the sample, as they will have absorbed the radiation of their specific frequency. If the radiation that emerges can be accurately measured, and the gaps identified, then the exact bonds in the sample can be identified.

A chart like the one below is produced. This one is for a ketone:

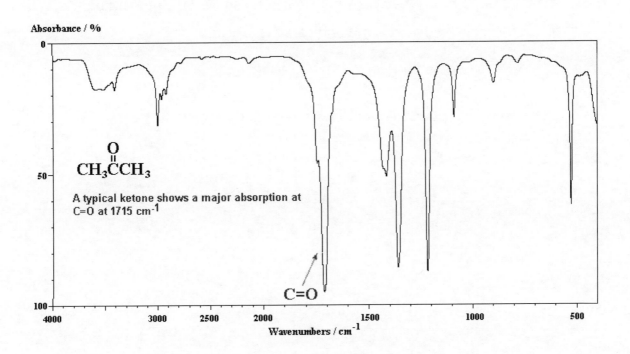

<u>Operation of the IR Spectrometer</u>

- A beam of radiation is passed through a sample.
- The radiation that emerges from the other side of the sample is collected and analysed. The missing radiation frequencies are the frequencies of the bonds in the sample.
- The machine plots a graph of the intensity of the radiation emerging from the sample against the frequency of radiation.
- The frequency is expressed as a wavenumber measured in cm^{-1}

The graphs produced can help a chemist to identify the functional groups present in a sample.

Look at the chart above and note that the dips are called peaks.

- The O – H bond produces a broad peak at around 3230 and 2550 cm^{-1} when in alcohols.
- The O – H bond produces a very broad peak at around 2500 - 3000 cm^{-1} when in carboxylic acids.
- The C=O bond produces a peak between 1680 and 1750 cm^{-1}. This bond would be found in aldehydes, ketones and carboxylic acids.

The characteristic absorption frequencies are recorded in the table below.

Characteristic Infrared Absorption Frequencies

Bond	Compound type	Frequency range cm^{-1}
C—H	Alkanes	2850–2960
		1350–1470
C—H	Alkenes	3020–3080
		675–1000
C—H	Aromatic rings	3000–3100
		675–870
C—H	Alkynes	3300
C=C	Alkenes	1640–1680
C≡C	Alkynes	2100–2260
C=C	Aromatic rings	1500, 1600
C—O	Alcohols, ethers, carboxylic acids, esters	1080–1300
C=O	Aldehydes, ketones, carboxylic acids, esters	1690–1760
O—H	Monomeric alcohols, phenols	3610–3640
	Hydrogen-bonded alcohols, phenols	3200–3600
	Carboxylic acids	2500–3000
N—H	Amines	3300–3500
C—N	Amines	1180–1360
C≡N	Nitriles	2210–2260
—NO$_2$	Nitro compounds	1515–1560
		1345–1385

Fingerprints

On an IR spectrum chart, there are typically a great many peaks below around 1500 cm^{-1}. These peaks are caused by vibrations of the molecules as a whole and they can be used to identify the molecules present in the sample. These are as unique as a fingerprint.

3.7 – Optical isomerism

Compounds that contain an asymmetric carbon atom form sterioisomers that differ in their effect on plane polarised light. This type of isomerism is called optical isomerism.

This is another area which we have looked at previously so this should be good revision.

Optical isomers can occur when a substance has 4 different groups attached to one of its carbon atoms. This can result in two substances that are mirror images of each other.

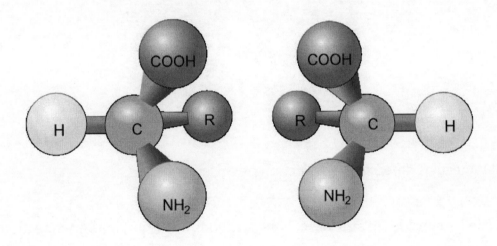

Chirality

Optical isomers are chiral, which is to say they are either left or right handed. The carbon atom that is bonded to the four different groups is called the chiral centre. Chiral atoms cannot be superimposed on each other, in the same way that left and right hands cannot be superimposed. Optical isomers that are mirror images like this are sometimes called **enantiomers**.

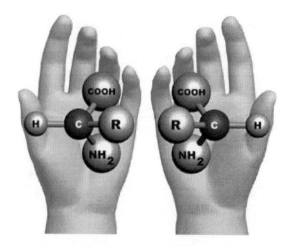

Chiral molecules differ in their effect on polarised light.

Light can be considered as a wave with vibrations occurring in every direction at right angles to the direction of movement of the light. If this light is passed through a polarising substance, then all of the planes of light are eliminated with the exception of the vertical plane.

This light is now considered to be vertically polarised and it will have a different impact on different optical isomers.

If we pass this light through a solution of one type of the optical isomer, the light will be rotated clockwise. This is called the positive isomer.

The other isomer will cause the light to be rotated in an anti-clockwise direction. This is called the negative isomer.

A **racemate** is a solution that is an equal mixture of left and right handed **enantiomers** (optical isomers).

In any normal reaction that produced enantiomers, unless the conditions of the reaction are designed to favour either the left or right hand optical isomer, both will form in approximately equal numbers.

Optical Isomers in the Drug Industry

In the drug industry, optical isomers are often produced because of the complexity of the chemicals involved. Sometimes a racemate mixture is acceptable, but at other times only one of the enantiomers is required and conditions in the reaction must be adjusted to ensure this occurs.

In the case of a painkiller like ibuprofen, a racemate mixture is acceptable. With some other drugs, one of the enantiomers will be an effective medicine, the other may be toxic.

3.8 – Aldehydes and ketones

Aldehydes, ketones, carboxylic acids and their derivatives all contain the carbonyl group which is attacked by nucleophiles. This section includes the addition reactions of aldehydes and ketones.

We have already encountered aldehydes and ketones earlier. Look back over those sections to make sure you are familiar with them.

Pay particular attention to:

- The naming system (up to 6 carbon atoms long)
- Understanding that aldehydes are readily oxidised to carboxylic acids
- The Fehling's solution and Tollens' reagent tests for aldehydes and ketones

Hazards of using HCN and KCN

A number of reactions in chemistry will use either hydrogen cyanide (HCN) or potassium cyanide (KCN) as a reactant. They are useful substances because they will generally attack a carbonyl group and add a CN group to a substance. They are, however, extremely dangerous.

Potassium cyanide will generally exist in crystal form and in appearance is much like common salt. Unfortunately, it is highly toxic. If the crystals become moist they will release hydrogen cyanide gas, which is also highly toxic (and smells of almonds).

Activity 82 – What do you remember about the reduction of aldehydes and ketones?

Reduction of Aldehydes and Ketones

We looked at this earlier too, but by way of a reminder: primary alcohols are oxidised to the equivalent aldehyde.

These can then be further oxidised to carboxylic acids. The two reactions are:

❶

$$CH_3 - \overset{\overset{\displaystyle H}{|}}{\underset{\underset{\displaystyle H}{|}}{C}} - OH \ + \ [O] \ \longrightarrow \ CH_3 - C\overset{\displaystyle O}{\underset{\displaystyle H}{\diagup}} \ + H_2O$$

ethanol   ethanal

❷

$$CH_3 - C\overset{\displaystyle O}{\underset{\displaystyle H}{\diagup}} \ + \ [O] \ \longrightarrow \ CH_3 - C\overset{\displaystyle O}{\underset{\displaystyle OH}{\diagup}}$$

ethanal   ethanoic acid

Secondary alcohols are oxidised to ketones.

This reaction requires the use of a suitable oxidising agent, like potassium dichromate (VI), for example. [O] is acceptable in the equation to demonstrate this oxidising agent.

Ketones are not easily oxidised to carboxylic acids.

Tertiary alcohols are not easily oxidised.

In terms of a mechanism, aldehydes are reduced (using NaBH₄ in aqueous solution) as follows:

$$CH_3-C \overset{O}{\underset{H}{<}} \quad + \quad 2[H] \quad \longrightarrow \quad CH_3-\overset{OH}{\underset{H}{C}}-H \qquad (\ CH_3CH_2OH\ )$$

Ketones are reduced as follows:

$$\overset{CH_3}{\underset{CH_3}{>}}C=O \quad + \quad 2[H] \quad \longrightarrow \quad CH_3-\overset{OH}{\underset{CH_3}{C}}-H \qquad (\ CH_3CHCH_3\ )\ \underset{OH}{}$$

Study the red H atoms (the square brackets are there to draw attention to them; they are not referring to concentration as is normally the case with square brackets).

Nucleophilic Addition of HCN to Aldehydes and Ketones

You will also need to understand the mechanism for the addition of HCN to both an aldehyde and a ketone. When hydrogen cyanide groups attack either an aldehyde or a ketone, they will attack the C = O double bond. They act to break this bond; they then themselves split into H^+ and CN^- and bond to the ions that form on the C and O when the double bond has broken.

HCN attacks an aldehyde as follows:

$$CH_3-C \overset{O}{\underset{H}{<}} \quad + \quad HCN \quad \longrightarrow \quad CH_3-\overset{OH}{\underset{H}{C}}-CN$$

HCN attacks a ketone as follows:

$$\overset{CH_3}{\underset{CH_3}{>}}C=O \quad + \quad HCN \quad \longrightarrow \quad CH_3-\overset{OH}{\underset{CH_3}{C}}-CN$$

Both reactions produce substances called hydroxynitriles.

3.9 – Carboxylic acids and derivatives

Carboxylic acids are weak acids but strong enough to liberate carbon dioxide from carbonates. Esters occur naturally in vegetable oils and animal fats. Important products obtained from esters include biodiesel, soap and glycerol.

3.9.1 – Carboxylic acids and esters

Carboxylic acids have the functional group:

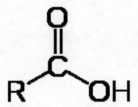

This is often written as –COOH, and it only ever occurs at the end of a carbon chain.

Carboxylic acids have two functional groups:

- C = O, as is found in aldehydes and ketones
- -OH as is found in alcohols

Activity 83 – Carboxylic acids are weak acids. What is a weak acid?

Answer to Activity 83:

Weak acids are acids that do not dissociate fully when at equilibrium in an aqueous solution. The dissociation reaction is as follows (for ethanoic acid):

$$CH_3COOH(aq) \rightleftharpoons CH_3COO^-(aq) + H^+(aq)$$

Carboxylic acids are weak acids. When they react with carbonates they will liberate CO_2 from them.

If we pour, for example, dilute ethanoic acid onto sodium carbonate crystals, the crystals will fizz as CO_2 is liberated. Eventually, if enough is added, you will get a colourless solution of sodium ethanoate, according to the following reaction:

$$2CH_3COOH + Na_2CO_3 \rightarrow 2CH_3COONa + H_2O + CO_2$$

Carboxylic Acids Producing Esters

Carboxylic acids can also be used to produce esters. Esters are chemicals that have a hydrocarbon group replacing the hydrogen of the –COOH group as follows:

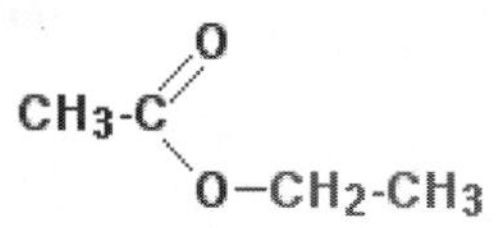

ethyl ethanoate

Esters can be manufactured by heating a carboxylic acid with an alcohol, in the presence of a strong acid catalyst. The catalyst employed is typically concentrated sulphuric acid (H_2SO_4).

The rate of the esterification reaction is slow, and it is also reversible. An example is to react ethanoic acid with ethanol in the presence of sulphuric acid to produce ethyl ethanoate as follows:

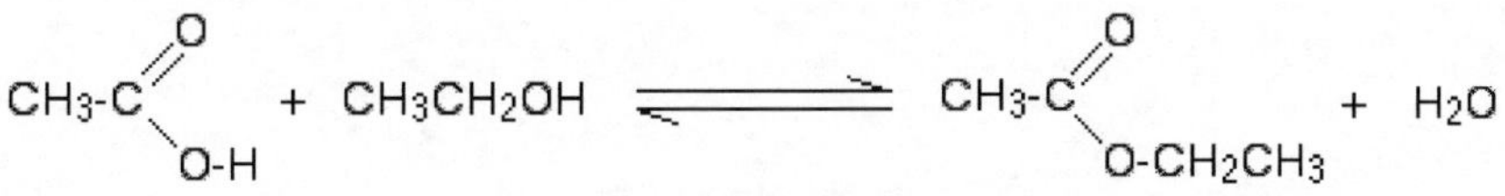

$$CH_3\text{-}C\!\!\begin{array}{c} \diagup O \\ \diagdown O\text{-}H \end{array} + CH_3CH_2OH \rightleftharpoons CH_3\text{-}C\!\!\begin{array}{c} \diagup O \\ \diagdown O\text{-}CH_2CH_3 \end{array} + H_2O$$

If you are conducting this experiment in a laboratory, you will know when the ester is being produced because it has a distinct and pleasant odour.

Uses of Esters

Esters are very useful commercially and can be used in a range of products, including:

- Solvents
- Plasticisers
- Perfumes
- Food flavourings

Animal fats and vegetable oils are both esters of propane-1,2,3-triol (also known as glycerol and illustrated below).

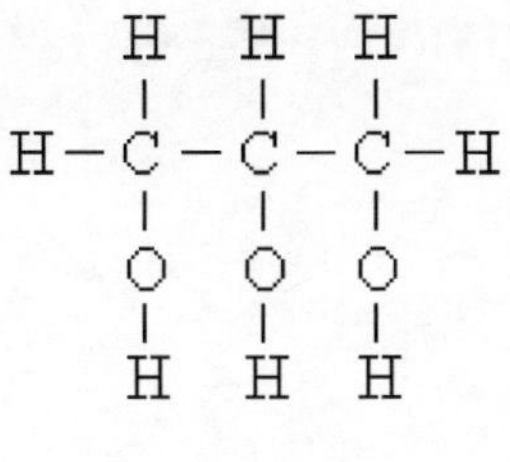

$$\begin{array}{ccc} H & H & H \\ | & | & | \\ H-C- & C- & C-H \\ | & | & | \\ O & O & O \\ | & | & | \\ H & H & H \end{array}$$

Fats and oils are very similar substances; the only difference between them is that oils are liquid at room temperature, while fats are solid.

Oils and fats contain three molecules of relatively long carbon chain carboxylic acids (C_{12}-C_{18} typically). These are called fatty acids. Since these are based on glycerol, they are called triglycerides.

Both fats and oils can be hydrolysed in acid conditions to give a mixture of propane-1,2,3-triol and the component fatty acid, as in the generic reaction:

$$
\begin{array}{l}
CH_2OOCR \\
| \\
CHOOCR \quad + \quad 3H_2O \longrightarrow \\
| \\
CH_2OOCR \\
\text{Oil or fat}
\end{array}
\quad
\begin{array}{l}
CH_2OH \\
| \\
CHOH \quad + \quad 3RCOOH \\
| \qquad\qquad\quad \text{Fatty acid} \\
CH_2OH \quad \text{(Waxy solid used in} \\
\text{Glycerol} \quad \text{candle manufacture)}
\end{array}
$$

Fats can also be hydrolysed by boiling them with sodium hydroxide to produce glycerol and a mixture of three sodium salts (soaps) as follows:

$$
\begin{array}{l}
CH_3(CH_2)_{16}COOCH_2 \\
| \\
CH_3(CH_2)_{16}COOCH \quad + \quad 3NaOH \longrightarrow \\
| \\
CH_3(CH_2)_{16}COOCH_2 \\
\\
\text{a typical fat or oil}
\end{array}
\quad
\begin{array}{l}
\\
3CH_3(CH_2)_{16}COONa \quad + \\
\\
\text{a typical sodium salt} \\
\text{found in soap}
\end{array}
\quad
\begin{array}{l}
CH_2OH \\
| \\
CHOH \\
| \\
CH_2OH \\
\\
\text{glycerol}
\end{array}
$$

Activity 84 – Write a paragraph on what you remember about biofuels from the AS section.

Biodiesel

Most experts today believe that we have an overreliance on oil which is, after all, a non-renewable fuel and is therefore a finite resource.

One possible solution to this is the manufacture of biodiesel, which we looked at briefly at AS. Revise that section now to make sure you are familiar with the concept of biodiesel and how it is produced.

Vegetable oils can be reacted with methanol to produce esters of long chain carboxylic acids (biodiesel) and glycerine as follows:

Triglyceride   Methanol   Ester   Glycerine

Activity 85 – What are the potential problems with biofuel production?

3.9.2 - Acylation

You will remember that the acyl group is as follows:

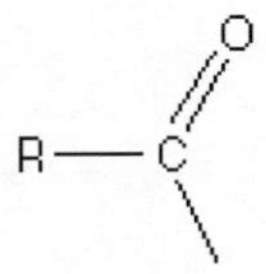

R—C(=O)—

Note that the carbon has a bond to nothing; this obviously would not exist but is an illustration that the carbon could be bonded to a number of chemicals to make very different substances.

An acyl chloride, for example, would look like the following:

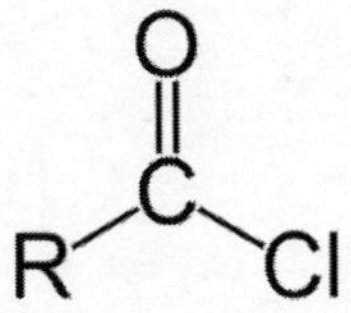

R—C(=O)—Cl

Note, of course, that the R group could be quite large or quite small.

The acyl group will have a slight positive charge on the carbon atom, and a slight negative charge on the oxygen atom (because of the electronegativity of the oxygen atom).

This leaves the group open to nucleophilic addition reactions with a substance bearing an unbonded lone pair of electrons.

Mechanisms of Reactions

The general mechanism for the nucleophilic addition-elimination reactions of carboxylic acid derivatives is:

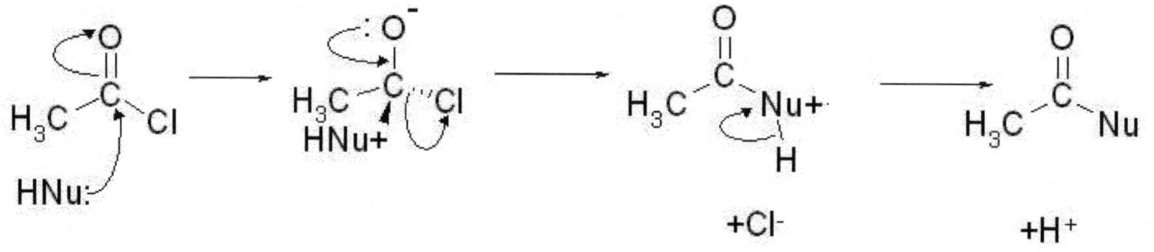

The mechanisms for the reactions of the acyl group tend to follow the same lines. This is the nucleophilic addition-elimination reaction of ethanoyl chloride and water:

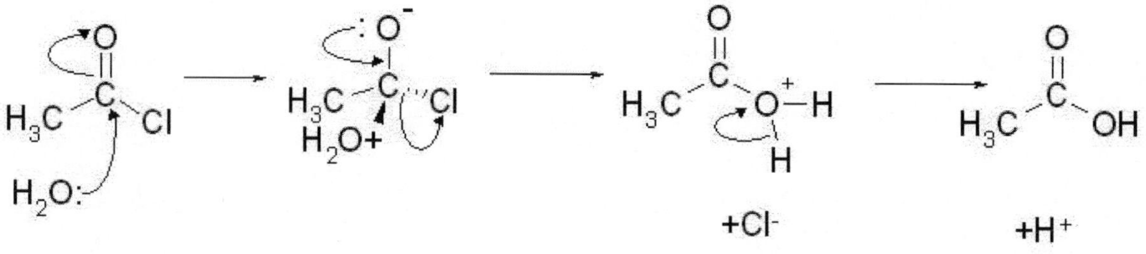

This is the nucleophilic addition-elimination reaction of ethanoyl chloride and an alcohol:

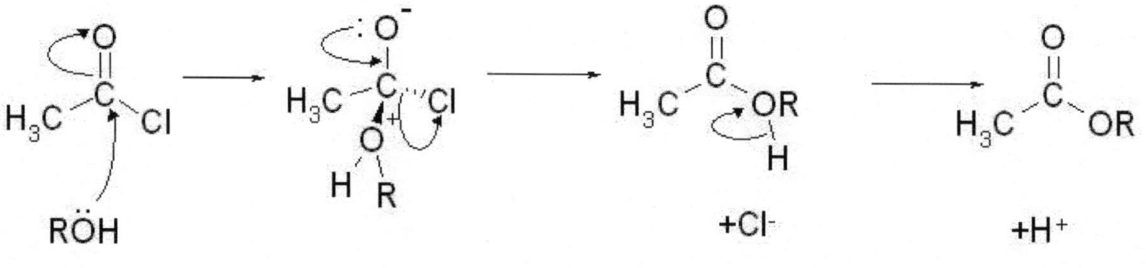

This is the nucleophilic addition-elimination reaction of ethanoyl chloride and ammonia:

This is the nucleophilic addition-elimination reaction of ethanoyl chloride and an amine:

Uses of the Acylation Reactions

Ethanoic anhydride is a chemical that is manufactured on a very large scale worldwide.

ethanoyl chloride   ethanoic anhydride

Ethanoic anhydride has a number of advantages over ethanoyl chloride:

- It is cheaper
- It is less corrosive
- It is unreactive with water
- It has safer by-products

Perhaps its major usage is in the manufacture of the drug Aspirin.

Required practical 10:

Preparation of:

- **A pure organic solid and test its purity**
- **A pure organic liquid**

3.10 – Aromatic Chemistry

Aromatic chemistry takes benzene as an example of this type of molecule, and looks at the structure of the benzene ring and its substitution reactions.

3.10.1 – Bonding

We have encountered benzene earlier the course, but here we must look more closely at the bonding in that structure.

The benzene ring.

The simplified representation of the benzene ring.

Arenes are a family of compounds whose structure is based upon a benzene ring. Benzene itself is the simplest arene.

You will note that a benzene ring is an unsaturated molecule (it has 3 double bonds). However, it is a remarkably stable structure due to the special nature of those bonds.

Activity 86 – Are you aware of any other arenes?

Answer to Activity 86:

We have encountered one other arene so far in this course, phenol, but here are some examples of others:

Phenol   o-Chlorophenol   *m*-Chlorophenol

p-Chlorophenol   2,4 -Dichlorophenol

Arenes are given the generic name "aromatic compounds" because of the sweet smell they give off.

The benzene structure is a flat, regular hexagon of carbon atoms, each of which is bonded to a single hydrogen atom.

The bond length of the C – C bonds is intermediate between what we would expect for a C – C single bond and a C = C double bond.

The C – C bond length in a benzene ring is shorter than a typical C – C bond in a hydrocarbon, but longer than the C = C bond.

Molecule	General Formula of Class	C — C Bond Length (Å)
Ethane	$CH_3 - CH_3$	1.54
Ethene	$CH_2 = CH_2$	1.33
Ethyne	$CH \equiv CH$	1.21

This can be explained by using the theory of delocalised electrons.

Each carbon atom in benzene has three covalent bonds: 1 to a hydrogen atom and one to each of the carbon atoms next to it in the ring.

Each carbon atom, therefore, has a spare electron which inhabits a p orbital. These p orbitals overlap and the electrons in them are delocalised. These delocalised electrons form a region of high electron density above and below the ring.

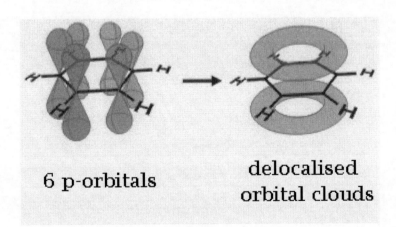

6 p-orbitals   delocalised orbital clouds

Delocalisation Stability

The benzene ring structure is remarkably stable because of these delocalised electrons.

The delocalisation of the electrons means that, on average, each C – C bond has a total of three electrons, meaning that they are somewhere between a single and a double bond. This fact is implied by the bond length also being between the two, as we saw above.

Thermo-Chemical Evidence for Stability

If we look at the enthalpy change for the hydrogenation of cyclohexene (a ring with only 1 double bond) to cyclohexane, we see:

$+ H_2 \rightarrow$ $\Delta H = -120$ kJ mol^{-1}

We might reasonably assume that the enthalpy change for cyclohex-1,3-diene (to cyclohexane) would be double this figure, as it has two double bonds that need to be broken, and it is close to that:

$+ H_2 \longrightarrow$ + cyclohexane; $\Delta H_1 = -120$ kJ mol^{-1}

$+ 2H_2 \longrightarrow$ + cyclohexane; $\Delta H_2 = -232$ kJ mol^{-1}

We might further assume, therefore, that the figure for benzene would be around 360kj mol^{-1} (3 x -120) as it should have three double bonds:

+ 3H$_2$ → $\Delta H = 3 \times (-120 \text{ kJ mol}^{-1})$
= -360 kJ mol^{-1}

What we actually find through experimentation, however, is that the enthalpy change for the hydrogenation of benzene is:

+ 3H$_2$ ⟶ $\Delta H = -209 \text{ kJ mol}^{-1}$

Benzene   Cyclohexane

Why is the real value lower that the theoretical value based upon the hydrogenation of cyclohexene?

It is now known that the explanation for this is that benzene does not contain three double bonds in the traditional way. The electrons in the ring are delocalised and are spread in clouds above and below the ring, as we have seen. This means that the C – C bonds in benzene are stronger than single bonds, but weaker than double bonds, hence the peculiarity in the enthalpy values.

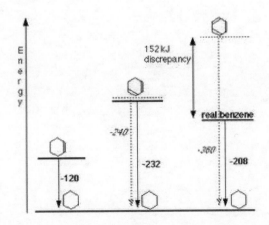

3.10.2 – Electrophilic substitution

You know that benzene is unsaturated, but that it does not react like an alkene.

The most common reaction of benzene is an electrophilic substitution, where an atom or group replaces one of the hydrogen atoms. This means that the ring system and the system of delocalised electrons remains unchanged.

If you wanted to break the ring structure, then you would need a lot more energy to break the bonds.

The delocalised electrons have a high electron density, and thus a negative charge, and therefore attract electrophiles (E^+ in the illustration below).

The converse is also true, of course; the delocalised electron cloud is also attracted to the positively charged electrophile.

One of the carbon atoms will form a bond with the electrophile, but to do this it needs to draw an electron from the delocalised cloud.

If this occurred it would destroy the delocalised system, so to maintain the stability of that system, the carbon will lose a hydrogen in the form of an H^+ ion.

The sum of this reaction is for the H^+ to be replaced in the benzene ring by the E^+ ion.

Nitration

Nitration involves the substitution of an NO_2 group into the benzene ring in place of a hydrogen atom.

The NO_2^+ group acts as an electrophile (as in the E^+ in the illustration above) and is first generated by the reaction of a mixture of nitric acid and sulphuric acid in a two stage process.

Stage 1:

$$H_2SO_4 + HNO_3 \rightarrow H_2NO_3^+ + HSO_4^-$$

The sulphuric acid is a stronger acid than nitric acid and it donates a proton (H^+) to the nitric acid.

Stage 2:

$$H_2NO_3^+ \rightarrow NO_2^+ + H_2O$$

The $H_2NO_3^+$ ion then loses a water molecule to leave the NO_2^+ ion, called either the **nitronium ion** or the **nitryl cation**.

NO_2^+ is an electrophile and is attracted to the delocalised electrons of the benzene ring. The substitution occurs in two stages.

Activity 87 – Draw the product you would expect to ultimately form from the nitration of benzene.

Stage 1:

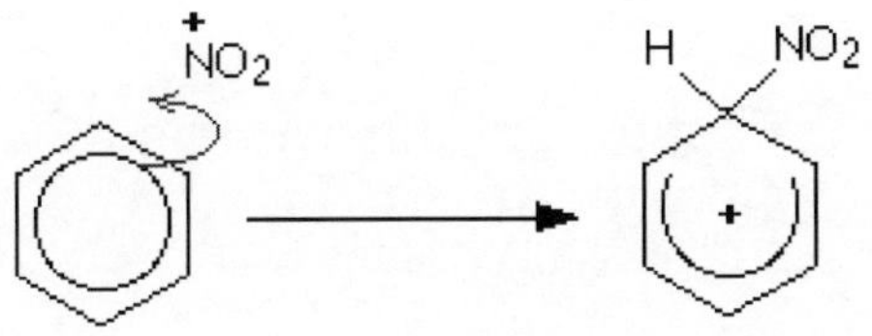

In stage 1, one of the carbon atoms loses an electron to the nitronium ion. This electron comes from the delocalised cloud, destabilising that system.

Stage 2:

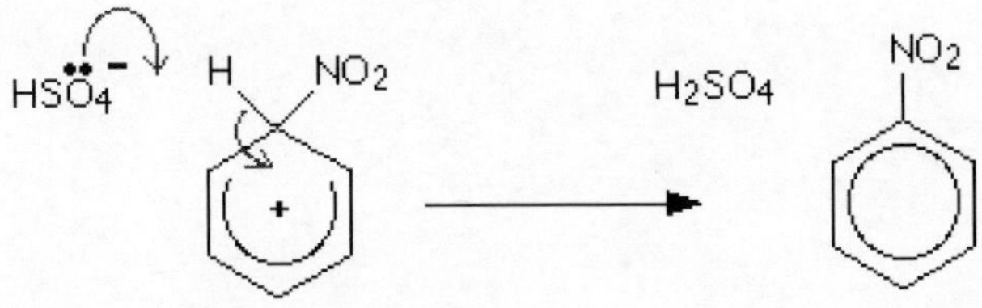

In order to regain the stability of the cloud, the carbon loses an H^+ ion, which reacts with the HSO_4^- that forms during the production of the nitronium ion. Sulphuric acid is, therefore, produced as a by-product of the nitration of benzene.

Uses of the Nitration Reaction

The nitration reaction has a number of commercial uses, notably the production of explosives like TNT. Nitration is also the first step in the production of amines, which can themselves be used to manufacture dyes.

Friedel-Crafts Acylation Reaction

Friedel-Crafts reactions use aluminium chloride as a catalyst ($AlCl_3$).

The acylation mechanism is a substitution one, with an RCO group substituting an H atom on the benzene ring.

The RCO (acyl) group has the structure:

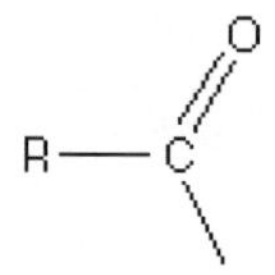

The acyl group is often formed from acyl chlorides (we will use ethanoyl chloride in the example) reacting with $AlCl_3$:

$$CH_3COCl + AlCl_3 \rightarrow CH_3CO^+ + AlCl_4^-$$

The mechanism for this is:

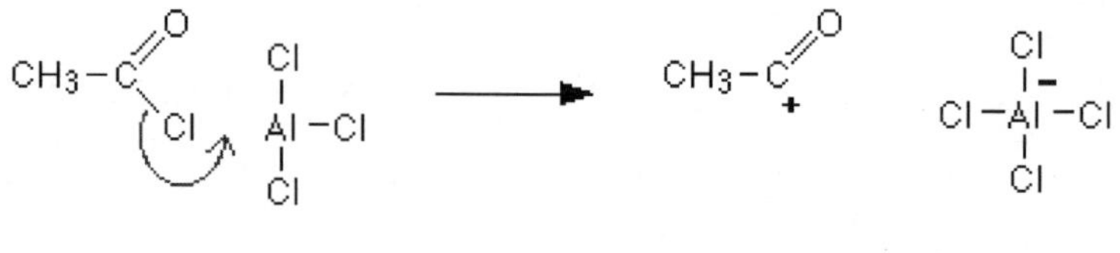

This reaction occurs because the aluminium atom in the aluminium chloride has only 6 electrons in its outer shell and readily accepts a lone pair from the chlorine atom in the ethanoyl chloride.

Activity 88 – How can the aluminium chloride be a catalyst if it is altered in the reaction?

Answer to Activity 88:

The $AlCl_4^-$ reforms into aluminium chloride by reacting with H^+ ions to produce hydrochloric acid. The aluminium chloride is therefore reformed and the net effect is for it not to be used or changed, therefore acting as a catalyst.

$$AlCl_4^- + H^+ \rightarrow AlCl_3 + HCl$$

The Friedel-Crafts acylation reaction occurs in two stages.

Stage 1:

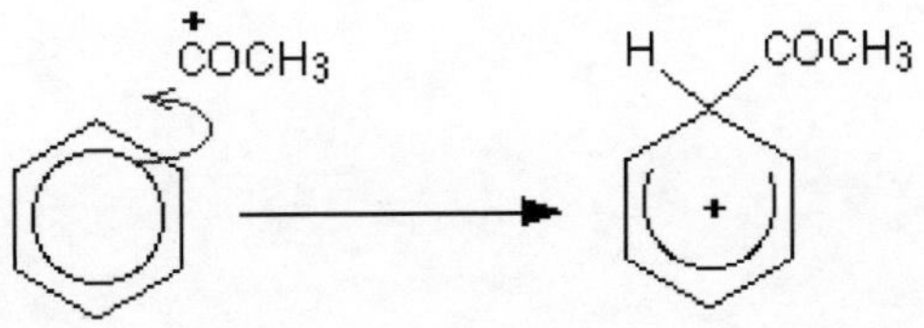

Stage 2:

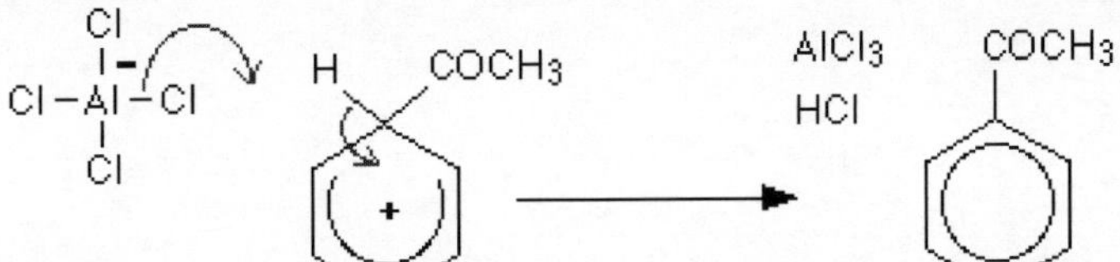

Acylation reactions are a very useful step in the formation of other aromatic compounds.

3.11 - Amines

Amines are compounds based on ammonia where hydrogen atoms have been replaced by alkyl or aryl groups. This section included their reactions as nucleophiles

3.11.1 - Preparation

Primary Amines – Reduction of Nitriles

Primary aliphatic amines can be produced from haloalkanes in a two stage process as follows:

Stage 1:

$$RBr + CN^- \rightarrow RCN + Br^-$$

The haloalkane will react with a cyanide ion in an aqueous ethanol solution. The cyanide ion replaces the halide in a nucleophilic substitution reaction to form a nitrile. Note that the carbon to nitrogen bond in the cyanide is a triple bond.

Stage 2:

$$RCN + 2H_2 \rightarrow RCH_2NH_2$$

Nitriles (RCN) can be reduced to primary amines by hydrogenation (in the presence of a catalyst).

Activity 89 – In your own words, describe the differences between an electrophilic and a nucleophilic reaction.

<u>Phenylamine</u>

Phenylamine can also be manufactured in a two stage process.

Stage 1:

In stage 1, the benzene is reacted with a mixture of nitric and sulphuric acids at 333K. This produces nitrobenzene.

Stage 2:

The nitrobenzene is then reduced to phenylamine in the presence of tin and hydrochloric acid, which acts as a reducing agent:

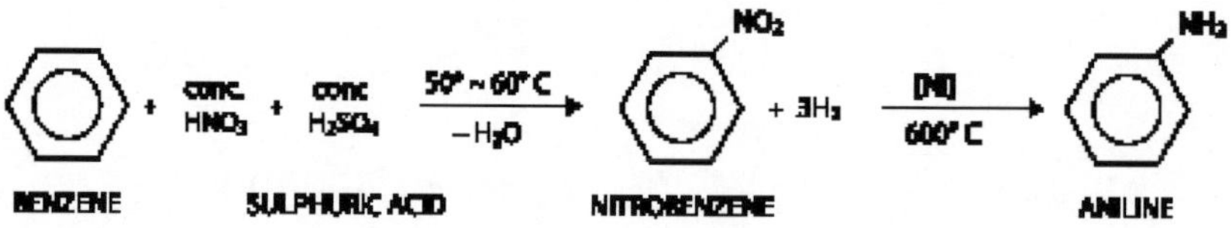

3.11.2 – Base properties

Base Properties (Brønsted-Lowry)

Amines are a family of chemicals that are based upon the ammonia molecule.

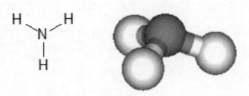

Ammonia has this particular structure because of the lone pair of electrons on the nitrogen atom.

Amines are typically divided into three groups:

1) Primary amines
2) Secondary amines
3) Tertiary amines

Primary Secondary Tertiary

$$R - NH_2$$

Secondary:
$$\overset{\displaystyle R}{\underset{\displaystyle }{R - NH}}$$

Tertiary:
$$\overset{\displaystyle R}{\underset{\displaystyle }{R - N - R}}$$

Naming amines...

1° **propylamine**
$$CH_3 - CH_2 - CH_2 - NH_2$$

2° **N - ethyl butylamine**
$$CH_3 - CH_2 - \underset{\displaystyle CH_2 - CH_2 - CH_2 - CH_3}{NH}$$

3° **N - ethyl - N - methyl propylamine**
$$CH_3 - CH_2 - \underset{\displaystyle CH_2 - CH_2 - CH_3}{N} - CH_3$$

As we said, amines are based upon the ammonia molecule, and as such have a lone pair of electrons (on the nitrogen atom). Amines, therefore, can act as proton acceptors. This ability makes them Brønsted-Lowry bases.

Base Strength

The strength of the base depends on how readily it will accept a proton (H^+). Both ammonia and amines have a lone pair of electrons that will act to attract an H^+ ion.

Alkyl groups release electrons from themselves towards the nitrogen atom. This is called **the inductive effect**. The inductive effect increases the electron density on the nitrogen group and this makes it even more attractive to H^+ ions; this makes it a stronger proton acceptor, and therefore a stronger base.

Secondary amines have two alkyl groups pushing electrons towards the nitrogen atom and are therefore greater proton acceptors than primary amines (as there are even more electrons being pushed towards the nitrogen, therefore more strongly attracting H^+ ions). Secondary amines are therefore stronger bases than primary amines.

Tertiary amines are *not* stronger bases than primary or secondary amines because they are not soluble in water (generally). They are therefore the weakest bases.

The aryl group (the benzene ring) acts to withdraw the electrons from the nitrogen atom in a phenylamine. This is because they are drawn towards the sea of delocalised electrons on the benzene ring, adding to the stability of the structure. This means that they are less attractive to protons and are therefore weak bases.

3.11.3 – Nucleophilic properties

The lone pair of electrons on the nitrogen atom of an amine will attack positively charged carbon atoms, and therefore will act as nucleophiles.

The mechanism for the nucleophilic substitution of a haloalkane is:

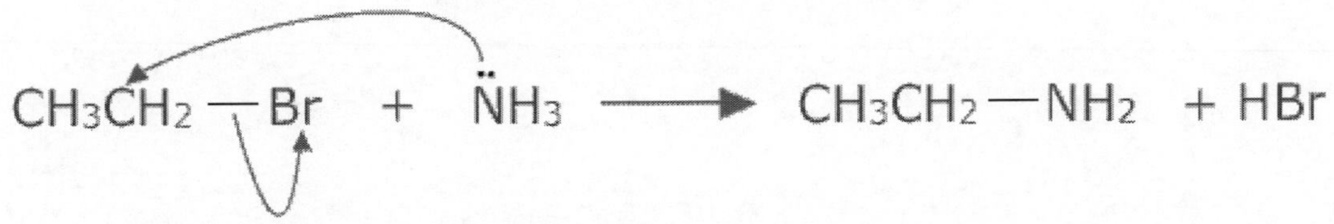

$$CH_3CH_2 - Br \ + \ \ddot{N}H_3 \longrightarrow CH_3CH_2 - NH_2 \ + \ HBr$$

Primary amines are produced when a haloalkane reacts with ammonia.

The reaction occurs in two stages, as illustrated below.

Stage 1:

$$NH_3 \ + \ C_2H_5Cl \rightarrow C_2H_5NH_3^+ \ + \ Cl^-$$

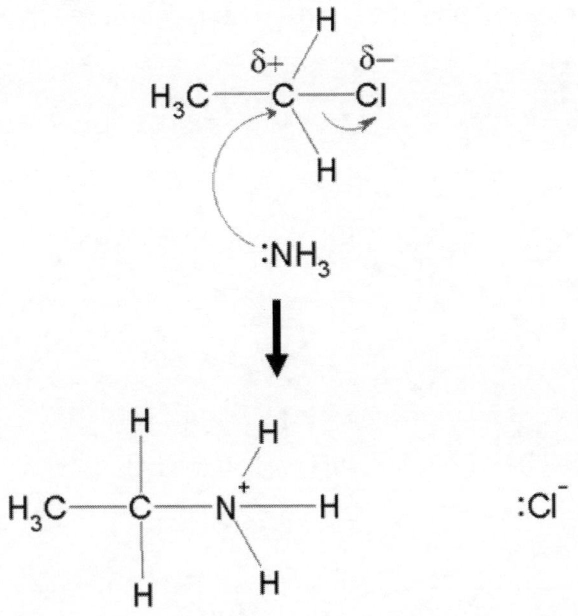

$$H_3C \overset{\delta+}{\underset{}{-}} \overset{H}{\underset{H}{C}} \overset{\delta-}{-} Cl$$

:NH₃

$$H_3C - \overset{H}{\underset{H}{C}} - \overset{+}{\underset{H}{N}} \overset{H}{-} H \qquad :Cl^-$$

Stage 2:

$$C_2H_5NH_3^+ + Cl^- + NH_3 \rightarrow C_2H_5NH_2 + NH_4^+ + Cl^-$$

The primary amine produced above is also a nucleophile, and it will also react with the haloalkane to produce a secondary amine. The generic reaction is as follows:

Stage 1:

$$RNH_2 + RX \rightarrow [R_2NH_2]^+ + X^-$$

Stage 2:

$$[R_2NH_2]^+ + X^- + NH_3 \rightarrow R_2NH + [NH_4]^+ + X^-$$

The secondary amine will then also react to give a tertiary amine. The generic formula being:

Stage 1:

$$R_2NH + RX \rightarrow [R_3NH]^+ + X^-$$

Stage 2:

$$[R_3NH]^+ + X^- + NH_3 \rightarrow R_3N + [NH_4]^+ + X^-$$

The tertiary amine will then react to produce a quaternary ammonium salt:

$$R_3N + RX \rightarrow [R_4N]^+ + X^-$$

Quaternary salts can be used as cationic surfactants in fabric softeners and hair conditioners.

Activity 88 – In your own words, describe the differences between an electrophile and a nucleophile.

3.12 - Polymers

The study of polymers is extended to include condensation polymers. The ways in which condensation polymers are formed are studied, together with their properties and typical uses. Problems associated with the reuse of both addition and condensation polymers are considered.

3.12.1 – Condensation polymers

Not all polymers are produced by an addition polymerisation reaction; some are produced using a reaction called a "condensation polymerisation" reaction.

With the condensation polymerisation reaction, a small molecule (water or hydrogen chloride, for example) is produced as a by-product, hence the name "condensation polymerisation".

Condensation polymerisation reactions require either:

- A diol and a dicarboxylic acid
- A dicarboxylic acid and a diamine
- Two amino acids

This is because, after two molecules have reacted together, there needs to be two reactive functional groups at either end of the growing chain to continue the reaction and the growth of the polymer chain.

Nylon is an example of a condensation polymer. To manufacture nylon, you require two monomers: 1,6 diaminohexane (also called hexamethylenediamine) and hexanedioic acid (also called adipic acid):

$$H_2N-CH_2-CH_2-CH_2-CH_2-CH_2-CH_2-NH_2 \quad \text{and}$$
Hexamethylenediamine

$$HO-\overset{\overset{\displaystyle O}{\|}}{C}-CH_2-CH_2-CH_2-CH_2-\overset{\overset{\displaystyle O}{\|}}{C}-OH$$
Adipic acid

These two monomers react together as below:

$$nHO-\overset{\overset{\displaystyle O}{\|}}{C}-(CH_2)_4-\overset{\overset{\displaystyle O}{\|}}{C}-OH + nH_2N-(CH_2)_6-NH_2 \longrightarrow$$
Adipic acid   Hexamethylene diamine

$$\left[-\overset{\overset{\displaystyle O}{\|}}{C}-(CH_2)_4-\overset{\overset{\displaystyle O}{\|}}{C}-NH(CH_2)_6-NH-\right]_n + 2\,nH_2O$$

However, the term nylon is only partly correct. Nylon is actually a trade name and not the correct chemical name. Nylons are actually forms of poly(amide) and there are many different kinds. However, having said this, we will continue to use the term "nylon" as it is almost always used.

The one thing we must say is, given that there are so many nylons, they do have to be distinguished in some way. The nylon produced in the above condensation reaction is typically called nylon 6,6. This is because both of the monomers have a 6 carbon chain.

Other nylons can also be produced using the generic condensation reaction below (also noting water as the by-product):

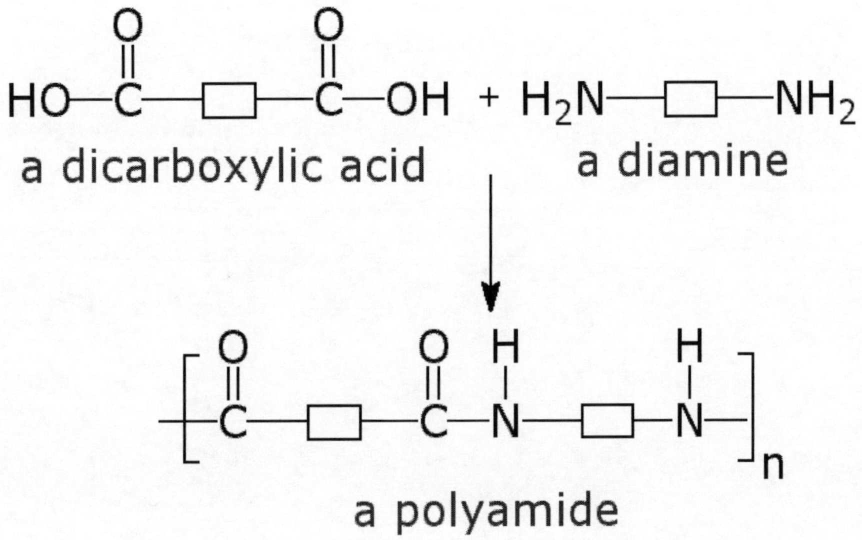

a dicarboxylic acid   a diamine

a polyamide

The blocks in the diagram above represent the CH_2 group repeated a number of times. In nylon 6,6 these would each be $6 \times CH_2$ groups. Kevlar is another example of a polyamide.

Esters can also be polymerised when reacted in a condensation polymerisation reaction with a dicarboxylic acid to produce polyesters, for example, terylene:

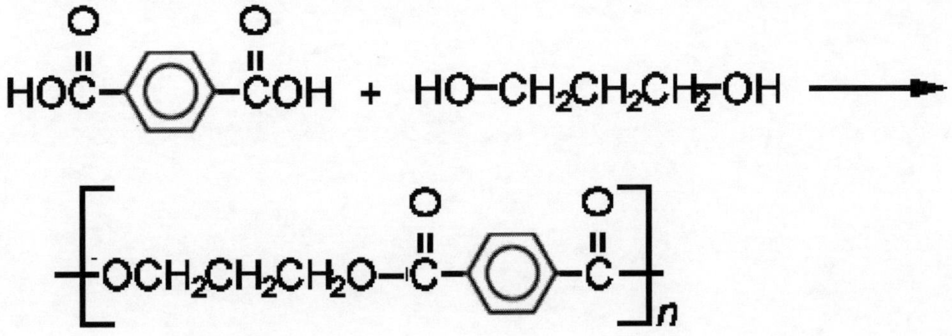

3.12.2 – Biodegradability and disposal of polymers

Polyalkenes have a structure consisting of a backbone of a long chain alkane.

Alkanes have strong, non-polar C–C and C–H bonds, making them very unreactive molecules. This is commercially very useful, but unfortunately means that they do not break down easily as they are not attracted by other chemicals, enzymes etc. In short, they are not biodegradable. A plastic bag will exist for thousands of years, much as it was when manufactured.

For the most part, addition polymers are either disposed of in landfill sites, burnt or recycled into other forms.

When polyalkenes are disposed of by burning, this produces energy, carbon dioxide and water. If the combustion is incomplete, however, then toxic carbon monoxide is also produced. The carbon dioxide that is produced is also a greenhouse gas, and thus an undesirable by-product.

More complex polymers, like polystyrene for example, can release other toxic chemicals when they are burnt.

Polyesters and polyamides can be broken down by hydrolysis and are, therefore, biodegradable.

Activity 92 – Do you think plastics can be recycled?

Recycling

Many plastics *can* now be recycled.

Unwanted plastic products can now be collected, sorted and remoulded into other products that can be sold to consumers.

This can be an expensive process and the economics do need to balance out. Whatever the cost, however, it is undoubtedly better for the environment for plastic to be recycled instead of put in landfill or incinerated.

Advantages of recycling:

- Almost all plastics ultimately come from crude oil, and this is a finite resource that is fast running out. The more we recycle, the longer that resource will last
- Landfill sites are limited and expensive
- Recycling is certainly better for the environment

Disadvantages of recycling:

- There are costs and difficulties associated with the collection and sorting of the different forms of plastic
- It is often labour intensive
- It can be expensive

Activity 93 – List some products made from recycled plastic:

3.13 – Amino acids, proteins and DNA

Amino acids, proteins and DNA are the molecules of life. In this section, the structure and bonding in these molecules and the way they interact is studied. Drug action is also considered.

3.13.1 – Amino acids

Acid and Base Properties

Amino acids are called the building blocks of life because they are the molecules that proteins are made from.

Amino acids have two functional groups in their structure:

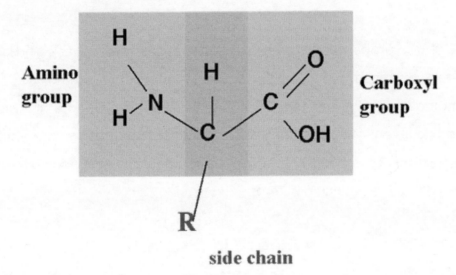

side chain

Amino acids sometimes refers to α amino acids. All 20 naturally occurring important amino acids are α amino acids.

An α amino acid occurs where the amino group is on the carbon atom next to the carbonyl group, as illustrated above.

The two functional groups in an amino acid mean that it will have some of the functions of an acid and some of the functions of a base.

The carboxylic acid functional group has a tendency to lose a proton (H^+) and act as a proton donor (acid) in an aqueous solution:

The amine group has a tendency to act as a proton acceptor, and therefore to act as a base.

Because of these properties, an amino acid can act as both a weak acid and a weak base. When dissolved in a highly acidic solution, the amino acid forms its corresponding cation. Dissolved in a highly alkaline solution, it will form its corresponding anion. At some intermediate point, amino acids can form both. We call these **zwitterions**. That is to say that they have a permanent + and − charge, but the overall charge on the molecule is zero.

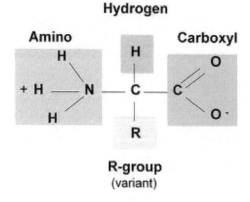

Amino Acid Structure

3.13.2 - Proteins

Amino acids link together to form peptides.

- Molecules that contain up to around 50 amino acids are called **polypeptides**
- Molecules where there are more than around 50 amino acids are called **proteins**

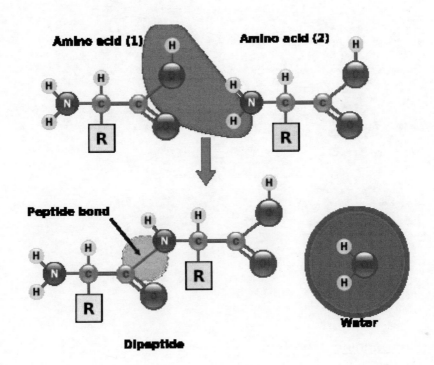

As you can see in the above illustration, the amine functional group of one amino acid will bond to the carboxylic acid functional group of another to form what is called a **peptide link** or a **peptide bond**.

When only two amino acids react together (as above) they form a dipeptide, so called because it consists of only 2 amino acids. When a dipeptide is formed, it retains the amine functional group at one end of the molecule and the carboxylic acid functional group at the other end. This allows for another amino acid to be added to either end of the structure, and this process can continue until the chain consists of a large number of amino acids. Eventually, when large enough, this becomes a protein.

Hydrogen Bonding in Proteins

Proteins are complex molecules with complex structures. These structures are held in place by hydrogen bonds. The shape of a protein is vital to its function within the body. Many proteins are of a spiral or helical shape, and hydrogen bonds hold together the structure as follows:

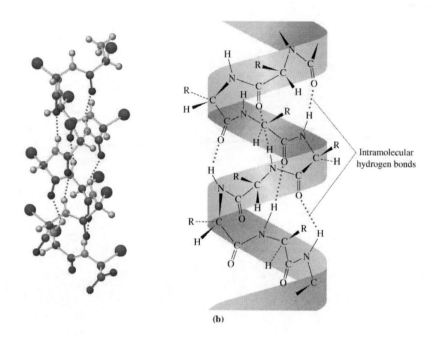

(b)

Sulphur-sulphur bonding in proteins

There is another feature in proteins which is also covalently bound. It involves the amino acid cysteine.

$$CH_2SH$$
$$|$$
$$NH_2\text{-}CH\text{-}COOH$$

cysteine

If two cysteine side chains end up next to each other because of folding in the peptide chain, they can react to form a **sulphur bridge**. This is another covalent link and so some people count it as a part of the primary structure of the protein.

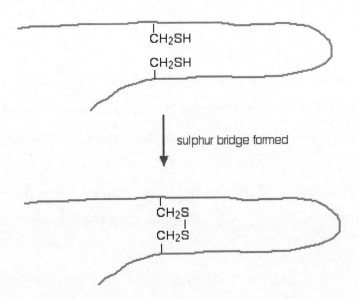

Sulphur-sulphur bonds affect the way the protein folds and thus their structure.

Hydrolysis of Peptide Bonds

If we take a protein and boil it with hydrochloric acid of concentration 6 mol dm^{-3} for around 24 hours, the structure breaks down to all of the constituent amino acids. The peptide bonds are hydrolysed by the acid.

The amino acids that are produced can be separated and identified using paper chromatography.

Note also that some enzymes will partially hydrolyse some proteins within the body.

Chromatography

Chromatography is not a single analytical technique. There are a range of different techniques that fall under this umbrella, but they all rely upon the sample under test being dissolved in a solvent and this resulting solution moving over a solid.

The **mobile phase** is the solution of sample and solvent. The more soluble the test sample, the more rapidly and easily it will move with the solvent.

The **stationary phase** refers to the solid material that the mobile phase must pass over or through. The stationary phase will hold back the component parts of the solution that are attracted to it. The more attraction a substance has for the stationary phase, the slower it will move across it.

Column Chromatography

Column chromatography uses a powder as the stationary phase. This powder is typically either:

- Silica
- Aluminium oxide
- A resin

This powder is placed into a tube (column) and the solution is added to the top of the column. The constituent parts of the solution move through the stationary phase at different rates and can be collected (separately) in a beaker (or several beakers) below the column.

Column chromatography works through the balance between two mechanisms:

- The solubility of the moving phase
- The retention in the stationary phase

Gas-Liquid Chromatography

Gas-liquid chromatography is usually called GC chromatography. In GC chromatography, the stationary phase is a powder coated with oil. A long capillary tube (up to 100m long and ½ mm in diameter) is either filled with this powder, or the inside of the tube is coated with it.

The mobile phase is typically an unreactive gas, frequently either nitrogen or helium. After the sample is injected into the gas, it moves along the capillary tube and the mixture separates out. Some of the component parts of the mixture will move along the tube at different rates, and some will be retained by the oil, with each component being affected to a different degree.

The different components of the sample will exit the capillary tube at different times, and therefore each has a different retention time within the tubing.

GC chromatography is an extremely useful tool for separating out volatile liquids.

Look at the example GC chromatogram below. The chart that is produced measures abundance against retention time within the tubing.

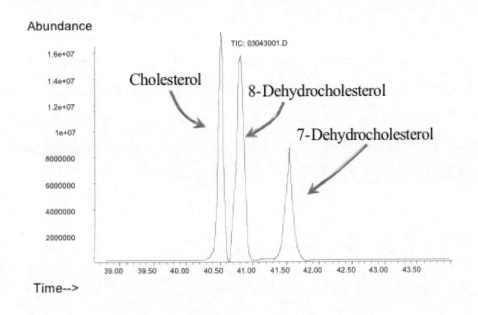

<u>R_f values</u>

Some compounds in a mixture travel almost as far as the solvent does; some stay much closer to the base line. The distance travelled relative to the solvent is a constant for a particular compound as long as you keep everything else constant - the type of paper and the exact composition of the solvent, for example.

The distance travelled relative to the solvent is called the R_f value. For each compound it can be worked out using the formula:

$$R_f = \frac{\text{distance travelled by compound}}{\text{distance travelled by solvent}}$$

For example, if one component of a mixture travelled 9.6 cm from the base line while the solvent had travelled 12.0 cm, then the R_f value for that component is:

$$R_f = \frac{9.6}{12.0}$$
$$= 0.80$$

In the example we looked at with the various pens, it wasn't necessary to measure R_f values because you are making a direct comparison just by looking at the chromatogram.

You are making the assumption that if you have two spots in the final chromatogram which are the same colour and have travelled the same distance up the paper, they are most likely the same compound. It isn't necessarily true of course - you could have two similarly coloured compounds with very similar R_f values. We'll look at how you can get around that problem further down the page.

Amino acids

In some cases, it may be possible to make the spots visible by reacting them with something which produces a coloured product. A good example of this is in chromatograms produced from amino acid mixtures.

Suppose you had a mixture of amino acids and wanted to find out which particular amino acids the mixture contained. For simplicity we'll assume that you know the mixture can only possibly contain five of the common amino acids.

A small drop of a solution of the mixture is placed on the base line of the paper, and similar small spots of the known amino acids are placed alongside it. The paper is then stood in a suitable solvent and left to develop as before. In the diagram, the mixture is M, and the known amino acids are labelled 1 to 5.

The position of the solvent front is marked in pencil and the chromatogram is allowed to dry and is then sprayed with a solution of **ninhydrin**. Ninhydrin reacts with amino acids to give coloured compounds, mainly brown or purple.

The left-hand diagram shows the paper after the solvent front has almost reached the top. The spots are still invisible. The second diagram shows what it might look like after spraying with ninhydrin.

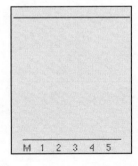

before spraying with ninhydrin

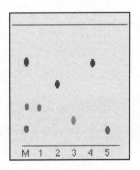

after spraying with ninhydrin

There is no need to measure the R$_f$ values because you can easily compare the spots in the mixture with those of the known amino acids - both from their positions and their colours.

In this example, the mixture contains the amino acids labelled as 1, 4 and 5.

And what if the mixture contained amino acids other than the ones we have used for comparison? There would be spots in the mixture which didn't match those from the known amino acids. You would have to re-run the experiment using other amino acids for comparison.[10]

[10] http://www.chemguide.co.uk/analysis/chromatography/paper.html

3.13.3 – Enzymes

Enzymes act as catalysts in living organisms. They enable or speed up chemical reactions without themselves being changed or used up. They act on a wide range of intracellular and extracellular reactions that determine structures and functions from the cellular to the whole-organism level. Enzymes are globular proteins, and as such are soluble in water. Enzymes are involved in almost every reaction that occurs in all living organisms. Enzymes can help to break down complex chemicals too, such as in digestion (catabolic enzymes). Enzymes can also have the opposite effect and can help build complex chemicals, such as in cell repair (anabolic enzymes). Enzymes are always very specific in their function. A single type of enzyme will only catalyse one type of reaction and this specificity makes them invaluable to life on earth. Enzymes need specific conditions in order to work at their optimum efficiency. Enzymes are very sensitive to changes in pH, temperature and pressure, just like other proteins. Enzymes may operate by reducing the activation energy needed to start a chemical reaction. The activation energy is the initial input of energy needed to start a reaction. Once a reaction has started, it takes far less energy to keep it going (see graph). There are two theories as to how enzymes work, but both agree on one thing, which is that the enzyme provides a surface for the reaction to take place.

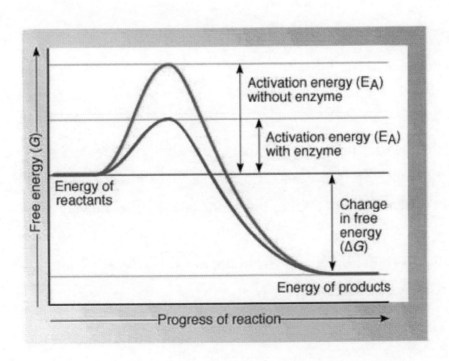

The Lock and Key Theory

Enzymes have very specific shapes because of their tertiary structure. This complex tertiary structure provides an activation site where chemical reactions between substrates occur. It is the unique shape of each enzyme's active site that makes them specific to certain reactions.

The lock and key theory proposes that the active site on an enzyme is a rigid shape, much like a lock. The substrate is essentially like a key which fits perfectly into that lock (the lock being the activation site). The substrate is then held at the activation site by ionic and hydrogen bonds whilst the reaction takes place.

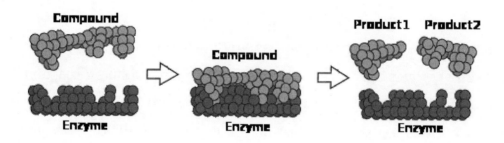

This theory explains why enzymes are so specific and also explains why even the smallest change in the shape of the enzyme will render it useless (because the substrates will no longer "fit" the activation site).

What this theory does not explain is that substrate molecules will not just happen to be oriented correctly to slip easily into the "lock" of the enzyme. This would be like throwing keys at a lock and hoping one lands facing the right way.

Activity 10 – In your own words explain what the activation energy of a reaction is and how enzymes affect it:

The Induced Fit Theory

The induced fit theory is similar to the lock and key theory in every way but one. In the induced fit theory the enzyme does not require the substrates to fit perfectly into the activation site. In this theory the activation site will change shape slightly to accommodate the shape of the substrate.

Once the substrate is in place, the enzyme will form itself around the substrate and therefore become the correct shape to facilitate the reaction. This would be like a piece of clothing that moulds to the body of the wearer.

As the substrate and enzyme are slightly distorted, the potential energy is reduced. This, in turn, lowers the activation energy for the reaction that will take place.

Once the reaction has occurred, the product no longer fits in the active site of the enzyme and it is, therefore, ejected. The enzyme then returns to its original shape ready for the next substrate molecule.

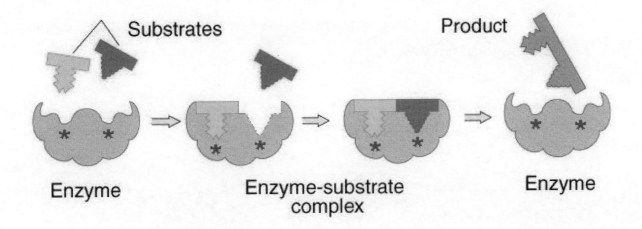

Factors Affecting Enzyme Efficiency

Inhibitors

Enzymes need specific conditions in which to operate at optimum efficiency. As we noted earlier, if an enzyme encounters conditions beyond the optimum, their efficiency will either be impaired or the enzyme itself could be destroyed.

Inhibitors can affect enzyme efficiency too. There are two main types of these:

- Competitive Inhibitors - These are substances that compete with an enzyme's normal substrate. They will bind to the enzyme's active site and prevent the enzyme catalysing any reactions with its normal substrate. Because they are competing for the same active site, the effect competitive inhibitors have on reaction rate is connected to the concentration of both the inhibitor and the substrate. With a high enough concentration of substrate, the reaction should still be able to proceed at its optimal rate. Many antibiotics work this way.
- Non-competitive Inhibitors - These do not bind to the active site of an enzyme, but instead bind to the enzyme in a different place and, in doing so, cause the active site to change shape, rendering it useless. Many poisons, such as heavy metals, work in this way.

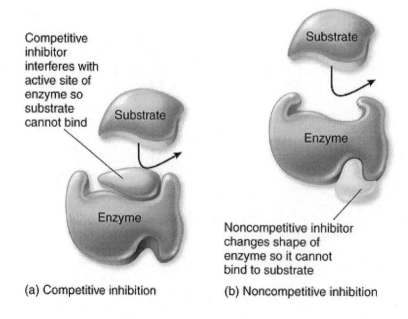

Competitive inhibitor interferes with active site of enzyme so substrate cannot bind

Substrate

Enzyme

(a) Competitive inhibition

Substrate

Enzyme

Noncompetitive inhibitor changes shape of enzyme so it cannot bind to substrate

(b) Noncompetitive inhibition

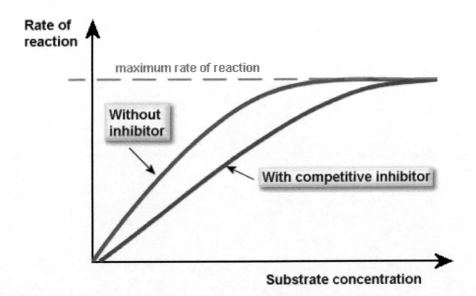

The presence of a non-competitive inhibitor affects reaction rate in a very different way to competitive inhibitors. Because it isn't competing for the same site, increasing the concentration of substrate will not bring the reaction rate back up to its optimal level. The reaction rate will plateau when all the enzymes that are not bound to the inhibitor are saturated with substrate. The graph below shows the effect of a non-competitive inhibitor on reaction rate. Non-competitive inhibition can also be a useful negative feedback tool in biological processes. This is referred to as end-product inhibition.

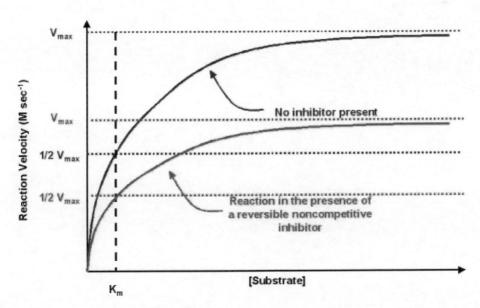

Computers can be used to help design drugs by taking into account the shapes of active sites etc.

3.13.4 - DNA

DNA, or deoxyribonucleic acid, is the hereditary material in humans and almost all other organisms. Nearly every cell in a person's body has the same DNA. Most DNA is located in the cell nucleus (where it is called nuclear DNA), but a small amount of DNA can also be found in the mitochondria (where it is called mitochondrial DNA or mtDNA). The information in DNA is stored as a code made up of four chemical bases:

- Adenine (A)
- Guanine (G)
- Cytosine (C)
- Thymine (T)

Human DNA consists of about 3 billion bases, and more than 99% of those bases are the same in all people. The order, or sequence, of these bases determines the information available for building and maintaining an organism, similar to the way in which letters of the alphabet appear in a certain order to form words and sentences. DNA bases pair up with each other, A with T and C with G, to form units called base pairs. Each base is also attached to a sugar molecule and a phosphate molecule. Together, a base, sugar, and phosphate are called a nucleotide.

Nucleotides are arranged in two long strands that form a spiral called a double helix. The structure of the double helix is somewhat like a ladder, with the base pairs forming the ladder's rungs and the sugar and phosphate molecules forming the vertical sidepieces of the ladder.

An important property of DNA is that it can replicate, or make copies of itself. Each strand of DNA in the double helix can serve as a pattern for duplicating the sequence of bases. This is critical when cells divide because each new cell needs to have an exact copy of the DNA present in the old cell.[11]

---

[11] http://ghr.nlm.nih.gov/handbook/basics/dna

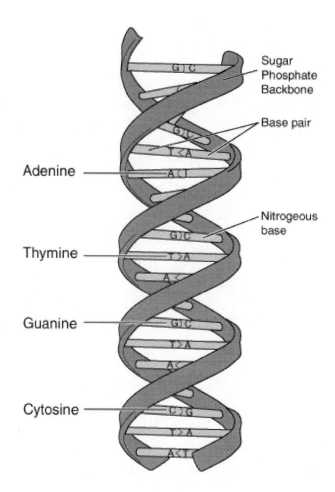

Sugar Phosphate Backbone

Base pair

Adenine

Nitrogeous base

Thymine

Guanine

Cytosine

DNA is a surprisingly simple molecule when we consider the complexity of the function it carries out. This simplicity led some scientists to initially doubt that it could possibly be the structure that carried the genetic code.

Nucleotides

Each nucleotide is made of three components. These are:

- Deoxyribose - This is a pentose sugar. It has 5 carbon atoms.
- A Phosphate Group - This helps the nucleotides to join together into a strand by forming phosphodiester bonds.
- A Nitrogen Containing Organic Base – There are four of these: cytosine and thymine are single ring bases, adenine and guanine are double ring bases. The structures of these bases are in the diagram below.

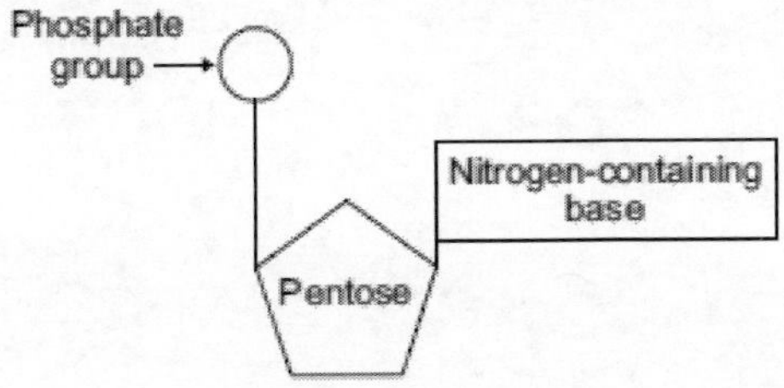

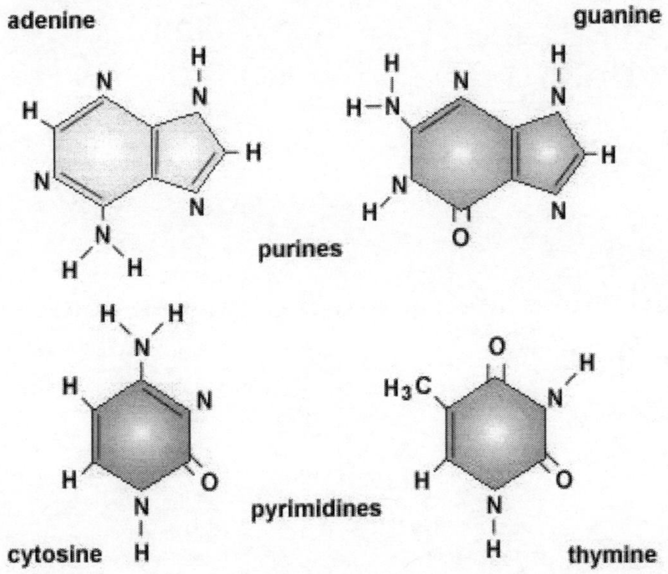

Nucleotides are formed by condensation reactions between their three component parts (a mononucleotide). The phosphate group on each mononucleotide can form a (phosphodiester) bond between one nucleotide and another to form a dinucleotide.

These bonds are what form the strand like structure of a polynucleotide. The phosphate group is attached to the number 5 carbon of the deoxyribose sugar, and forms the phosphodiester bond with the number 3 carbon on the deoxyribose molecule of the next mononucleotide. The organic base attached to each mononucleotide is used to link the two polynucleotide strands that are needed to create DNA's double helix structure.

RNA (which we will discuss in more detail later) contains the sugar ribose (another pentose). The structure of these sugars is illustrated below:

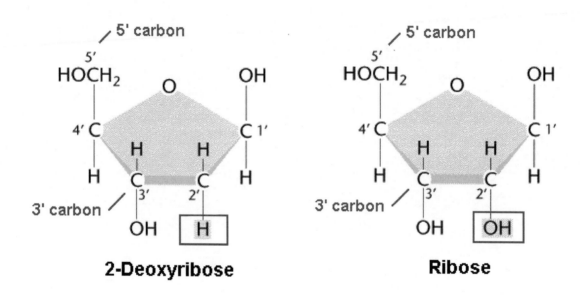

Activity 13 – Nucleotides are formed by condensation reactions. What are condensation reactions?

Activity 14 – DNA and RNA are polymers formed from nucleotides. What are polymers?

DNA Structure

DNA is made up of two polynucleotide strands joined together by hydrogen bonds formed between the bases on each nucleotide. As we noted earlier, these bases bond in a very specific way. Adenine and thymine always join together, using two hydrogen bonds. Cytosine and guanine always join together, using three hydrogen bonds.

This pairing of bases is only possible because each strand of the DNA molecule runs in opposite directions (they are anti-parallel). Think of the phosphdiester bonds we looked at earlier. A polypeptide chain has two distinct ends to it, the three prime (3') end, which terminates at the number 3 carbon on the deoxyribose molecule, and the five prime end (5') that terminates at the number five carbon on the deoxyribose molecule (and is connected to the phosphate group). So, in a molecule of DNA, one strand runs from 5' to 3' while the other strand runs from 3' to 5'.

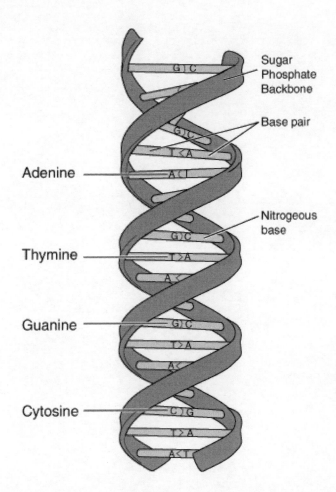

The double helical structure of DNA is dependent on this opposite or anti-parallel running of the two strands. It allows the bases to pair up correctly and so gives the molecule its standard structure. Each base pair is 0.34 nm apart, and one complete twist of the double helix contains ten base pairs.

3.13.5 – Action of anticancer drugs

Cell division and cancer

Cancer is a disease that is caused by a growth disorder within cells. Damage to the genes that control mitosis and the cell cycle can lead to cells replicating abnormally and at a very fast rate. This causes tumours to form. Doctors use drugs, known collectively as chemotherapy, that block or disrupt the cell cycle thus preventing their replication. There are a number of ways in which these chemotherapy drugs can work:

- Some drugs prevent DNA from replicating.
- Others inhibit spindle formation in metaphase of mitosis.

The problem is these drugs are non-specific and attack all the cells, healthy or unhealthy. They work better on cells that replicate quickly, like cancer cells, or hair cells, or sperm cells.

We encountered square planar shapes of molecules earlier; cisplatin is a square planar structure and is one of the most successful cancer drugs on the market.

$$
\begin{array}{ccc}
Cl & & NH_3 \\
 & Pt & \\
Cl & & NH_3
\end{array}
$$

Cisplatin

Cisplatin prevents DNA replication in cancer cells by a ligand replacement reaction with DNA in which a bond is formed platinum and a nitrogen atom on guanine. Many drugs, like cisplatin, have negative side effects but society as a whole must analyse if the negative side effects are outweighed by the positive impact.

3.14 – Organic synthesis

The formation of new organic compounds by multi-step syntheses using reactions included in the specification is covered in this section.

<u>Applications</u>

We will now look at methods of synthesising specific target molecules. Synthesis is a common industrial problem and one that chemists are frequently asked to resolve.

Consider, for example, a situation where a new wonder drug has been discovered that will cure cancer; how to synthesise that drug on an industrial scale is the next major problem that must be solved.

<u>Organic Synthesis</u>

To work out a synthesis scheme, you can first write down the formula of the starting molecule (A), and of the desired end product (X).

One method is then to write down all of the compounds that can be prepared from A and all of the compounds that can lead to X.

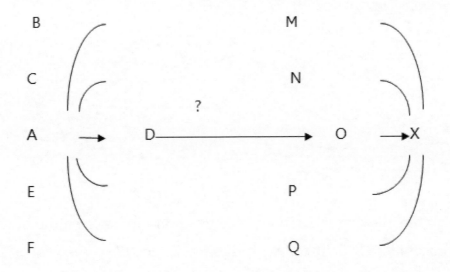

By doing this, you may be able to determine that actually C can lead to Q and, therefore, develop a method of synthesis that has several stages to it, but eventually produces the product, X.

Note that for the exam you will need to recall the reactions for all of the functional groups you have encountered. These include the conditions for the reactions where given (e.g. temperature, catalyst etc.).

<u>Interrelationships between Functional Groups</u>

This can be complex:

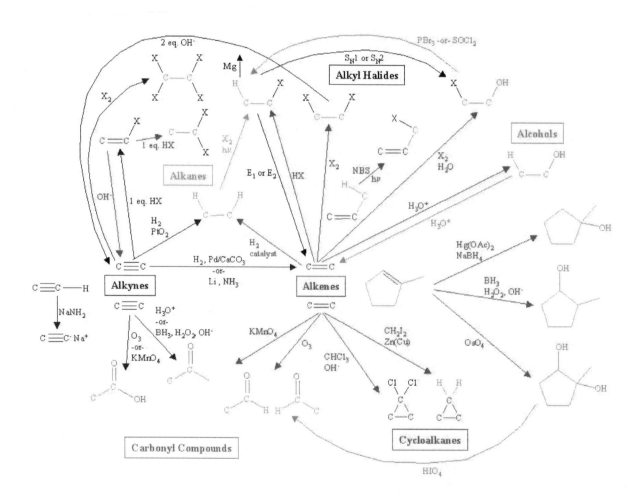

As you can see, there is an enormous interrelationship between the function groups we have encountered on the course. This makes the job of synthesising a new chemical challenging and very interesting.

Reagents in Organic Chemistry

There are a range of reagents that are commonly used in organic chemistry to perform a range of functions:

- **Oxidising agents**: Potassium dichromate (VI) ($K_2Cr_2O_7$), when acidified with dilute sulphuric acid, will oxidise primary alcohols to aldehydes, and aldehydes to carboxylic acids. It will oxidise secondary alcohols to ketones.

- **Reducing agents**: Sodium tetrahydridoborate (III) ($NaBH_4$) will reduce C=O bonds but not C=C bonds. In aqueous solution, it will attack polar bonds but not non-polar ones (as in C=C) because of the production of an H^- nucleophile. This H^- is not attracted to the electron rich C=C bond. Hydrogen with a nickel catalyst will reduce the C=C bond, but not the C=O bond. Tin and hydrochloric acid will reduce $R–NO_2$ to $R–NH_2$.

- **Dehydrating agents**: Alcohols can be converted to alkenes by passing the vapour over heated aluminium oxide or by acid catalysed elimination reactions.

Reaction Schemes

Consider the reaction to produce propanoic acid from 1-bromopropane.

Activity 94 – Draw these two molecules.

Answer to Activity 94:

1-bromopropane:

Propanoic acid:

To start the synthesis, we should do as we suggested earlier and consider first what products can be made from 1-bromopropane. Secondly, consider what substances can react to produce propanoic acid. The fact that there are the same number of carbon atoms in the chain makes the process a little less difficult.

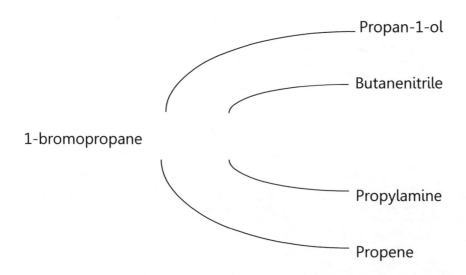

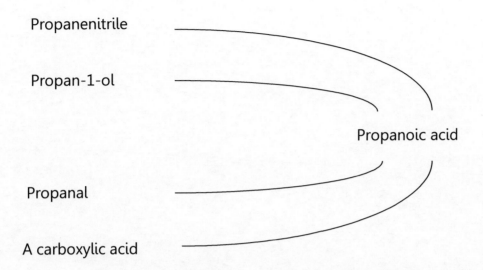

Propanenitrile

Propan-1-ol

Propanoic acid

Propanal

A carboxylic acid

We can see from these two reaction schemes that:

1-bromopropane → Propan-1-ol

(This is a reflux reaction with NaOH(aq))

and:

Propan-1-ol → Propanoic acid

(This is a reflux reaction with $K_2Cr_2O_7/H^+$)

Propanoic acid can, therefore, be produced from 1-bromopropane in a two stage reaction.

Activity 95 – Using the same process, how can we synthesise propylamine from ethene?

Answer to Activity 95:

Ethene:

H   H
 \   /
  C = C
 /   \
H   H

Propylamine:

$$H-\overset{\displaystyle H}{\underset{\displaystyle H}{C}}-\overset{\displaystyle H}{\underset{\displaystyle H}{C}}-\overset{\displaystyle H}{\underset{\displaystyle H}{C}}-NH_2$$

Ethene reactions:

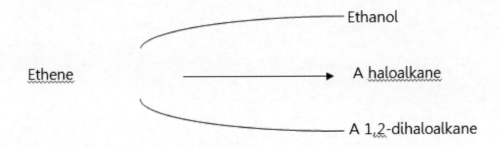

Ethene ⟶ Ethanol / A haloalkane / A 1,2-dihaloalkane

Synthesis of propylamine:

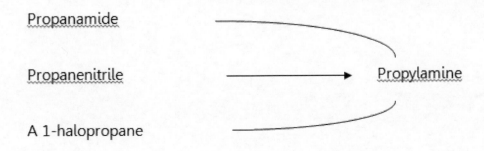

Propanamide / Propanenitrile / A 1-halopropane ⟶ Propylamine

In these reactions, nothing immediately presents itself as offering a 2 stage reaction process from ethene to propylamine.

However, we know that:

A haloalkane + CN^- → Propanenitrile

$CH_3CH_2Cl + CN^- → CH_3CH_2C≡N + Cl^-$

We can, therefore, suggest a three stage process:

Stage 1:

$CH_2CH_2 + HBr → CH_3CH_2Br$

Stage 2:

$CH_3CH_3Br + KCN → CH_3CH_2C≡N$

The KCN will be in dilute sulphuric acid.

Stage 3:

$CH_3CH_2C≡N + H_2 → CH_3CH_2CH_2NH_2$

This reaction takes place with a nickel catalyst.

3.15 – Nuclear magnetic resonance spectroscopy

Chemists use a variety of techniques to decide the structure of compounds. In this section, nuclear magnetic resonance spectroscopy is added to mass spectrometry and infrared spectroscopy as an analytical technique. The emphasis is on the use of analytical data to solve problems rather than on spectroscopic theory.

Nuclear magnetic resonance spectroscopy (NMR) is a powerful tool in organic chemistry because it can help to identify the structure of even very complex compounds.

A magnetic field is applied to a sample, which in turn is surrounded by a source of radio waves and a radio receiver.

An energy change is therefore generated in the nuclei of the sample (remember each molecule will have a lot of atoms and therefore a lot of different nuclei).

The nuclei emit electromagnetic radiation, which in turn can be detected by a computer.

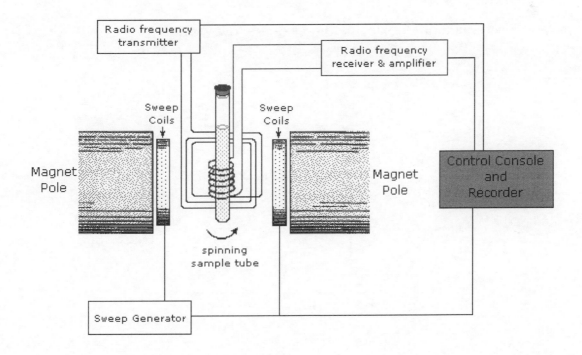

Nuclei with odd mass numbers spin; this spin gives them a magnetic field which can be detected. (An odd mass number means C^{13} not C^{12}, and H^1 not H^2.)

If we consider C^{13} for a moment, then we can see that not all C^{13} atoms in a molecule will resonate at the same magnetic field strength. This is because some of those C^{13} nuclei will be shielded to differing degrees by electrons, due to their relative positions in the molecule.

The NMR machine produces a graph of the energy absorbed from the radio signal against chemical shift (a property related to the resonance frequency of the nuclei) measured in parts per million (ppm).

The range runs from the chemical shift of a substance called tetramethylsilane (TMS), which is considered to be the zero point.

The symbol generally used for chemical shift is the Greek letter delta (δ).

δ is the difference between the resonance frequency of the nucleus in question compared to that of TMS. With C^{13}, for example, the δ value ranges from zero to 200.

An NMR spectrum might look something like the following:

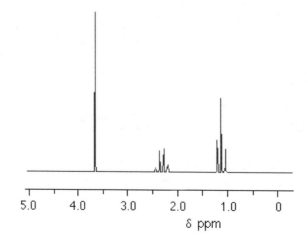

high resolution nmr spectrum for methyl propanoate, $CH_3CH_2COOCH_3$

The important thing to note on an NMR spectrum is that the nucleus of every C^{13} and every H^1 will resonate at a different frequency, and therefore exhibit a different chemical shift, depending on their position in the molecule.

A C^{13} spectrum for ethanol is illustrated below:

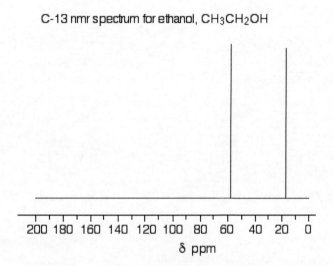

C-13 nmr spectrum for ethanol, CH_3CH_2OH

We can see from the illustration above that the CH_3 and CH_2 have different δ values.

The different values for δ in the table below can be explained because of the electronegativity of the substances bonded to the carbon. Oxygen, for example, is strongly electronegative and draws the electrons away from the carbon atom, therefore essentially "de-shielding" the carbon and allowing it to resonate more and thus have a higher δ value.

In other compounds where the carbon is bonded to atoms that are less strongly electronegative, then the carbon will still be shielded by electrons as they have not been drawn away to another atom.

Note that the machine can look for the C^{13} spectrum or the H^1 spectrum, and they are different. We will look at C^{13} specifically first.

carbon environment	chemical shift (ppm)
C=O (in ketones)	205 - 220
C=O (in aldehydes)	190 - 200
C=O (in acids and esters)	170 - 185
C in aromatic rings	125 - 150
C=C (in alkenes)	115 - 140
RCH_2OH	50 - 65
RCH_2Cl	40 - 45
RCH_2NH_2	37 - 45
R_3CH	25 - 35
CH_3CO-	20 - 30
R_2CH_2	16 - 25
RCH_3	10 - 15

Activity 97 – Look at the C^{13} NMR spectrum below and, using the information in the table above, identify the peaks. The substance is:

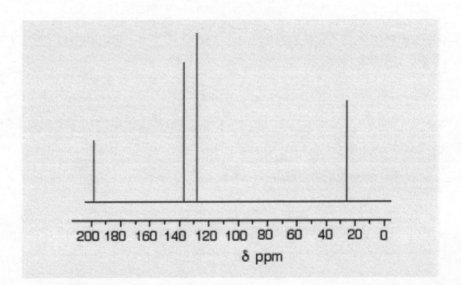

Answer to Activity 97:

- The peak around 200 ppm is the C = O bond
- The peak around 140 ppm is the C = C bond
- The peak around 130 ppm is the C = C bond

(Note there are two peaks because there are carbon atoms at either end of the C = C double bond and they both have a different amount of shielding.)

- The peak around 25 ppm is the C – C bond that connects the methyl group

We have seen, therefore, that the C^{13} NMR spectrum depends on the electronegativity of the bonds, and upon shielding from other atoms in the molecule; it depends, essentially, upon the molecular environment.

We will now look at the proton NMR. This is an NMR which looks at H^1 rather than C^{13}.

Proton NMR

With proton NMR, it is the H^1 nucleus that we are examining, rather than the C^{13}. This is easier to achieve, because whilst only around 1% of carbon atoms are C^{13}, almost all hydrogen atoms in an organic compound will be H^1.

The results are obtained by dissolving the sample in a proton free solvent, e.g. deuterated solvents and CCl_4.

The principles are basically the same as with the NMR spectroscope. The magnetic field causes the H^1 bonds (this time) to resonate, and the amount of resonance depends on the shielding from the surrounding groups.

The greater the electron density around the atom, the lower the chemical shift and, therefore, the lower the δ number.

The values for chemical shift in a proton NMR are rather lower than those in the C^{13} NMR, typically between 0 and 10.

If all of the hydrogen atoms in an organic molecule are in the same environment and condition, then we will get a single peak on the spectrum. Methane is a good example of this, as all of the hydrogen atoms are bonded to a carbon, and none is any more shielded than any of the others.

If we look at a slightly different compound, methanol (CH_3OH) for example, we see two peaks. To understand the spectrum, we should look at the structure of methanol:

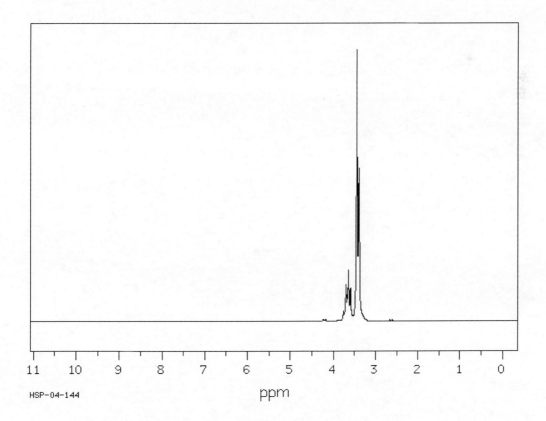

HSP-04-144

The peak at around 3.6 must come from a hydrogen that has less shielding than the hydrogen at around 3.4. We can also deduce that the peak at around 3.4 is from many more hydrogen atoms, simply because it is a much larger peak.

Looking at methanol, there is a single hydrogen bonded to the oxygen atom. We know that oxygen is an electronegative atom and will draw electrons towards itself, thus removing some of the shielding from that hydrogen, hence the peak.

We can also see from the structure that there are three hydrogen atoms bonded to the carbon of the CH_3 group. These three will all have the same shielding, as they are all essentially in the same environment. The three combined will also produce a larger peak, the one at 3.4.

In a proton spectra, the area of the peak is related to the number of hydrogen atoms that produced it. There are three times as many hydrogen atoms in the CH_3 group than in the OH group. The CH_3 peak is therefore three times the area.

TMS

We noted earlier that the chemical shift value uses tetramethylsilane (TMS) as a standard value, essentially the zero point on the spectrum.

TMS is similar to methane in that, with methane, each of the hydrogen atoms are in exactly the same environment and therefore produce a single peak.

$$CH_3 - Si - CH_3$$
$$\begin{array}{c} CH_3 \\ | \\ H_3C - Si - CH_3 \\ | \\ CH_3 \end{array}$$

The chemical shift values of any other compound are measured against TMS, and the TMS values are therefore the standard and, by definition, zero. A small amount of TMS can be added (it is a liquid under normal conditions) to the sample under test. This will produce a peak at a particular point on the spectrum, and this peak can be used to calibrate the readings (as it can be called the zero point) with the other peaks then relative to the TMS peak.

TMS also has other advantages in that it is inert, non-toxic, liquid at RTP and easy to remove from the sample when the testing is complete.

Spin-Spin Splitting

If we were to zoom in to most peaks on an NMR spectrum, we would see that they are split into particular patterns; this is called **spin-spin splitting**. (Sometimes it is called spin-spin coupling, but the AQA specification uses the term splitting.)

This occurs because the applied magnetic field on any given hydrogen atom is affected by the magnetic field of neighbouring hydrogen atoms. This information can be invaluable in working out a complex structure.

The n+1 Rule

If there is 1 hydrogen atom on an adjacent carbon, this will split the NMR peak into two, with each of the two peaks of the same height.

If there are two hydrogen atoms on adjacent carbon atoms, this will split the peak into three, in the height ratio 1:2:1.

If there are three hydrogen atoms on adjacent carbon atoms, this will split the peak into four, in the height ratio 1:3:3:1.

The n in the n+1 rule refers to the number of hydrogens on adjacent carbon atoms. These hydrogens will split a peak into n+1 smaller peaks.

Solvents for Proton NMR

NMR spectra are normally conducted in solution. The solvent must be proton free (no hydrogen atoms) otherwise these would interfere with the spectrum. The most commonly used solvent is tetrachloromethane (CCl_4). Other solvents could contain deuterium (an isotope of hydrogen). This has the chemical symbol D.

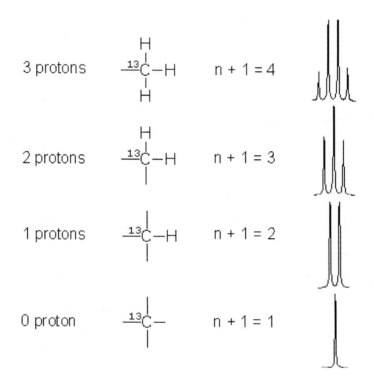

3.16 - Chromatography

Chromatography provides an important method of separating and identifying components in a mixture. Different types of chromatography are used depending on the composition of mixture to be separated.

Chromatography is not a single analytical technique: there are a range of different techniques that fall under this umbrella, but they all rely upon the sample under test being dissolved in a solvent and this resulting solution moving over a solid.

The **mobile phase** is the solution of sample and solvent. The more soluble the test sample, the more rapidly and easily it will move with the solvent.

The **stationary phase** refers to the solid material that the mobile phase must pass over or through. The stationary phase will hold back the component parts of the solution that are attracted to it. The more attraction a substance has for the stationary phase, the slower it will move across it.

Column Chromatography

Column chromatography uses a powder as the stationary phase. This powder is typically either:

- Silica
- Aluminium oxide
- A resin

This powder is placed into a tube (column) and the solution is added to the top of the column. The constituent parts of the solution move through the stationary phase at different rates and can be collected (separately) in a beaker (or several beakers) below the column.

Column chromatography works through the balance between two mechanisms:

- The solubility of the moving phase
- The retention in the stationary phase

Gas-Liquid Chromatography

Gas-liquid chromatography is usually called GC chromatography. In GC chromatography, the stationary phase is a powder coated with oil. A long capillary tube (up to 100m long and ½ mm in diameter) is either filled with this powder, or the inside of the tube is coated with it. The mobile phase is typically an unreactive gas, frequently either nitrogen or helium. After the sample is injected into the gas, it moves along the capillary tube and the mixture separates out. Some of the component parts of the mixture will move along the tube at different rates, and some will be retained by the oil, with each component being affected to a different degree. The different components of the sample will exit the capillary tube at different times, and therefore each has a different retention time within the tubing.

GC chromatography is an extremely useful tool for separating out volatile liquids. Look at the example GC chromatogram below. The chart that is produced measures abundance against retention time within the tubing.

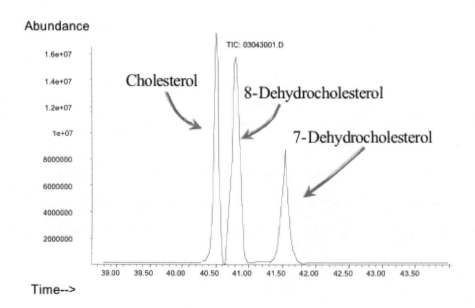

Required Practical 12:

Separation of species by thin-layer chromatography

Mathematical Requirements

In order to be able to develop your skills, knowledge and understanding in chemistry, you need to have competence in the appropriate areas of mathematics as indicated below.

Overall, at least 20% of the marks in assessments for chemistry will require the use of mathematical skills. These skills will be applied in the context of chemistry and will be at least the standard of high tier GCSE Mathematics.

The list of examples below is not exhaustive and is copied directly from the specification.

6.1 Arithmetic and numerical computation

	Mathematical skills	Exemplification of mathematical skill in the context of chemistry
MS 0.0	Recognise and make use of appropriate units in calculation	Students may be tested on their ability to: • convert between units eg cm^3 to dm^3 as part of volumetric calculations • **give units for an equilibrium constant or a rate constant** • understand that different units are used in similar topic areas, so that conversions may be necessary, eg entropy in $J\ mol^{-1}\ K^{-1}$ and enthalpy changes in $kJ\ mol^{-1}$.
MS 0.1	Recognise and use expressions in decimal and ordinary form	Students may be tested on their ability to: • use an appropriate number of decimal places in calculations eg for pH • carry out calculations using numbers in standard and ordinary form eg use of Avogadro's number • understand standard form when applied to areas such as (but not limited to) K_w • convert between numbers in standard and ordinary form • understand that significant figures need retaining when making conversions between standard and ordinary form eg $0.0050\ mol\ dm^{-3}$ is equivalent to $5.0 \times 10^{-3}\ mol\ dm^{-3}$.

	Mathematical skills	Exemplification of mathematical skill in the context of chemistry
MS 0.2	Use ratios, fractions and percentages	Students may be tested on their ability to: • calculate percentage yields • calculate the atom economy of a reaction • construct and/or balance equations using ratios.
MS 0.3	Estimate results	Students may be tested on their ability to: • **evaluate the effect of changing experimental parameters on measurable values eg how the value of K_c would change with temperature given different specified conditions.**
MS 0.4	Use calculators to find and use power, **exponential and logarithmic functions**	Students may be tested on their ability to: • carry out calculations using the Avogadro constant • **carry out pH and pK_a calculations** • **make appropriate mathematical approximations in buffer calculations.**

6.2   Handling data

	Mathematical skills	Exemplification of mathematical skill in the context of chemistry
MS 1.1	Use an appropriate number of significant figures	Students may be tested on their ability to: • report calculations to an appropriate number of significant figures, given raw data quoted to varying numbers of significant figures • understand that calculated results can only be reported to the limits of the least accurate measurement.
MS 1.2	Find arithmetic means	Students may be tested on their ability to: • calculate weighted means eg calculation of an atomic mass based on supplied isotopic abundances • select appropriate titration data (ie identification of outliers) in order to calculate mean titres.
MS 1.3	Identify uncertainties in measurements and use simple techniques to determine uncertainty when data are combined	Students may be tested on their ability to: • determine uncertainty when two burette readings are used to calculate a titre value.

6.3 Algebra

	Mathematical skills	Exemplification of mathematical skill in the context of chemistry
MS 2.1	Understand and use the symbols: $=$, $<$, $\ll$, $\gg$, $>$, $\propto$, $\sim$, equilibrium sign	No exemplification required.
MS 2.2	Change the subject of an equation	Students may be tested on their ability to: • carry out structured and unstructured mole calculations eg calculate a rate constant k from a rate equation.
MS 2.3	Substitute numerical values into algebraic equations using appropriate units for physical quantities	Students may be tested on their ability to: • carry out structured and unstructured mole calculations • carry out rate calculations • calculate the value of an equilibrium constant K_c.
MS 2.4	Solve algebraic equations	Students may be tested on their ability to: • carry out Hess's law calculations • calculate a rate constant k from a rate equation.
MS 2.5	Use logarithms in relation to quantities that range over several orders of magnitude	Students may be tested on their ability to: • carry out pH and pK_a calculations.

6.4 Graphs

	Mathematical skills	Exemplification of mathematical skill in the context of chemistry
MS 3.1	Translate information between graphical, numerical and algebraic forms	Students may be tested on their ability to: • interpret and analyse spectra • determine the order of a reaction from a graph • derive a rate expression from a graph.
MS 3.2	Plot two variables from experimental or other data	Students may be tested on their ability to: • plot concentration–time graphs from collected or supplied data and draw an appropriate best-fit curve.
MS 3.3	Determine the slope and intercept of a linear graph	Students may be tested on their ability to: • calculate the rate constant of a zero-order reaction by determination of the gradient of a concentration–time graph.
MS 3.4	Calculate rate of change from a graph showing a linear relationship	Students may be tested on their ability to: • calculate the rate constant of a zero-order reaction by determination of the gradient of a concentration–time graph.
MS 3.5	Draw and use the slope of a tangent to a curve as a measure of rate of change	Students may be tested on their ability to: • determine the order of a reaction using the initial rates method.

6.5 Geometry and trigonometry

	Mathematical skills	Exemplification of mathematical skill in the context of chemistry
MS 4.1	Use angles and shapes in regular 2D and 3D structures	Students may be tested on their ability to: • predict/identify shapes of and bond angles in molecules with and without a lone pair(s), for example NH_3, CH_4, H_2O etc.
MS 4.2	Visualise and represent 2D and 3D forms including two-dimensional representations of 3D objects	Students may be tested on their ability to: • draw different forms of isomers • identify chiral centres from a 2D or 3D representation.
MS 4.3	Understand the symmetry of 2D and 3D shapes	Students may be tested on their ability to: • describe the types of stereoisomerism shown by molecules/complexes • identify chiral centres from a 2D or 3D representation.